NEGRO YOUTH
AT THE CROSSWAYS

NEGRO YOUTH
AT THE CROSSWAYS

Their Personality Development
in the Middle States

E. FRANKLIN FRAZIER

WITH AN INTRODUCTION BY ST. CLAIR DRAKE

Prepared for The American Youth Commission
AMERICAN COUNCIL ON EDUCATION

SCHOCKEN BOOKS · NEW YORK

Introduction to the 1967 Edition

BY ST. CLAIR DRAKE

In May, 1967, several young Negro men jumped down from the rail and began to run beside the horses exercising on the Kentucky Derby track in Louisville. They were adding the "run-in" to a roster of non-violent social action techniques that already included the "sit-in," the "wade-in," the "pray-in," and Freedom Riding. This was a distinctive contribution to a series of demonstrations their elders had been carrying on for a number of weeks against residential segregation in the city, and one that threatened to disrupt the Derby itself. A quarter of a century before these dramatic events occurred in Louisville, Kentucky, a team of social scientists had studied the Negro youth of that city under the direction of sociologist E. Franklin Frazier, and had concluded that "social movements in the strict meaning of the term exercise practically no influence on the personality of Negro youth." In fact, there were no social movements in Louisville. Times have changed!

A few days after the Louisville race track episode, Stokeley Carmichael, *enfant terrible* of the civil rights movement, announced that he was selecting Washington, D.C., as his special target for a Black Power organizational drive. The nation's leaders were understandably apprehensive, for over three-quarters of Washington's young people are Negroes, and their frustration and hostility have occasionally exploded in a minor riot and find continuous expression in acts of delinquency. The same research team that visited Louisville more than twenty-five years ago also visited Washington. It reported that no organization had stirred Negro youth there into disciplined social action, except for a tiny minority involved in a picketing-for-jobs campaign that offered an outlet for "some of the latent mili-

tancy and resentment of Negro youth toward discrimination."
Hostility is still, on the whole, latent in Washington, D.C., but
it is not likely to remain so.

The reissue of *Negro Youth at the Crossways* makes a document available that aids us in understanding why certain types
of communities have not been at the forefront of the civil rights
movement, but have recently become centers of activity. Research on these two cities was sponsored by the American Youth
Commission of the American Council on Education in 1939, in
order to "determine what kind of person a Negro youth is or is
in the process of becoming as a result of the limitations which
are placed upon his or her participation in the life of the communities in the border states." This book is a research report
on reactions to those "limitations" in the years when a crippling
depression was just about to end and World War II was about
to begin. It provides a meaningful baseline from which to
measure change, as well as cues for interpreting the meaning
of change. The Negro youth so vividly portrayed here "in the
process of becoming" are now a part of the adult population of
Washington and Louisville. They are among the fathers and
mothers, aunts and uncles, of a new generation that stands at
the "crossways." And some of them, no doubt, helped to swell
the crowd during the March on Washington in 1963, or have
recently been following Martin Luther King's brother on the
Louisville streets.

The major problems of youth in the United States today
center around various types of alienation, and are often, indeed,
the afflictions of the affluent. Only one in five American families
is defined as "poor" today. It was a very different story at the
end of the 1930's, for on the eve of World War II, when the
need for special research on America's young people was felt,
tens of thousands of them were in Civilian Conservation Corps
camps or were on various projects—in school and out—of the
National Youth Administration. The New Deal had provided
these forms of "made work" and, thus, some temporary economic stability for the children of the unemployed who were
themselves on WPA, PWA, and other such agencies.

Hope was widespread that "recovery" would eventually come

to eliminate these government-provided jobs. But Negroes, who were suffering most severely from the depression, were not very hopeful about their future when and if "recovery" did come. "Last hired and first fired" was the epigrammatic way Negro adults summed up their previous work experiences, and they saw no reason to expect anything different this time. Adult attitudes toward their fate were often echoed by their children, as in the case of a teen-age boy (a member of a cadet corps at school) who was overheard by one of Professor Frazier's research workers saying to another boy:

> I want to get in the army ... *I wish there'd be a good war. We'd get a break then. Negroes got the best breaks during the last war, and the white people will probably need us more this time than they did before.* James and me will probably be used to train other men and we'll be right over here doing it. (Italics added.)

Within a few years his wish came true, and by 1944 most able-bodied Negro males were either in the armed forces or working in war-related industries—even if they weren't the best ones. Over two decades later this point of view is still prevalent among Negroes, and certain respectable and responsible social scientists (among them Daniel Moynihan) point to the army as the only place where Negro men can feel fully free and equal to whites!

Negro youths "at the crossways" were found to be less militant, on the whole, than their counterparts in the large Northern urban ghettos, yet only a few youths anywhere—black or white —were participating in radical activities during the depression years. A few hundred young Negroes were active in left-wing groups such as American Youth for Democracy (AYD) and the Southern Negro Youth Congress (SNYC), and a slightly larger number belonged to NAACP Youth Councils which had been recently organized. Also, in several communities—including Washington—successful "Don't Spend Your Money Where You Can't Work" campaigns had opened up a few jobs in the ghettos by picketing and boycott, but young people did not form the backbone of these movements. Even the 1935 riot in Harlem was not primarily an outburst of youth. It is to the credit of the American Youth Commission that it did not wait for Watts-type explosions to stimulate research on the hopes and fears of young Negroes, or to try to gather information on their attitudes toward themselves, their own racial group, and white people. Sound planning for the future demanded such information and the educators recognized that fact.

Two Negro scholars chose to study Negro youth in the lower South. One of these, a sociologist, designed, supervised, and wrote what became a race-relations classic on rural Southern youth: Charles S. Johnson, *Growing Up in the Black Belt*. The other, a social anthropologist, invited a white psychologist to cooperate with him, and together they produced an important volume on the effects of caste and class discrimination upon Negro youth in urban areas of Louisiana and Mississippi: *Children of Bondage,* by Allison Davis and John Dollard.

The scholar who had been most influential in developing and popularizing the caste-class frame of reference for analyzing Negro-white relations in the United States, W. Lloyd Warner, collaborated with one of his graduate students, Buford H. Junker, and a Negro psychoanalyst, Walter A. Adams, in exploring the inner life of ghettoized youth in Chicago. The result of their efforts was *Color and Human Nature.*

Lying between the plantations of the Deep South and the massive ghettos of the North were numerous Negro communities of the "upper" South, among them the nation's capital. E. Franklin Frazier selected two of these cities—Washington, D.C., and Louisville, Kentucky—for intensive study and chose to call his book *Negro Youth at the Crossways*. Robert L. Sutherland, the Youth Commission's Associate Director for Studies of Negro Youth, noted in his Preface that "the author found many of these youth facing dilemmas that are a part of the transition from a southern rural to a middle states urban way of living. . . . Dr. Frazier's account stays close to the daily experiences of individuals and is grounded on the hard facts of the economic and social existence of typical communities." The author was well prepared by temperament and training for producing that kind of study.

E. Franklin Frazier was himself a son of the "crossways." Born in Baltimore, Maryland, he attended segregated elementary and high schools there, and then went on to get his bachelor's degree from a Negro institution in the area, Howard University in Washington, D.C. When he was asked to carry out the Youth Commission study he was head of the Department of Sociology at his Alma Mater (a post he held until his death in 1962). Known for his sense of humor and his appreciation of the ironies of human existence, Frazier would no doubt have referred to himself as a Prodigal Son of the area if he had been asked to comment upon his career. From Howard University he went North, to secure a master's degree from Clark University in Massachusetts; and he traveled widely in Europe and the Deep South before returning "home."

When he came back, he was a maverick neo-Marxist and remained one until his death, staying on the staff of *Science and Society* and refusing to trim his ideological sails regardless of pressures, whether from leftists who wanted him to toe a line or conservatives who feared that his radicalism might hurt Howard. Ensconced in one of the educational citadels of the Negro upper-middle class, Frazier never ceased to criticize and satirize the "black bourgeoisie" for what he considered its false values. He also ridiculed what he considered an escapist fantasy, "salvation by Negro business." He was convinced, too, that Negro businessmen, preachers, politicians, and even professors had a vested interest in preserving segregation and would probably sabotage any serious attempts to pull down the ghetto walls.

But Frazier was also what Negroes call a "race man." He didn't believe in sitting by waiting for economic forces to abolish segregation. He felt that Negroes, themselves, had to organize as a battering ram, forming coalitions with white allies (especially labor unions), probing, pushing, protesting, and constantly developing self-confidence and solidarity. He, himself, did not walk picket lines. He saw his own scholarly work as a contribution to the shattering of the myth of Negro inferiority. His own life and work show some of the ambivalence toward being a Negro in America that emerges as one of the most characteristic traits of the Negro youth at the crossways about whom he wrote. As the possibilities of integration grow nearer, this type of ambivalence grows stronger among all Negroes.

Frazier's ideological and intellectual orientation took form in the crisis period that followed World War I. He was working on his master's degree at Clark when race riots erupted throughout the United States in 1919, and his attention became focused upon the people of the Great Migration to the North and the consequences of their coming. He quickly defined his role as that of a participant-observer, accepting a post as Research Fellow at the New York School of Social Work in 1920. The next year he traveled to Denmark as a Fellow of the American-Scandinavian Foundation, beginning a quest for intellectual tools to help him understand and interpret what was happening to the Negro in America. The choice of a comparative frame of reference against which to view the race problem in America stayed with him throughout his life, and he eventually visited South America and the Caribbean. One of his best books is a study of race relations within a global context, *Race and Culture in the Modern World.*

Frazier was convinced that ghetto problems in the North could never be solved so long as the South made life for Negroes unbearable there. Booker T. Washington's "Let down your bucket where you are" philosophy had died with its originator in 1915. So, when Frazier was offered an appointment to direct the newly founded Atlanta School of Social Work in 1922, he took it and headed for the Deep South. But a man of Frazier's temperament could not survive in a Negro educational institution in the Georgia of the 1920's, for he was as proud of his reputation as a fighter as he was of his status as a scholar, and he was always forthright and outspoken. Legend has proliferated about the circumstances of his retreat from Atlanta, with Frazier emerging from the telling as a sort of combative hero, fighting a rear-guard action against the Ku Klux Klan. Whatever the facts of his leaving, he decided to go to Chicago in 1928, to continue a scholarly project in which he was involved, and to get his Ph.D.

During his five years at Atlanta, Frazier became convinced that the key to understanding the adjustment of the Negro to life in America lay in the knowledge of the history, structure, and dynamics of the Negro family. The eminent sociologist Robert Ezra Park, of the University of Chicago, had already taken him under his wing (as he had Charles S. Johnson before him) and Frazier elicited sympathetic support for a large-scale study of the Negro family. He presented the first installment for his Ph.D. thesis, *The Negro Family in Chicago,* in 1931.

There were no posts available at white universities for brilliant Negro scholars in those days, so Frazier accepted a position at Fisk University in Tennessee. It was inevitable that he would eventually leave Fisk, however, for he was a scholar who liked to work on his own, and the team research of Charles S. Johnson's social science institute was not to his taste. Coming to Howard in 1934 not only gave him an opportunity to develop a sociology department along lines of his own choice, but also placed him in a position to observe and participate in the activities of a large Negro community. While affiliated with Howard, he wrote a definitive social history, *Race and Culture in the Modern World,* and *The Negro Church in America,* as well as two lighter memoranda for the Carnegie-Myrdal work *An American Dilemma:* "Recreation and Amusement Among American Negroes" and "Stories of Experiences with Whites." He also served a term as president of the American Sociological Society. He was granted leave for three years (between 1951 and 1954) to accept an appointment in Paris as Chief of the Division of Applied Social Science of UNESCO, and wrote *Black Bourgeoisie* while there.

The American Youth Commission study was his first piece of research after going to Howard. When Frazier began this study he had just published *The Negro Family in the United States,* referred to by Ernest A. Burgess, a University of Chicago sociologist, as "the most valuable contribution to the literature on the family in twenty years." His special interest in the family is apparent in this study of the personality of Negro youth, but the book also reflects a wide range of interests the author had developed over a period of two decades, during which he had published widely in journals and magazines on subjects such as "Durham: Capital of the Black Middle Class" (1925) ; "The

American Negro's New Leaders" (1928); "The Garvey Movement" (1926); "Graduate Education in Negro Colleges and
Universities" (1932); "Children in Black and Mulatto Families" (1933); "Traditions and Patterns of Negro Family Life
in the United States" (1934). In 1936 he had been invited by
the City of New York to perform a post-mortem on the race riot
of 1935, and a portion of this research was published as "Negro
Harlem: An Ecological Study" (1937). Writing about Negro
youth in border communities gave him an opportunity to inte-
grate these diverse interests into a study of the impact of the
total community upon personality formation.

Frazier's study of the Negro family in Chicago was concerned
primarily with ecology, how different types of families and of
family disorganization were distributed spatially within the
Black Belt. He demonstrated conclusively that family stability
increased with the distance people lived from the center of the
city. The ecological approach was the favorite method of the
so-called Chicago School of Sociology at the time. When he
published *The Negro Family in the United States,* however,
it was clear that he was an apprentice no longer. The influence
of the Chicago School was still there but primarily in the emphasis upon social processes—the study of competition, conflict,
accommodation, and assimilation; but the emergence of a system of social stratification among Negroes was the primary
focus. Frazier had synthesized the points of view of several
groups of scholars into something uniquely "Frazierian." This
synthesis carried over into the Youth Commission study.

The author presents a short and useful section on the social
ecology of Washington and Louisville at the outset, but he
selected family and church as two crucial institutions for analysis,
and the neighborhood and school as two situations in which
values derived from home and church are tested as youth struggles for an identity. Like the other authors writing in the Youth
Commission series, he organized the research in such a way as
to contrast variations in life styles, attitudes, and world views of
youth at various class levels within the Negro subculture. That
not all Negroes are alike was a point stressed (and quite delib-
erately) in all of these studies.

Frazier's research strategy rejected the use of formal questionnaires. Instead, young Negroes from various social strata were encouraged to talk freely, and with a minimum of guidance from the interviewers, about their world and their place in it as they perceived it. Spontaneous and incisive comments about their life chances, about the white world which impinged upon them, and the segregated Negro world within which they lived most of their lives, were gathered by a group of seven interviewers in Washington and two in Louisville. They talked to, and listened to, 123 boys and 145 girls, stimulating them to express themselves freely and frankly on a number of specific topics. Three out of four of the young people came from homes where their parents, when employed, earned their living with their hands—most of them as laborers or domestic servants. The sample was representative of the occupational structure of the two communities.

Frazier had demonstrated his statistical sophistication in *The Negro Family in Chicago* and his handling of historical sources and life-history material in *The Negro Family in the United States*. In the youth study he preferred to employ another sociological style: the use of interview material to illustrate themes such as "Negroes Don't Stick Together," "The Lighter Ones Stick Together,""Hear and Not Hear," "Don't Be a Monkey for Whites," and to document social class differences in behavior and attitude. One reviewer for an academic journal was critical of this method and wrote that "the book evidently is intended to give 'insight.' It certainly doesn't give us much basis for generalization." But another professional colleague, reviewing for an equally prestigious journal, felt that "as all other publications by Frazier, the present one is characterized by its competence, readability, and scholarship. . . . It is worth its weight in gold." *The Annals of the American Academy of Political and Social Science,* which presents scientific data for the "influentials" and "opinion makers" in the country, considered *Negro Youth at the Crossways* "a mature book . . . a scholarly, candid, and penetrating analysis without sacrificing an iota of spontaneity or of human interest." And that is what the author meant the book to be, one written for the public—not for his more pedantic peers.

But the theoretical aspects of the problem are not ignored. They are presented in appendices, in one of which Frazier states his rejection of racial biological determinism, instinct psychology, orthodox Freudianism, and Pavlovian concepts in favor of the view that "in studying motives, wishes, attitudes, and traits of personality, we are dealing with emotions and impulses which have been organized and directed toward goals in the course of social interaction." What one learns from family, church, and peers are all factors in the individual's choice of goals, but Frazier reminds us that it is in a "more or less isolated social world with its peculiar social definitions and meanings and with its own social evaluations and distinctions that the personality of the Negro takes form and acquires meaning." (Appendix A: A Statement of the Relation of Culture and Personality in the Study of Negro Youth.) He utilized the concepts of comparative sociology to explain the prevalence of indices of social disorganization, commenting that "the Negro community in the border city exhibits all the characteristic pathological features of social life which one would expect among a racial minority of rural background and low economic status, and subject to all forms of economic and social discriminations." And he adds a very significant demographic variable: an unbalanced sex ratio. Incidentally, Negro women still greatly outnumber Negro men in Washington. (Appendix B: Supplementary Information on the Institutions, Social Movements and Ideologies, and Social Pathology of the Negro Community in Washington, D.C.).

But it is the case material itself that reveals with dramatic effect the impact of the social milieu upon these young people. Those from upper-class homes were confident that they would some day find useful and pleasant employment in professional and semi-professional pursuits (as Frazier states it, "behind the walls of segregation"). But the dominant mood of the lower-status youngsters was not so optimistic, and was evaluated by the author as one of "distrust and animosity" toward higher-status Negroes as well as toward whites. A thirteen-year-old illustrates the point with a somewhat bitter comment:

About one hundred to one the odds are against me in favor of the white boy. It doesn't matter how smart I am, what kind of family I'm from, what I know, or what I can do, my chances are slim compared with a boy with a white face. Negroes don't have the chances they ought to have—whites take care of that. That's one group that looks out for themselves.

Lower-class boys tended to take the position of a ten-year-old who said: "It doesn't make any difference to me what people think about the type of work I'm doing, just so I'm making a lot of money." Not caring where the money came from led some boys at this status level to blur the distinction between the legal and the illegal insofar as source of income was concerned, while holding to middle-class values in other respects. One boy shared his dream in these words:

I just want that job and a chance to earn good money. Any job will do that will provide that. I want to have a home of my own and, if possible, go into some business or racket. Liquor, numbers, or women, all the same to me. You know I used to be known as a bad egg around these parts and I've got a reputation to live up to. I've got to do something!

A more conventional view than the "money at any price" philosophy was expressed by a nineteen-year-old lad who commented:

I always wanted to be a mechanic . . . I believe the Negro's best chance in life is work with his hands. These so-called successful Negroes aren't doing a thing but 'jibing.' They get by with a lot of mouth, the kind of pull you can get with the rackets and paying your way through. I don't have any such friends and my folks don't have the money.

Merely reading such comments at random generates insight and evokes empathy, but the most rewarding approach to the book might be to begin with the Introduction and Chapter I ("The Negro Community"), followed by a study of Appendix B on Washington, and the Summary and Conclusion. Within the frame of reference provided by these sections, the substantive chapters will make sense read in any order, in whole or in part, as illustrative case material.

Some sociologists make a fetish of keeping their work "value-free." Frazier operated in a different tradition, that stated in C. Wright Mills' famous motto, "I do not claim to be detached; I try to be objective." For instance, Frazier had well-known strong feelings against one lingering legacy of slavery: Washington, New Orleans, Charleston, and several other Southern communities were notorious for the extent to which lighter-skinned Negroes felt superior to those of darker complexion. This is something most Negroes prefer not to talk about publicly. Frazier dragged it into the open because he felt that it had a damaging effect upon the personality of darker Negroes. The respondents were encouraged to talk about the matter. Yet, his treatment is restrained. He doesn't moralize or preach. He simply analyzes the historical roots of such attitudes and lets the "victims" tell their own poignant stories of how they are affected. He then puts the matter in perspective by pointing out that charges of such color discrimination were made almost entirely by girls against female school teachers. It falls into a broader context when he notes that "in the larger metropolitan areas a fair complexion has less value than in Washington," and that "within the larger Negro world status is determined by a form of competition in which individual success counts for more than skin color." To use modern slang, Frazier "keeps his cool," sure that the old upper class in Washington which perpetuates such snobbery will eventually be pushed aside in the inexorable competitive process. Today, with hundreds of Negro women of all complexions employed at clerical and managerial levels in government offices, the darker girls have successful role models and perhaps fewer of them feel the sting of this particular form of prejudice than a quarter of a century ago.

This study reveals that in-group color prejudice (even in Washington) was far less damaging in its consequences than white prejudice and discrimination against Negroes, who, at the time, were not even allowed in downtown movie houses. One of the more subtle effects of white dominance was revealed in the striking finding that "the majority of the Negro youth of all classes believe that God is white." The low self-esteem implicit in such a belief profoundly affected the personality of these young people. One youngster actually said, "I wish the ground would swallow me up," and another soliloquized, "I'm beginning to hate the fact that I'm a Negro. Yet, I know I might just as well be satisfied because, like a leopard, I can't change my spots." But the temper of the times has changed. The emergence of nearly forty independent African states and a vigorous civil rights movement have changed the image of the Negro and the Negro's image of himself. One result of these changes has been a lessening of actual discrimination. Concurrently, there has been an upsurge of race pride that ultimately gave rise to the Black Power movement, one wing of which has reconstructed the image of the deity, proclaiming that "God is black!" The psychological roots of the demand for Black Power are laid bare in this volume.

The generation portrayed in this study has grown up. The chances are that most of them, now men and women, are employed somewhere, even if not in the kinds of jobs they wanted or dreamed about—some even in positions better than they expected. Participation in the affluent society must have assuaged many racial wounds. But their children, and those of more recent migrants, on the whole have not been so favored. The unemployment rate among Negro young people is more than twice that for whites, and in some urban areas over a third of the Negro youngsters cannot find employment at any wage level they consider equal to their worth. The reasons for this state of affairs are complex, but can always be traced back to race prejudice and discrimination, indirectly if not directly: to neglected Negro schools that did not prepare them adequately for a time when pencil-and-paper tests are often the prerequisite for even menial jobs; to broken homes that did not motivate them (many of them the result of racial economics that depressed the status of Negro husbands vis-à-vis their wives) ; and to doors slammed too often in the face. Also, the successful parents have often repeated tales of their own unhappy experiences with "the man" (Whitey), and these feed the feelings of impotence and weaken self-confidence. To understand the youthful experiences of the fathers and mothers helps us to explain the attitudes of the children.

The distinguished psychoanalyst Harry Stack Sullivan cooperated with Frazier, whose social interactionist theory of personality development he shared. Sullivan interviewed twenty subjects and discusses one case in detail (Chapter VIII: Warren

Wall). He compared these border-city cases with others he had studied in the Deep South. In his view, *all* Negroes in America find their pursuit of success goals interfered with by the entrenched system of racial discrimination, and their sense of worth damaged by derogatory appraisals of Negroidness. To use a phrase coined by another analyst, Abram Kardiner, they all bear "the mark of oppression." Sullivan felt that the most general stigmata were a heavy load of anxiety and the adoption of compensatory and substitutive behavior, leading to a pronounced "immaturity" of personality. Because he lives in a world that sets up a goal of being something he is not allowed to become, "the border Negro struggles with rage where the Southern Negro suffers from fear." Sullivan assailed white America for allowing a system to continue that results in a "general very early distortion of personality, presumably by almost ubiquitous racial factors."

For the young people who express themselves through the pages of this book, what Sullivan calls "rage" was very deeply suppressed, sublimated in religious and social ritual, or manifested in criminal behavior by a few. Even grumbling about their fate had a subdued character. They did not find their catharsis through social movements, nor did they seek to reconstruct their world by social action. But the resentment was clearly there. It is obvious that Frazier wished they would act otherwise, comparing the border states unfavorably with the northern ghettos for lack of aggressive social movements, and commenting upon the "confusion of ideologies" that inhibited action.

During the early 1960's, however, Negro youth in the Deep South and in the Northern black ghettos began to rattle the bars and batter down the walls—non-violently through SNCC and CORE and the Southern Christian Leadership Conference, but more recently with arson and looting. Out of their ranks the cry for Black Power burst forth. The youth of the border cities cannot remain isolated from these currents and will become increasingly involved. Meanwhile, Washington has almost become a "black" city as the white middle class has withdrawn to the suburbs, leaving it to Negro Americans. The "black bourgeoisie" has increased in size, but not in influence or power—only in its ability to acquire the material symbols of status. The black mass has increased in size, too, and its children are among the alienated.

The grosser evidences of discrimination in public accommodations and the denial of access to white-collar jobs have been wiped away, but the conditions Frazier describes as the "Social Pathology of the Negro Community" have become more serious, not less so. The Negro masses in Washington, like those elsewhere, have profited little from the "partial integration" that the civil rights movement achieved. Ghetto schools remain poor. Inadequate housing, overcrowding, unemployment or inadequate employment still generate family disorganization, juvenile delinquency, narcotizing anodynes, and hedonistic escape—which in turn bring those occasional disorders during which the police become community targets, and riots often result. And there is no political outlet, for Southern Congressmen will not allow Home Rule for the District of Columbia. There is a black majority, but no Black Power in the nation's capital. It is inevitable that this generation of young people will demand it, even though their more cautious elders, whom this book describes in the process of their "becoming," have not.

Except in the fields of employment and public accommodations, the youth at the crossways in the late 1930's was not demanding "integration." For a brief period in the late 1950's, some of them, as adults, did broaden the demand—in neighborhood and school—but their white neighbors fled. The Washington race relations story is the general American urban story in an exaggerated form. Now, in their disillusionment, many Negroes—particularly adults at lower-class and lower-middle-class levels—and the youth generally, are questioning whether or not "integration" should remain the goal of Negro social action at all. They believe that first priority should be given to stimulating racial pride and solidarity, to the cultivation of a "dignity" that does not "beg" for integration with those who spurn them, for the renovation of the ghetto, and for the winning and consolidation of Black Power. Some, like the Black Muslims, actually look at white society with contempt and revulsion, and call for deliberate "separation." Others say, "we do not fight for integration or segregation, but for the right, eventually, to choose."

The relaxed qualities of "soul" are sometimes contrasted positively with the white-derived middle-class goal of "striving." Against these tendencies to exalt the Negro subculture, Frazier opted for tearing down the ghetto walls—physical and psychological—even if it meant a victory for the kind of bourgeois society he, himself, despised. Segregation creates an "artificial situation in which inferior standards of excellence and efficiency are set up"—this was his insistent message. Today's young black militants would answer back, "our black community does not *have* to be inferior. We can transform pathology into health." Frazier would reply with words from this book: "Since the Negro is not required to compete in the larger world and to assume its responsibilities and suffer its penalties, he does not have an opportunity to mature" (still his view in the posthumously [1964] published *Negro Church in America*). He died before Martin Luther King and other civil rights leaders began to challenge the maturity of the nation's leaders in the field of international relations.

Frazier presented *Negro Youth at the Crossways* as a clinical case study of the results of enforced segregation and isolation from the American mainstream. It is a significant contribution to the lively contemporary dialogue.

CONTENTS

PREFACE

Iₙ ᴏᴛʜᴇʀ senses than geographical, Negro
youth are at the "crossways" in the middle states. This volume,
the result of investigations conducted by E. Franklin Frazier,
describes the personal experiences of Negro boys and girls living
in Washington, D.C., and Louisville, Kentucky; these communities were selected as examples of middle-area conditions.
The author found many of these youth facing dilemmas that
are a part of the transition from a southern rural to a middle
states urban way of living, dilemmas that are related to the shift
in family patterns from slavery to self-sufficiency, dilemmas that
grow out of the area's culturally middle position between North
and South, and dilemmas that are related to Negro youth's new
economic freedom.

From the first pages of the volume, real youth speak their
minds on all of these matters, and what they say is checked with
the results of expert observers and interviewers who comprise
the research staff. Dr. Frazier's account stays close to the daily
experiences of individuals and is grounded on the hard facts
of the economic and social existence of typical communities.

The study is not dominated by any school of thought, nor
does it depend for its findings upon any one scheme of analysis
or method of inquiry. It makes use of many ways of determining the socio-psychological effects of being a Negro upon the
personality development of the individual boy or girl. The
author inquires: What are the typical situations these youth
face? What adjustments do they make? What frustrations do
they suffer? Does being a Negro mean something different if one
is born into a high social position within his own group or into a
low one? How do youth organizations in Negro communities
reflect the minority status of their members? These and other
questions of importance to those concerned with the relations of

personality and culture and to those interested in race relations are dealt with in this volume.

The attention given to community background, the analysis of conflict situations, the insight into the intimacies of personal relations, and the consideration of broader factors such as occupation, race tradition, and educational experience all attest the candor, breadth of scholarship, and objectivity of the author. E. Franklin Frazier, born in Baltimore, Maryland, was educated at Howard and Clark universities, from which he received his B.A. and M.A. degrees; at the New York School of Social Work; and at the University of Chicago, from which he received his Ph.D. in 1931. His academic experience includes teaching and administrative positions in public and private schools in Alabama, Georgia, Virginia, Maryland, and North Carolina, and professional work in his own field of sociology at Morehouse College in Georgia, Fisk University in Tennessee, and Howard University in the District of Columbia, where he has been the head of the department of sociology since 1934. For five years he served as director of the Atlanta School of Social Work.

Dr. Frazier has held research positions with the University of Chicago, the Social Science Research Council, and Mayor La Guardia's Commission on Conditions in Harlem. His publications include *The Negro Family in Chicago* and *The Negro Family in the United States,* as well as contributions to other volumes. Dr. Frazier has been awarded a John Simon Guggenheim fellowship for the year 1940-41 to make a study of the Negro family in Brazil and the West Indies.

ROBERT L. SUTHERLAND
Associate Director for Studies of Negro Youth

AUTHOR'S ACKNOWLEDGMENTS

THE AUTHOR is indebted to Edward B. Reuter and Ruth Shonle Cavan, who formulated the outline for the interviews, for their counsel and advice during the conferences which preceded the inauguration of the study. He also profited by the stimulating discussions in the periodic conferences of the area study directors which were from time to time called by Robert L. Sutherland. To Harry S. Sullivan, who graciously gave time from his schedule of duties to assist in the interviewing and in the discussion of various aspects of our cases, the author makes this acknowledgment of appreciation.

Certain members of the staff, the personnel of which is given at the end of the volume, deserve special mention for their cooperation in making this study possible. A word of appreciation is due first to Charles H. Parrish, instructor in sociology at the Louisville Municipal College for Negroes, who supervised the field work in Louisville and organized the materials on the Negro community. Appreciation is here expressed to Zulme S. MacNeal, who in addition to her work as secretary for the entire project typed interview materials as well as the entire manuscript. The author also wishes to thank Ruth Bittler not only for her work on community materials involving interracial relations but also for her services in helping in the analysis of the materials. To his secretary, Leora H. Nesbitt, the author is indebted for typing much of the final revision of the manuscript.

A final word of appreciation is due to the President and Trustees of Howard University who granted permission for the author to undertake the study and provided office space as well as the use of equipment.

E. FRANKLIN FRAZIER

INTRODUCTION

On the corner of two of the most run-down streets in the roughest neighborhood of the Southwest section of Washington, D.C., two Negro youth were lolling about the entrance to a funeral parlor. Freddie, fifteen, the younger of the two, was very black with an ashen complexion, five and a half feet tall, and weighed 130 pounds. His pearly white teeth, always visible through his pleasing smile, more than compensated for his unprepossessing appearance. Although he was constantly active, he carried himself with a slow shuffle which marked him as being lazy. Freddie had unusually good manners and was a great favorite at a near-by settlement house. Dick, seventeen, whose father was a janitor, was of very dark complexion with broad, blunt features and kinky hair. He stood five feet, eight inches and weighed about 150 pounds. He was an officer in the high school cadet corps and was proud of the status which it gave him as well as the uniform which it permitted him to wear. Dick always wore the numerous medals and pins which he had won at school and church, though some were supported only by threadbare and faded ribbons.

Freddie and Dick were waiting for the third member of the inseparable trio, Charlie, nineteen, who was helping his father, the undertaker, with some chores connected with the business. In fact, Charlie's house had become the "stamping ground" for the trio, who usually ambled over there to play checkers after spending a few hours each day at the settlement house. While waiting for the third member of the trio, Freddie and Dick spent their time conversing.[1]

Freddie—Today I played tennis for the first time this year and I sure got the hell beat out of me. I know I can play Ping-

---

[1] Their conversation was recorded by a former settlement worker who was friendly with the boys and had their confidence.

pong well, but it seems like you have to keep up tennis the same way.

Dick—You ain't so hot anyway. When I get a chance I'll come out and show you how the game's played.

Freddie—I've got to buy me another racket. I'm trying to get Charlie to sell me one of his. He's the only one of us who ever gets anything. And he's swell enough to share anything he owns. See that funeral there? Well, tomorrow Charlie will have a new suit, a new racket, and a lot of other things, and then we'll all have fun.

Dick—I'll be glad when I can have boys of my own like Mr. X [a former Negro settlement worker]. I want them to be good students in school, be perfect physically, and go to West Point. How am I going to do that? Well, I plan to have them born somewhere outside of Washington and see to it that the state senator and congressman sends him or them to the Academy. I think the army is the greatest thing a Negro can get into. That's one place where a Negro can get the respect a white man can get. Down at camp white soldiers almost broke their arms and legs snapping to attention and saluting to Negro officers. Look at Colonel Davis! He gets over $60 a week, room and board! His son is a Lieutenant at Camp Benning. White men look up to Negro officers and like it.

Freddie—I thought you wanted to get on the police force? You don't expect to get in with those flat feet, do you? Say, do policemen put in so many full hours a day or do they split their time up? Do they carry their "gats" around with them when they're off duty? I sure wouldn't want to be a policeman even off duty without a gun. Not as bad as the "niggers" are down here.

Just then Charlie, a very dark boy about six feet tall and weighing 160 pounds, emerged from the funeral parlor. He is very conscious of his appearance, always being sure that his curly black hair is in place and that his clothes are never ruffled. Charlie enjoys the reputation of being one of the best dressed boys in Southwest. In his officer's uniform during high school days, he was the idol of the girls and an object of envy among the boys. Since he is a splendid athlete and good boxer, the young men in this section respect his prowess. As soon as he rejoined his comrades, he began talking of his work with his father.

Charlie—I've been working on one stiff all evening. I heard you all talking and I couldn't stay in any longer. I'm trying to get both of these guys here to go to camp with me this summer. I'll get my commission after this year. Even the President's name will be on it.

Freddie—It sure is funny that the colored tennis courts are the last ones to be fixed up. We like tennis as well as the "pecks," and the courts at the other end of the Mall have been finished for white people and they've been playing on them for over a week. We used to be able to get permits to play on any courts; now the Mall courts are the only ones we can use and they fix them up last. Just goes to show you just what it means to be a "nigger."

Charlie (Turning to the former settlement worker)—As soon as we can get on the courts we want you. We haven't forgotten the "horse shoes" you had last year. Too bad you won't try to take it out on me in Ping-pong. On a table I'm a champion and I know it.

Dick—Well, gang, it's about time we go girl hunting. I ain't had no stuff all week. [Laughter]

Charlie—Don't pay him no mind. Both Dick and Freddie are at the age where their brains have gone down in their pants and when they can't find anything else to do they are running around with girls or talking about them. I like to talk about them, too, and these guys come to me for advice. What can I tell them they don't know?

Freddie (Addressing the former settlement worker)—You know we haven't had any chance to talk to anyone who seems to understand or who would not get all insulted by questions since you left the settlement house, and we just like to talk about things that bother us when you're around.

Dick—See that row of houses in this block? Well, there is a gang of good-looking "broads" through here, and all you've got to do is stop and open your car door and you've got you a "broad."

Freddie—We had a swell time when you were down here. Miss R can't seem to get along with anyone else and they haven't enough spunk to even get equipment they need. We could have a swell time if the House would give us a break. There's nothing else down here to do except run around with fast women and go to the show. We don't go to the beer joints and poolrooms, so there ain't much left. I suppose we'd be doing a lot of things we shouldn't if Charlie's father didn't let us hang around here.

Dick—I've tried to get a job all year, but any I found meant I had to give up school and I sure don't want to do that if I can help it.

Freddie—Well, you're a fool. You can always go to school but you can't always get a job. I wish I had a chance at a job. Last week I didn't have any shoes and I was out the whole week. I couldn't go to school barefooted, could I? I wanted to stay out this week and do some placard work with Mr. X, but he wouldn't let me. I wish he'd change his mind, because I could use the money.

Charlie—You're still in school, aren't you, Mr. X? I don't see any sense in a man going to school when he's as old as you. Take old lady R for example; by the time she gets out she'll be old enough to lay down and die. I stopped school when I finished high school last year and I've made more money with my little education than she's made with all her education. This is our fourth funeral this week—so I'll just wait—the old lady will be along soon. If Southwest and tightness don't kill her, Howard[2] will.

Dick—Well, I want to go to school as long as I can. I'd even like to go to college. But I don't guess it's much use, though. A colored man's best chance is to go in the army. I've always wanted to go to West Point, but I guess it's too late now. My folks won't be able to send me and unless I can earn some money that's out entirely.

Charlie—I want to get in the army, too. I was a captain in the cadet corps at school and I'll be a noncommissioned officer in the Reserve Corps this summer. I wish there'd be a good war. We'd get a break then. Negroes got the best breaks during the

[2] Howard University.

last war, and the white people will probably need us more this time than they did before. James and me will probably be used to train other men and we'll be right over here doing it.

[Here the boys began to engage in youthful boasting concerning their sexual prowess. During their conversations about sex matters, Charlie made the statement that "all Negroes are intercourse crazy" and that he got his "share."]

Charlie—That white fellow, Dr. Y, is a funny old coot. He asked so many damn fool questions that I got sick of him for a while. Then, I heard about the money he gave Bill and Henry and how he treated the fellows who went up to see him at Howard—I took a new interest in him. I could stand a lot of questioning for $5.00.

Freddie—I liked him all right, I thought he was one of the nicest white men I'd ever met. I didn't understand a lot of his questions or what he was driving at. It is unusual to have a white man really interested in Negroes. At first, I didn't trust him and even when I'd seen him a number of times I was suspicious. I just couldn't help feeling uncomfortable around that white man. Those I've known were either hard-boiled employers or white men who want to push Negroes around. You just can't learn to trust white people by one nice one. I guess there are others but I'll bet they're far between.

Dick—I liked him from the start. I thought he was a very funny guy. I was all right with him till he started asking questions about girls and my relations with them—how I found out I was a Negro and all that; I felt very uncomfortable. I don't like to talk to white people about what Negroes do like that. They sort of expect it anyway and it just makes us all look that much worse. I can talk to Mr. X or some other Negro I like or trust about such things—but it just seems out of place to tell such things to white people. You know in the first place that you wouldn't be expected to ask the same questions of them and, second, you just about know what they're expecting for answers. But he was smart, though, and when we got on the army and athletics we got along swell. I didn't hear about all that money that he passed around or I'd been there, too.

Charlie—I wish my old man would make enough money so I could take some nice long trips. I haven't been out of this city in years. It sure gets tiresome staying in one place, doing the same things, seeing the same old "broads."

Freddie—You're lucky! My old man has a fairly good job, but he doesn't make enough money for me to expect to take any trips. Every once in a while I think about just getting out on my own and seeing the world. Well, I've got sense enough to know I couldn't get far without money. So I just put it off each time.

Dick—You guys got a lot to kick about. I don't have a father and I don't have a job. My mother has to support me. I'd like to leave home, too—and some day I will—but I can't go as long as my mother depends on me to stick around. These freights that go by look awful tempting, though.

Charlie—Dick has already made up his mind to send a son of his to West Point. How do you expect to do it, Hoghead?

Dick—They've still got senators and congressmen, haven't they? Well, if a boy of mine could be smart in school and make good grades and was physically perfect, they couldn't keep him out of West Point. I'll see that my wife gives birth to him in some state outside the District. All my life I have dreamed of going, and wished it might be possible. Now I know how slim my chances are. I'm no brilliant student at school but I could be if I was working toward something. It's all just because I'm a black boy instead of a white one that makes the difference. White people don't care what you are as long as you're not a "nigger."

Freddie—Well, you'll have to be satisfied with the Citizens' Training Camp. They ought to make you a general—you and Charlie both like it so well. I like to drill—I think I'd like the camp, too, but army life, never! Say, it's about time you're returning Mr. X's book I loaned you, Hoghead. If you don't get it back to him, he probably won't let me have another. You know how I hate to read schoolbooks. I read the same trash that you guys do, but that's different. I was supposed to read and report on *The Last of the Mohicans, Lady of the Lake,* and *Robin Hood;* but I never got to read them, and I'd have flunked sure, if Mr. X hadn't loaned me a book with all those stories in it, in a very few sentences.

Dick—Well, I like to read and as a rule I just can't find enough good books to read. The public library hasn't many and they're old as hell—and I haven't any of my own. I wish I could find some good adventure and detective stories.

Charlie—That's kid stuff—I haven't read a book since I graduated last year—and I wouldn't waste my money to go to college. I read the newspapers and a few magazines but otherwise you can keep that reading "jibe." Reading a lot of books is the same as those phoney medals Hoghead wears. [Smiles]

Dick—Don't let these medals bother you, pal. I'm proud of them and you'd be, too, if you had them. I got this one for marksmanship, this for being a member of the winning squad last year, and this one for distinguished service on patrol duty. That's more than you've got. Your father ought to be pretty near through now. Let's see if we can start that checker game. I can't beat you guys at tennis and Ping-pong and I may be a chump at those games, but at this I'm champ and you guys know it.

Much of the spontaneous conversation of these three Negro youth is the same as that of white youth in similar circumstances. There is the usual interest in athletics and games, the same difference of opinion concerning the relative advantage of continuing their education or entering immediately upon a business career, the longing of boys of this age for new experiences as an escape from routine and familiar places, and a type of interest in sex often found in slum areas. One observes, too, that the oldest of the trio is conscious of having reached the age when one begins to lose interest in the type of fiction, "kid stuff" as Charlie calls it, which still appeals to Dick, two years his junior. But one is struck by the fact that an ever recurring subject in their conversation is the fact that they are Negroes. In fact, consciousness of being Negroes seems to cast a shadow over their hopes and ambitions. As Dick, who has dreamed all his life of going to West Point, remarks: "Now I know how slim my chances are. I'm no brilliant student at school but I could be if I was working toward something. It's all just because I'm a black boy instead of a white one that makes the difference." Although Dick has projected his ambition upon his unborn sons, the prospect of a career in the army is not merely a fulfillment of an ambition for himself or children, but the army is a place where the Negro can acquire status and secure the respect of white people.

The experience of being a Negro has bred in these youth a suspicion and wariness in regard to white people. A Negro must be on his guard when he talks to them, especially when it concerns the more intimate aspects of his behavior. Not only should he not share his most intimate experiences with white people, but he must not reveal certain things about his conduct which would only confirm what they think of Negroes. One must even suspect the motives of friendly white people; for, as Freddie remarks, one "can't learn to trust white people by one nice one." However, one notes that whereas the Negro must erect these defenses against white people, he must take unusual precautions against such people "as bad as the niggers" in Southwest. The very use of the word "nigger," though accepted good-naturedly within the group, smacks of the white man's appraisal of the Negro. Nor can one overlook Charlie's remark that "all Negroes are intercourse crazy," which, if it does not represent the white man's appraisal of Negroes, at least differentiates them from white people.

Consciousness of their status as Negroes and the discriminations which they suffer because of their racial identity not only influences their attitudes toward white people and toward themselves but also affects their attitudes toward broader issues facing mankind generally. War, with its horrors and suffering, is viewed from the standpoint of its effect upon the treatment and the status of Negroes. Dick, who thinks that "white people don't care what you are as long as you're not a nigger," wishes for a "good war" because he believes that the Negro would get a break. Behind his desire for a war in which he hopes the status of the Negro will be improved, there may lurk impulses toward aggression fostered in a world of frustrated hopes and ambitions.

Of the more subtle effects of being a Negro upon their developing personalities their conversation reveals little. Freddie's reply to Dick that he "will have to be satisfied with the Citizens' Training Camp" seems to express an attitude of accommodation to discrimination. But one cannot be sure to what extent such verbal responses are an indication of freedom from inner conflicts or feelings of revolt. On the other hand, one may be sure, their feelings and emotions as well as their rationalizations and overt responses to the situation in which Negroes find themselves have been conditioned by their experiences within the more or less isolated world of the Negro.[3] Consequently, before attempting to analyze the specific effects of family, school, church, and other social influences upon the organization of their personalities in regard to their status as Negroes, we shall first explore the general culture of the Negro world into which these youth are born.[4]

[3] See Appendix A for a statement of the conception of personality basic to our analysis.

[4] A note here on the methods and materials used in this study will enable the critical reader to judge the value of the data upon which it is based as well as the validity of its generalizations and conclusions. First, it should be pointed out that the youth who served as subjects were not selected according to statistical methods of sampling. Groups of youth were chosen in such numbers with respect to the occupation of their parents and residence in the city as to correspond roughly to the distribution of the Negro population according to socio-economic groupings and according to residence in the five zones of settlement. (See Tables II, III, and IV in Appendix C.) The youth selected were members of such groups as Boy and Girl Scout troops, dramatic, social, and recreational clubs connected with the settlement houses, the Y.M.C.A. and Y.W.C.A.; groups of upper-class youth in the high schools; a group of delinquents, a group of domestic workers, and a club from a Baptist Sunday school. A small number of youth were picked up at random on the playgrounds and on the streets. The 28 boys and 33 girls who were studied in Louisville as a check on the Washington materials were selected on the basis of materials which had been collected on the social stratification of the Negro community. The work in Louisville was carried on under the direction of Charles H. Parrish, instructor in sociology at the Louisville Municipal College for Negroes. Throughout the study, materials from Louisville as well as those from Washington are used as a basis of analysis since there were no significant differences between the cases secured in these two border cities. Secondly, this study is based almost entirely upon documents which were secured through interviews with the youth and their parents. Young colored men and women who had completed college and had had some graduate training in addition to experience in interviewing were used as interviewers. They were provided with a guided interview outline which the directors of the study in the four areas had assisted Ruth Shonle Cavan in preparing. The interviewers were required to memorize the outline and to make trial interviews which were discussed with the director before they entered upon the regular field work. The interviews were read by the director who constantly conferred with the interviewers during their contacts with the subjects, some of whom were interviewed as many as five or six times. Although the white psychiatrist had contacts with about twenty boys, he devoted most of his time to one subject; the results of these contacts are given in the chapter in which the case of Warren Wall is presented. In addition to the background materials which the author had already accumulated, much of the data on the community, especially those on race relations, were secured by a white investigator who had access to the other side of the color line.

PART I

FACTORS AFFECTING THE PERSONALITY OF NEGRO YOUTH

CHAPTER I

THE NEGRO COMMUNITY

THE BORDER states, the area with which our study is concerned, became differentiated from the old South during the growth of the cotton kingdom. Although, as the cotton kingdom moved westward, slavery was introduced into Missouri, it never thrived there as in the old South. Nor did great plantations with hordes of Negro slaves find a congenial soil in Kentucky. Likewise, in Maryland, where slavery was confined to the eastern tidewater area, the slave system was fast disappearing at the outbreak of the Civil War. There had never been more than a sprinkling of slaves in Delaware and the District of Columbia. The failure of the cotton kingdom to become established in the border states determined their attitude toward secession. Consequently, though Lincoln's "border state" policy was not entirely successful, Missouri, Maryland, and Kentucky did not secede, and the loyal western third of Virginia was admitted to the Union in the same year in which the Emancipation Proclamation was issued.

CHARACTER OF THE NEGRO POPULATION IN THE BORDER STATES

To the Negro, the differentiation of the border states from the old South has had a peculiar significance. Before emancipation even the Negro slave felt that the "peculiar" institution was milder in the border states than in the old South. After the Negro became a freedman and a citizen, he was even more conscious of the differences which affected his status in the two sections. In the border states he has enjoyed a greater security of life and property and his children have had a better opportunity to get an education. Though he has been segregated and denied certain civil rights, caste-like restrictions such as characterize the old South have been less rigid and racial antipathies have been less violent. The record of lynchings for the fifty-five year period from 1882 to 1936 shows that in Mississippi alone the number of lynchings has been double that of the six border states combined. Only in Kentucky has the number of lynchings been comparable to that in the states of the old South. As regards educational opportunities, one finds that in 1930 the percentage of Negro children from 7 to 13 years of age attending school in the border states ranged from 91.1 per cent in Kentucky to 96.6 per cent in the District of Columbia, whereas in no state in the old South did the percentage reach 90. Moreover, in most of the states of the old South the percentage of illiteracy in the age group 10 to 14 was from two to four times as high as in Kentucky which had the highest rate among border states.[1] Besides having superior educational advantages, the Negro in the border states has been able to exercise what is generally regarded as the mark of citizenship, namely, the right to vote. It is not strange then that the Negro in the border states may deny that he is a southerner or in speaking disdainfully of the South may declare that he will never go South "where Negroes are not treated as men."

In 1930 there were about a million Negroes, or approximately 9 per cent of the Negroes in the United States, in the six border states, that is, Delaware, Maryland, West Virginia, Kentucky, Missouri, and the District of Columbia. Unlike the Negroes in the old South, the Negro population in the border states, exclusive of the District of Columbia, constitutes a relatively small part of the total population. In Kentucky and Missouri, Negroes constitute one out of sixteen; in West Virginia, one out of twelve; in Delaware, one out of seven or eight; and in Maryland, one out of six. In the District of Columbia, where the population is entirely urban, the proportion of Negroes amounts to slightly more than one out of four. Moreover, from 1910 to 1930 the proportion of Negroes in the population of these states remained practically unchanged. Then, too, whereas in the old South the vast majority of the Negroes live in the state of their birth, a comparatively large proportion of Negroes

---

[1] Horace Mann Bond, *Education of the Negro in the American Social Order* (New York: Prentice-Hall, Inc., 1934), p. 184.

in the border states are migrants. In West Virginia, Missouri, and the District of Columbia from 50 to 60 per cent are migrants, while in the remaining three states from a fifth to a third were born outside of the state in which they reside.

In regard to some other characteristics, the Negroes of the border states are not so sharply differentiated from those of the old South. Since the Negro population of the border states is more urbanized than that of the old South, it is not surprising that there are fewer children in the population of the border states. The slightly lower birth rates and slightly higher death rates in the border states than in the old South are also probably due to the urbanized character of the Negro population in the former area. On the surface, home ownership and the marital status of the Negro population in the border states are not different from those of Negroes in the old South. If, however, we take the proportion of families with women heads as an indication of broken family life, the border states appear to a greater advantage than the old South. This difference is especially marked among rural families in the two areas. On the other hand, one would hesitate to attribute any particular significance to the fact that Delaware and Maryland have higher illegitimacy rates than the states in the old South since this is offset by lower rates in West Virginia and Kentucky.

The most important single factor which differentiates the Negro population of the border states from that of the old South is the degree of urbanization. In this respect, the Negro population of the border states occupies a position between the Negro population in the North and the South. In the six border states as a whole, including the completely urbanized population of the District of Columbia, three out of four of the Negro inhabitants are city dwellers. Although only a fourth of the Negro population in West Virginia is urbanized, the majority of the rural Negro population is in industrialized areas. In Kentucky and Maryland slightly more than half, and in Delaware slightly less than half of the Negroes live in cities. In Missouri three out of four Negroes live in cities, over 40 per cent of the Negroes in the state being in the city of St.

Louis. Because of the urban character of the Negro population in the border states, this study is concerned with the Negro adolescent in two urban areas.

THE NEGRO COMMUNITY IN THE BORDER CITY

In the border and southern cities, the Negro population does not show the same degree of segregation and compactness as the Negro communities in the cities of the North. In the northern city the Negro, like the immigrant, has settled first in the deteriorated slum areas surrounding the financial and business centers. As business and industry have encroached upon these slum areas, the Negro population has expanded into contiguous areas. But border cities tend to exhibit the same pattern in regard to location of their Negro populations as southern cities, where historical rather than economic factors have determined to a large extent the location of Negro residence districts. In Washington, D.C., and Louisville, Kentucky, the two border cities chosen for study, the Negro population is widely scattered.

DISTRICT OF COLUMBIA

The Negro has been identified with the nation's capital since its establishment in the District of Columbia. A Negro mathematician named Benjamin Banneker served on Major L'Enfant's commission which surveyed the city. In 1800, the year in which the seat of the federal government was established in Washington, there were 623 slaves and 123 free Negroes in a total population of 3,210.[2] Though slavery on the whole was not particularly harsh at the seat of the federal government, Washington achieved a bad reputation because it served as a depot for the interstate slave traffic. During the sixty years from 1800 to 1860 the slave population of the entire District of Columbia rose from 783 to 3,185, while the free Negro population increased from 3,244 to 11,131. The greatest increase in the free Negro population was in the city of Washington proper, where the free Negroes from the South sought a more congenial environment.

---

[2] William Henry Jones, *The Housing of Negroes in Washington, D.C., a Study in Human Ecology* (Washington: Howard University Press, 1929), p. 27. In 1800 Washington was only a part of the District of Columbia.

Growth of the Negro Population Following the Civil War

Following the Civil War, Washington was considered to be a promised land by the freedmen. Here, under the protection of the government that had been responsible for their emancipation, the Negroes expected to enjoy the full benefits of freedom. Table I indicates the rapid growth of the Negro population in the capital from 1860 to 1930. The most rapid increase took place between 1860 and 1870, when thousands of

TABLE I

TOTAL POPULATION AND NEGRO POPULATION OF THE DISTRICT OF COLUMBIA, 1860-1930[a]

Year	Negro	Total
1860	14,316	75,080
1870	43,404	131,700
1880	59,596	177,624
1890	75,572	230,392
1900	86,702	278,718
1910	94,446	331,069
1920	109,966	437,571
1930	132,068	486,869

[a] *Negroes in the United States 1920-1932* (Washington: U. S. Bureau of the Census, 1935), pp. 9-10.

ignorant and impoverished Negroes flooded the District and naturally created a tremendous social problem. According to a report made to the Senate at the time by General O. O. Howard of the Freedmen's Bureau, many of the refugees were crowded into filthy, floorless hovels unfit for human habitation, for which they were forced to pay exorbitant rents. In order to relieve this situation the Freedmen's Bureau provided tenements in public buildings and fitted up barracks in and near Washington. Yet the sordid realities of living in the nation's capital failed to dissipate the illusion that drew thousands of emancipated blacks to Washington. Some of those seeking a refuge in the capital following Reconstruction were the educated and more prosperous leaders who fled from the wrath of southern whites when "white supremacy" was re-established in the South.

Although the Negro inhabitants before the Civil War were badly enough housed, it was not until after the Civil War that the alleys of Washington became the special abode of Negroes.[3] In 1872 it was estimated that 3,000 whites as against 22,000 or about half the Negroes lived in alleys. Forty-one years later, the Negro population in the alleys, according to a police census, had declined one-half and the white population to less than a thousand. In 1927, a firsthand investigation of 206 alleys in which 2,489 houses were located in 1912, revealed that only 150 of these alleys were inhabited and that they contained 1,495 houses.[4] During the depression, many of the uninhabited alleys once again became a refuge for dispossessed families. According to the estimates of the Alley Dwelling Authority made in 1937 there were 176 inhabited alleys containing 2,500 houses.

From time to time, welfare workers and humanitarians have protested against the condition of the Negro in the alley, but the power of landlords has been sufficient to halt periodic attempts to condemn alley dwellings. Consequently, many impoverished and ignorant Negroes have continued to live in the alleys until the inauguration of a more enlightened social policy. This has appeared in the creation of the Alley Dwelling Authority in 1934 which has cleared up many of the worst sore spots and has built several low-cost housing projects for Negroes. That the Authority succeeded during the single fiscal year ending June 30, 1937, in demolishing 77 houses offers a fair promise that the aim of the Alley Dwelling Act to rid the District of alley dwellings by 1944 will be accomplished.[5]

Areas Inhabited by the Expanding Negro Population

From the beginning of the Negro community in Washington some Negroes because of their thrift and intelligence

[3] *Ibid.*, p. 31.
[4] *Ibid.*, Appendix.
[5] Reports of Alley Dwelling Authority for the District of Columbia: 1934-35, 1935-36, 1936-37.

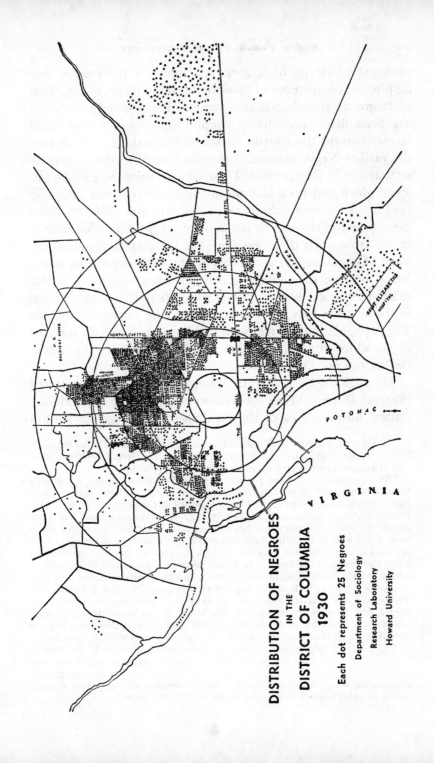

DISTRIBUTION OF NEGROES
IN THE
DISTRICT OF COLUMBIA
1930

Each dot represents 25 Negroes

Department of Sociology
Research Laboratory
Howard University

managed to escape from areas inhabited by the masses. But despite the competence of exceptional individuals, the location of Negro neighborhoods and homes, though widely scattered, has been determined by a complex of economic and social factors beyond the control of the individual. It appears that the earliest Negro communities were located in the Southwest section and in Georgetown. These communities were located in areas which had been abandoned by white residents generally because of the encroachment of commerce and industry. From these communities the Negro population has expanded mainly in a northwesterly direction along the thoroughfares and in the wake of commerce. It is not easy to trace the expanding population because the movement has not been as orderly as, for example, the expansion of the Negro population in Chicago or New York City.[6] Moreover, when the expansion of the Negro population has met with stubborn resistance on the part of the white community, it has overflowed into new communities on the outskirts of the city.[7]

Although the Negro population appears to be widely scattered over the District, heavy concentrations of Negroes encircle the central business area of the city.[8] (See map, page 9.) Within

[6] E. Franklin Frazier, "Negro Harlem: An Ecological Study," *The American Journal of Sociology,* XLIII (July 1937), 72-88; and *The Negro Family in Chicago* (Chicago: University of Chicago Press, 1932), pp. 91-97.

[7] The 1940 census gives the population of the District as 663,153; if the ratio between whites and Negroes is the same as in 1930, the Negro population is about 175,000. In 1930, Negroes resided in all of the 95 census tracts into which the District has been divided. In 53 of these tracts, Negroes comprised less than 5 per cent of the total population and their numbers did not exceed 500 in any single tract. There were 18 tracts in which they constituted from 10 to 20 per cent of the population and numbered from 500 to 1,500 persons. In the next 10 tracts in which they amounted to from 20 to 30 per cent of the population their numbers ranged from 1,000 to 3,000 in a single tract. In the 8 tracts in which they constituted a third to a half of the population, there were 1,000 to 4,000 Negroes. There were also 8 tracts with 3,000 to more than 5,000 Negroes constituting from a half to three-quarters of the inhabitants in the tracts. In each except one of the 9 remaining tracts, there were from 3,000 to more than 8,000 Negroes comprising more than three-fourths—90 per cent in four tracts—of the population.

[8] The city of Washington, which has been coterminous with the District of Columbia since 1895, was laid out in quadrants corresponding to the four points of the compass with the Capitol as the center; but in the natural organization which has grown up, the central business area is located roughly in the neighborhood of F and Thirteenth Streets, Northwest.

the central business section (designated as Zone I), covering a half-mile area and including nearly two census tracts, there were in 1930 only 330 Negroes but within the next three-quarter mile zone (Zone II) encircling the central business area

TABLE II

DISTRIBUTION OF THE NEGRO POPULATION IN THE DISTRICT OF COLUMBIA ACCORDING TO ZONES, 1930[a]

Zones[b]	Number	Per Cent
Zone I—½ Mile	330	0.2
Zone II—¾ Mile	48,447	36.7
Zone III—1 Mile	51,669	39.1
Zone IV—1 Mile	19,212	14.6
Zone V—To Boundary	12,410	9.4
TOTAL	132,068	100.0

[a] Figures compiled by the Department of Research and Statistics, Council of Social Agencies, Washington, D.C., from federal census data for 1930.

[b] The zones vary in width because the census tracts were grouped to correspond with the natural areas of Negro settlement.

there were 48,447 Negroes, or nearly three-eighths of the entire Negro population in the District. This zone embraces a large part of the old Southwest community described in a Senate Report as follows:

The Southwest section has been the "problem child" of Washington housing students for three generations. Separated from the Northwest by the Mall and bounded by waterfront on two sides, the Southwest is characterized by old and depreciated housing, the second largest number of inhabited alleys in any police precinct, and a fair percentage of old family residences whose owner-occupants, loyal to their neighborhood, see themselves more closely hemmed in each day by decaying housing. Census statistics show a steady diminution in the population of the Southwest. This reduction in population . . . has been halted, probably by the reduced economic status of families who moved to the Southwest in quest of lower rents.[9]

Fourth Street, running through the heart of this area, serves

[9] *Rent and Housing Conditions in the District of Columbia.* 73rd Congress, 2nd Session, 1934. Senate Document No. 125, Part 2, pp. 8-9.

as a business and an amusement center for the Negro population. This area is regarded by whites and Negroes as the "worst
place to live in Washington." Negro families that have moved
out of Southwest often prefer to forget this part of their history,
while Negroes in Southwest continue to speak contemptuously
of the "dicties" (snobs) in Northwest, where the majority of the
Negro population in this zone are located.

It is not, however, in the section of the Northwest area en-
compassed by the second zone that the so-called "dicties" live
because in this part of the Northwest area there are within sight
of the Capitol a large number of Negro families occupying
dilapidated dwellings in the side streets and alleys next to
white families. The section of the Northwest thus referred
to lies within the third and fourth zones of the area north of
Florida Avenue in which are located some better types of
middle-class neighborhoods and Howard University. The recreational and business center of Northwest is located in the U
Street area which is often referred to as "the center of Washington's Little Harlem." Going eastward on U Street from
Fourteenth Street, one finds whisky stores, Negro night clubs,
a government building, dance halls, poolrooms, the Republic
and the Lincoln theaters, the offices of Negro lawyers, physicians, and dentists, beauty parlors, barber shops, funeral homes,
and restaurants. At Twelfth Street is the Metropolitan Police
Boys' Club and at Eleventh Street is the only Negro bank in
Washington. During warm weather Negroes "cruise" in cars
along U Street, and laughing and chattering crowds cluster at
the corners. In fact, men and women from all walks of life may
be met along this main thoroughfare of Negro life in the
Northwest section.

The U Street area, however, is only the focal point of the vast
number of recreational, commercial, and industrial institutions
in the section of the Northwest Negro community located in
the third zone. In the same area one finds the American League
Baseball Park, a jumble of large and small businesses, a large
bakery, garages, lumber and coal yards, and warehouses. The
residences surrounding and sandwiched among these institutions

are generally run-down slum houses occupied by the poorer classes of Negroes. Nevertheless, on the fringe of this area, which merges with the Negro area in the next zone, are well-kept neighborhoods occupied by the professional classes and government workers.

The Negro population within the fourth zone dwindles to less than 20,000 and is scattered over a wide area. Three areas of concentration sharply differentiate this zone from the two preceding zones containing the bulk of the Negro population. First, there is the community in the Northeast section in which Kingman Park and the Langston low-cost housing project are located. This government subsidized low-cost housing unit occupied by wage-earning families is located close to a new Negro school and large recreation grounds. To the south, on the other side of Benning Road is Kingman Park, a part of which, it is reported, has been covenanted for white occupancy exclusively. The Negro section is occupied by upper-class families whose standards of living are reflected in their homes and the general tone of their neighborhoods. The second Negro community in the third zone is located north of Rhode Island Avenue in the Northeast section. In this area, known as Brookland, upper-class Negro families have bought and built comfortable and attractive homes despite opposition on the part of white residents. In this same zone, but in the Northwest section, a number of upper-class Negro families have secured comfortable homes west of Georgia Avenue and north of Fairmont Street.

The fifth or outermost zone encompasses the remainder of the District of Columbia. Although Negro residents of this area are widely scattered, there are two areas of concentration which form large and important communities. There is first the Deanwood section, which experienced rapid growth following the turn of the century. It was first settled by wage earners seeking cheap rent and land. Located to the east of Eastern Branch and its swampy lowlands and in the neighborhood of lumber mills and slaughter pens, Deanwood has lacked the desirable features generally associated with suburban developments. The old

Deanwood has remained practically a suburban slum with shacks and frame houses in need of paint and repair. Recently some real estate agents have developed to the east such areas as DePriest Village and Capitol View designed for Negro upper-class occupancy. Their bright new brick houses, occupied by government clerks, post office employees, teachers, and other professional workers, offer a striking contrast to Deanwood and the near-by shantytown of Marshall Heights.

LOUISVILLE, KENTUCKY

Unlike the rapidly increasing Negro population of the District of Columbia, the number of Negroes in Louisville increased only 6,000 during the twenty years from 1910 to 1930. Because of migrations to Cleveland, Chicago, and Detroit the Negro population had decreased 500 between 1910 and 1920. The increase during the next decade was due largely to an influx of migrants from the rural districts and small towns of the state. In 1930 the Negro population numbered 47,354, or 15.4 per cent of the total population of Louisville.

Although Negroes live in practically all sections of Louisville, there are areas of concentration similar to those found in other border cities. The areas of greatest concentration are just outside the central business zone. (See map, page 15.) One such area, known as "Downtown," is seven blocks wide—Broadway to Jefferson—and extends westward for a distance of twenty-five blocks—Sixth to Thirty-first Street. The approximately 20,000 Negroes in this area in 1930 constituted nearly two-thirds of the total resident population. Negroes are not, however, evenly distributed over this area, which for purposes of analysis may be divided into three zones indicating the westward expansion of the Negro community. Negroes have almost crowded out the entire white population in the first zone—Sixth to Fourteenth Street—the slum section just outside the central business area. Nearly three-fourths of the structures in this area are multiple dwellings and 30 per cent of them are unfit for use. Very few of the families, 3 per cent, are home owners, while half of the residents pay monthly rentals of less than $5.00. The highly mobile character of the residents in this

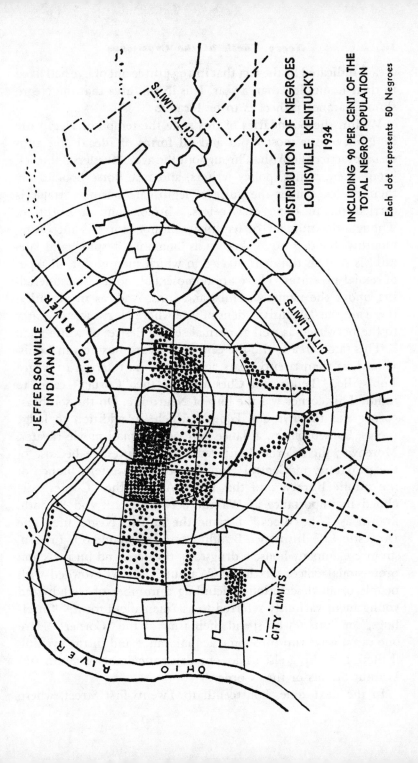

JEFFERSONVILLE
INDIANA

OHIO RIVER

OHIO RIVER

CITY LIMITS

CITY LIMITS

CITY LIMITS

DISTRIBUTION OF NEGROES
LOUISVILLE, KENTUCKY
1934

INCLUDING 90 PER CENT OF THE
TOTAL NEGRO POPULATION

Each dot represents 50 Negroes

area is indicated by the fact that in 1934 three out of five had lived in their homes less than a year. It is in this area that the Negro slum clearance project is to be located.

Within the boundaries of this zone the tempo of Negro life in Louisville is most rapid and all forms of illegal and anti-social practices flourish. Throughout the area "hustlers," thieves, "con" men, pimps, policy writers, and race horse bookies ply their trades. Under the guise of legitimate business, traffic is carried on in dope or "reefers," liquor, and prostitution. Though the number of legitimate liquor stores is increasing monthly, bootleg liquor known as "mammy," "splo," and "de-rail" is sold in the dens of vice to which men go for all types of sexual pleasures. There are homosexual "joints" masquerading under the names of clubs and inns. And, as in all cities, there are the "exclusive" dens of vice where Negro women cater to the perverted as well as normal sexual desires of white men.

This same area is also the center of Negro business in Louisville. Less than twenty years ago, when one referred to Negro Louisville, "Tenth and Chestnut" or the "Corner" came to mind. This corner was the hub of Negro life. On the southeast corner was the Pythian Temple which, in addition to lodge rooms, housed offices, a dance hall, and a small movie theater. Moreover, the "Corner" enjoyed a certain prestige because of the proximity of Central High School, the western branch of the public library, and the Y.M.C.A. But the "Corner" declined in importance as Walnut between Sixth and Seventh, known as "The Block," became the hub of Negro life. The Domestic Life Insurance Building and the Mammoth Life Insurance Company house a drugstore, theaters, and business and professional offices. Sixth and Walnut is always crowded with people of all descriptions, including a number of well-dressed young men, variously referred to as "men-about-town," "jitter-bugs," or "cats," who spend their time at the "Corner." Here one can always run into some acquaintance and in the evening if there is nothing else to do, one drifts inevitably to Sixth and Walnut Streets or the "Corner."

In the next zone, Fourteenth to Twenty-first Street, where

Negroes comprise three-fourths of the residents, one out of five of the structures is a multiple dwelling and only 13 per cent of the structures are unfit for use. Rentals are distinctly higher than in the first zone and home ownership amounts to 30 per cent. Located in this area are the Congregational Church, the most exclusive Negro church in Louisville, the Madison Street Junior High School, and the large elementary school whose principal was well-known in educational circles for over forty years. Until about twenty years ago the farthest extension of the Negro population westward did not go beyond this zone.

Since 1916 the Negro population has moved westward as far as Thirty-first Street, with a few Negroes finding a dwelling place in the alleys beyond. This third zone, from Twenty-first to Thirty-first Streets, where only a third of the residents are colored, is the most desirable residential district for Negroes. There are relatively few multiple dwellings and less than 3 per cent of the dwellings are unfit for use. Half of the families own their own homes and those who rent pay relatively high rentals. The westward movement of the Negro population, involving the higher social and economic classes, has come up against the exclusive white residential area known as "Shawneeland" at Thirty-first Street.

To the east of the central business district is a Negro slum area. The northern portion, sometimes referred to as "Uptown," is characterized by abject poverty and by high delinquency and crime rates. The southern portion of the area, known as "Smoketown," has on the whole a much better character. There are some home-owning families and rents are fairly high. In fact, some of the most prominent Negro families lived in this area before they found a more congenial environment west of the central business district. Within this area are such institutions as a junior high school, a branch library, and a neighborhood theater. Since the northern portion of the area has been chosen as the site of the four-million-dollar, white slum-clearance project, the Negro population will soon be moved.

Southwest of the central business area there is a string of Negro communities extending, with a single break, to the city limits. In the most westerly of these communities, California, there is a group of white-collar workers, doctors, teachers, and other professionals, many of whom own their homes. Just south of this area is a community known as "Cabbage Patch." Though a large section of this area has many undesirable features as a residential zone, a fairly large proportion, 31 per cent, of the families own their homes. Farther south is what is known as South Louisville. This community is composed almost entirely of home owners, the majority of whom are employed in the Louisville and Nashville Railroad shops.

Special mention can be made of only one other community, Parkland. The southern portion of this community, known as "Little Africa," was founded about half a century ago. In 1916 this community was described by a resident as follows:

> There are about 700 black homes, 400 black children of school age, one black county school, six black churches, six black groceries and the following list of black workmen: five bricklayers, six carpenters, nine concrete workers, one blacksmith, two paper hangers, three contractors and builders, three plasterers, two ice men, two farmers, and two doctors. It is a part of the city where the word "segregation" breeds no terror and conjures up no law suits. The people believe in pigs and chickens, gardens and children, churches and charity.

During the 'twenties this area was enlarged as the result of the development of an exclusive residential section by upper-class Negroes from the expanding "Downtown" community. The prestige of this new residential area was lowered, however, by the floods of 1937, which inundated the district and caused considerable damage.

There are other areas of Negro settlements in Louisville such as the Portland slum near the river, and the Bottom near the southeastern city limits, but 75 per cent of the Negro population is concentrated in the areas described above.

THE SOCIAL ORGANIZATION OF THE NEGRO COMMUNITY

The general pattern which the Negro community assumes in the border city results from the impact of economic and social forces upon the expanding Negro population. These forces tend to select and segregate various elements in the population, as the city expands, thus giving a definite character to different areas of the Negro community, and affecting the social structure and institutions that develop. Our description of this phase of the Negro community will be limited to the social stratification of the community.[10]

SOCIAL STRATIFICATION

The social stratification of Negro communities in the border cities today is the result of a long evolution extending back to pre-Civil War days. In the District of Columbia there was, as we have seen, a fairly large group of free Negroes before emancipation. These free Negroes, despite their often poor circumstances, felt themselves superior to the slaves, and their descendants took pride in their free ancestry.

Social Distinctions Following the Civil War

Following the Civil War, social distinctions in the Negro community were based to a large extent upon whether a person was of free or slave ancestry. A colored member of the community writing twelve years after the Civil War, probably to give vent to his own feelings rather than to enlighten later generations, satirized the existing distinctions as follows:

The upper class (i.e.) all Negroes who bought their freedom or were set free before the war of rebellion, undertook at an early day in the history of the Negroes of the District of Columbia to mark out the boundary and the habitation not only of the "free niggers" but also of those who but for a kindness of Mr. Lincoln might possibly have been grovelling in darkness and superstition to a greater extent than they are today. The objection raised against this last named class seemed to have arisen from the fact that the prolific and inventive genius of the immortal Ben Butler had transformed them into "contraband of war" a technicality—which shows not only wisdom and humanity but marvellous sagacity and hind sight. A Negro therefore who worked and bought himself from those whose only right to his carcass was the thief and robber's right considered himself more valu-

[10] See Appendix B for a description of institutions, social movements and ideologies, and social pathology of the Negro community.

able intrinsically, than the Negro whose liberty was given him at the demands of justice.[11]

The fact that in 1860, 40.4 per cent of the free Negroes were of mixed blood helped to mark off this group from the general body of Negroes of slave ancestry. Indeed, it appears that white ancestry was as important a consideration as free ancestry. According to our contemporary observer, there was an element in Washington colored "society" that was

> forever and ever informing the uninitiated what a narrow escape they had from being born white. They have small hands, aristocratic insteps and wear blue veins; they have auburn hair and finely chiselled features.[12]

These people, so we are informed, were opposed to manual labor and were constantly referring to their relationship to distinguished white families. "Blood will tell" was their motto; and because of their aristocratic heritage they regarded themselves as superior to the great mass of the Negro population and refused to associate with them.

Despite the satirical attitude of this observer, it appears that many of those of white ancestry had made considerable progress in taking over the culture and civilization of the white man. In this respect they were differentiated from the mass of crude and darker Negroes and formed a narrow circle which constituted an upper class. There were, of course, other distinctions, as, for example, so-called "first" families who enjoyed a certain distinction because of their close association with prominent white families in the capacity of valets and servants. This group was conservative and took over as far as possible the manners and ways of living of these white families. Then, too, even in the earliest stages of social stratification the occupation which one followed and the income which one received played some part in social distinctions. Consequently, one finds that throughout the evolution of social stratification, family and general culture, white ancestry and color, free ancestry, occupation and income have all played a role in differentiating an upper class

[11] Manuscript in the private collection of E. Franklin Frazier.
[12] *Ibid.*

from the great mass of the Negro population. In describing the more complex social stratification of the present Negro community, it will be necessary to disentangle as far as possible these various factors and to evaluate their role in present social distinctions.[13]

Social Stratification Today in the Negro Community

As the social structure has evolved, such social distinctions as free ancestry, white ancestry and color, and even family background and general culture have tended to become less important than distinctions based upon occupation, education, and income. One may get a general idea of the social stratification of border cities from the figures on the socio-economic groups in the District of Columbia and Louisville, Kentucky.[14] (See Table III and chart.) The lower class, at the base of the social pyramid in both cities, is composed of the large group of domestic workers and laborers. In Louisville almost half of the Negro population is dependent upon the earnings of common laborers; in the District of Columbia a little more than

[13] The development of the social stratification of the Louisville community has been similar on the whole to what we have found in Washington.

[14] Since in scientific discussions as well as in everyday speech the concept of social classes varies, it is necessary to indicate what is denoted by social classes in this study. Time and other considerations precluded an extended research into the nature of social stratification in the Negro community. Therefore, certain socio-economic groupings were combined to form the three classes which are used as a frame of reference for the data in this study. It was possible by this procedure to use objective indices in classifying the youth studied. However, it should not be inferred that the three classes are merely artificial constructions and that they have no relation to social stratification in the Negro community. On the contrary, the three classes as constructed include both the objective and subjective factors which are generally regarded as essential in the concept of social class. Roughly, they indicate the differentiation of the community along lines of economic and cultural advantages and standards of living as well as in regard to prestige, rank, and social participation. This fact was determined by the studies of Charles H. Parrish of the Municipal College for Negroes in Louisville, Kentucky, and the writer's investigations in the District of Columbia.

Attention should also be called to the different uses of the term "middle class" in this study. As indicated above, it refers to an intermediate class within the class structure of the Negro community. But the term is also used in its historic sense. When used in the historic sense, it refers, of course, to the aspirations and outlook of the propertied bourgeoisie which gained economic and social ascendancy during the nineteenth century. When the term is used in this sense, it is so indicated in the text.

Percentage of Negro Males in Each of the Seven Socio-Economic Groups in the District of Columbia and Louisville, Kentucky, 1930

	DISTRICT OF COLUMBIA	LOUISVILLE, KENTUCKY
PROFESSIONAL	3.0	3.8
PROPRIETORS, MANAGERS, OFFICIALS	2.6	2.4
CLERKS AND KINDRED WORKERS	8.5	2.8
SKILLED WORKERS, FOREMEN, etc.	7.4	5.9
SEMI-SKILLED WORKERS	19.0	18.9
SERVANTS	23.1	21.2
LABORERS	36.5	44.9

a third of the Negroes are so situated. In both cities slightly more than a fifth of the employed males are servants. The middle class includes both skilled and semiskilled workers. In the District of Columbia the group of skilled workers, representing 7.4 per cent of the total number employed, is larger than the same group in Louisville, partly because of the presence of the federal government. At the top of the social pyramid is the upper class, comprising the professional group, that is, physicians, dentists, lawyers, and teachers; the business group, including managers and officials as well as proprietors; and those engaged in clerical and similar occupations.

A description of the three social classes which our interviewers found were generally recognized by members of the Negro community itself will show to what extent these three social classes correspond to the different socio-economic groupings in the Negro community. In Louisville the three social classes are described by our interview documents as consisting of the following:

1. Upper Class

   Composed of a small group of professional persons, chiefly principals and teachers in the high schools, the faculty of Louisville Municipal College, pastors of prominent churches, the more successful physicians and dentists, and the executives of large Negro business enterprises.

   Next in order come the less successful professional people, elementary school teachers, business supervisors, proprietors of small businesses, and post office employees.

   Old family retainers, some hotel employees, domestic servants in the wealthier families, may be placed at the bottom of this upper class.

2. Middle Class

   This includes the skilled and most of the semiskilled industrial workers and the majority of female domestic servants.

3. Lower Class

Unskilled laborers and many domestic workers belong in this group. Tobacco workers are at the bottom of the social ladder.

TABLE III

NUMBER AND PERCENTAGE OF EMPLOYED NEGRO MALES IN EACH OF THE SEVEN SOCIO-ECONOMIC GROUPS IN THE DISTRICT OF COLUMBIA AND LOUISVILLE, KENTUCKY, 1930

Socio-Economic Groups	District of Columbia[a]		Louisville, Ky.[b]	
	Number	Per Cent	Number	Per Cent
1. Professional	1,242	3.0	630	3.8
2. Proprietors, managers, and officials	1,084	2.6	389	2.4
3. Clerks and kindred workers	3,554	8.5	452	2.8
4. Skilled workers and foremen	3,086	7.4	965	5.9
5. Semiskilled workers	7,945	19.0	3,106	18.9
6. Servant classes	9,658	23.1	3,480	21.2
7. Laborers	15,242	36.5	7,365	44.9
TOTAL	41,811	100.0	16,386	99.9

[a] *Social-Economic Groups in the District of Columbia.* Released by the Bureau of the Census, May 18, 1937.

[b] Classified according to the *Alphabetical Index of Occupations by Industries and Social-Economic Groups, 1937.* (Washington: U. S. Bureau of the Census, 1937).

In order to give a more concrete picture of the social stratification of the Negro community, it will be necessary to show how family status, education, color, occupation, income, and adherence to the moral codes of the community determine one's group affiliations and participation in the community.

The Lower Class

Because of their poverty, ignorance, and low incomes, the lower-class families in the Negro community are confined largely to slum and semislum areas. The lives of the more stable elements among them revolve around the church and to a less extent the lodge. Their intimate associations are limited to visiting with friends of their class, although their children are brought into a wider circle of participation in the school and in various recreational activities. Here one can see how much factors such as family status, occupation and income, and color affect social participation. The girl without family background, low in economic status, and dark in pigmentation may possibly secure recognition and status through outstripping her school-mates in her studies during school time or in athletics on the playground, but such "success stories" are not common. Usually, such a girl, in spite of her individual merit, will be excluded from intimate association with girls who have higher social and economic position, more secure family background, and lighter pigmentation. Even the girl of somewhat lighter complexion but from a low social and economic group will probably be barred from participation with the most exclusive groups; yet her chances of ultimately being accepted into the more exclusive groups are greater, especially if she displays the talent or cleverness which will enable her to marry a prosperous business or professional man. Of course, the position of the black boy from a family without "good background" and from low economic circumstances is far better than that of the girl from the same class. In the competitive life of the community the exceptional boy can fight his way to the top and, especially if he marries into a family with higher status, will be accepted despite his color.

The Middle Class

In the middle class, intermediate between the lower and upper, one finds the most energetic and ambitious elements in the Negro community. Members of this class, unlike the more accommodated mass beneath them, are often intensely self-conscious and seek assiduously to improve their status. They are careful not to be identified with the lower class and resent the assumption of superiority of the upper class. For a livelihood, their families are dependent upon wage earners in skilled and semiskilled occupations or domestic service. But often they or their children may invest these occupations with honorific titles or an importance that will raise their status. College students from this class have been known to change the designation of their father's occupation from "cook" to "restauranteur."

The general attitude of this class toward its position in the social pyramid will make understandable the role of such factors as family background, color, occupation, and income in social stratification.

Members of the middle-class families in the Negro community seek through education, the professions, or business to make themselves eligible for membership in the upper class. They may even disown their families if identification with them would prove a handicap because of their occupation, color, or morals. And since the upper class is often of fair complexion, the associates whom they seek in friendship and in marriage will most likely be of fair complexion. In such selections, it should be emphasized, they are not simply seeking to identify themselves with a group because of its light color but fundamentally because they wish to improve their status.

The Upper Class

We come finally to the upper class in the Negro community which has long had a reputation for snobbishness toward dark or pure-blooded Negroes. It is quite natural that a stranger to the Negro community viewing a social gathering of the upper class might conclude that a fair complexion determined admission to this class. But by observing and studying those who attend the most exclusive social functions of the upper class, one may gain an understanding of the relative importance of such factors as family and general culture, occupation and income, and personal achievement and morals in determining membership in this class. First, one will observe that the majority of those present are of decidedly fair complexion, with a minority of brown and a conspicuous few of dark complexion. The majority of those of fair complexion will possess a good family background, will be of professional and business standing, and enjoy good incomes, as well as a reputation for respectability. Among those of fair complexion will be a few, generally women, of lower-class origin, who because of education or a good marriage have secured admission into the upper class. The attitudes of this group toward the blacks will range all the way from a strong repulsion through neutrality to a positive preference. Frequently, it happens that those who have come up from the lowest strata exhibit the greatest snobbishness, probably because a fair complexion was so important in determining their class position. Among those of brown complexion will be a large proportion who have risen from the middle, or intermediate, class in the Negro community.

An outsider might well ask: How did the few extremely dark persons get into such a gathering? The answer probably is that their status reflects the influence of such factors as family background, occupation and income, and personal achievement; in the case of men their positions may be consolidated by the fact that their wives may have light complexions and a good family background. On the other hand, the dark women, with a few exceptions, will owe their admission to this exclusive group primarily to family background. In regard to their feelings, one will find that they are not unconscious of the snobbishness of some of their lighter associates and will often wish with their brown-skinned sisters that they had a light skin.

At one time in Washington the mulatto upper class was accused with much justice of extreme snobbishness and discrimination against the blacks when it was in their power to discriminate in regard to jobs. In retaliation, a newspaper, owned and edited by a black man who was a relative of a prominent Negro leader, carried on warfare against the light upper class. At the present time, however, it appears that a growing race consciousness and the rise of members of the darker lower classes have tended to neutralize the snobbishness of the light upper class. If light-skinned Negroes feel an antipathy toward the darker members of the community, they usually conceal it and only confess it among intimates.

The upper class in Negro communities in the border states is characterized by an essentially middle-class (that is, in the historic sense) outlook with an emphasis on pretension and display. Of course, one hears much talk about "culture," but this is not to be taken seriously. It generally turns out that "culture" is restricted to the social amenities, since it is diffi-

cult to find among this group many who read good books or
have a genuine appreciation of literature or art or music. Rather
it is in the matter of conspicuous consumption that the upper
class expresses most explicitly its position and role in the social
stratification of the Negro community. A teacher or a physician
in the Negro world is not simply a professional worker, but is
generally a member of an aristocracy which requires certain
standards of consumption. High standards of consumption are
often made possible by the fact that upper-class married women
in the border states, unlike those in the South, engage in professional and clerical occupations. Thus fine homes, expensive
clothes, and automobiles give an appearance of wealth which is
one of the chief values of this class. In order to maintain these
standards some families live beyond their means, or, as one investigator found, the head of the family engages in so-called
"sundown" occupations.[15] But it also happens sometimes that
the wife with a secure and fairly large income from teaching is
the main support of the family, while her husband, doctor or
businessman with low income, presents a "social front" for the
family. Though the upper class is relatively small in numbers,
it is important in the Negro community because it provides the
standards and values, and symbolizes the aspirations of the
Negro community; being the most articulate element in the
community, its outlook and interests are often regarded as
those of the community at large.

[15] "Many homes were found in which the head of the family worked regularly
at two jobs. This is especially true of those heads of homes that have government
positions. The early closing hours enable the employee to engage in another
occupation during the evening. Several government clerks were found practicing
law, selling real estate, printing, waiting on table, or working at gasoline filling
stations after the closing hours of the department in which they were employed.
These 'sundown occupations' greatly enhance the economic status of the family.
The average salary of Negro male government employees ranges from $125 to
$150 per month, which is by no means adequate to maintain the standard of
living which is characteristic of the average government clerk. Those who desire
the comforts of a well-appointed home, the luxuries of an automobile, frequent
entertainments, and membership in a number of social clubs are forced to
supplement their salaries received from the government by additional money
secured from spare-time jobs. It is often the case, therefore, that, instead of
the income of the head of the home being merely $150 a month, it approximates
$250 or $300 a month." William H. Jones, *The Housing of Negroes*, p. 117.

RELATION OF THE NEGRO COMMUNITY TO THE WHITE WORLD

The relations of the members of the Negro community in Washington to whites and the institutions of the larger community are governed by public opinion and the local folkways and mores rather than abstract legal enactments. Hence, despite the fact that Washington is under the federal government, race relations in the capital are typical of border cities.[16] According to the colored members of the community, race relations have grown worse in recent years; that is, Negroes enjoy fewer rights and privileges today than thirty or forty years ago. And when they undertake to fix a date for the change for the worse and attempt to place responsibility for the change, they usually say that it dates from the inauguration of President Wilson, and that his wife became the leader in the movement to segregate the Negro after her visit to the Bureau of Printing and Engraving, where she saw white and colored people working together. They are likely to add that the situation was worsened by the influx of southern whites during the Wilson administrations. A study of the situation reveals that although the influx of southern whites into the District has had something to do with the growing restrictions and discriminations which have occurred during the past twenty-five years, the pre-Wilson period in Washington was certainly not free from racial discriminations.

Discrimination in Employment

There is a color line in the industries of Washington as well as in the other relations of the races.[17] In the majority of in-

[16] It is in the border cities where the segregation of the Negro is not so firmly fixed as in the deep South that the major battles over the residential segregation of the Negro have been fought. Baltimore, Washington, D.C., Louisville and St. Louis have all been the scene of these struggles. In St. Louis the first popular vote on the residential segregation of the Negro in the United States occurred in 1916. It was in the Louisville segregation case that the Supreme Court handed down the unanimous decision that it was unconstitutional to prohibit Negroes by law from buying and occupying property. But only recently the right of white owners to covenant not to sell or rent to Negroes has been upheld by a court decision in the District of Columbia.

[17] See Lorenzo J. Greene and Myra Colson Callis, *The Employment of Negroes*

dustries employing Negroes and whites, Negro workers are restricted to unskilled or menial tasks, and the whites fill the
more responsible positions requiring skill and education. For
example, in paving construction where Negroes are employed
not only as laborers but as asphalt and concrete layers, the
whites are employed as shop mechanics and engineers, and in
a clerical and supervisory capacity. Also in the laundries, where
the majority of workers are Negro women, one finds that Negro
women are employed as feeders, shakers, catchers, and hand
ironers, while the whites are sorters, markers, seamstresses,
clerks, and drivers. The same color line is apparent in a coal
and oil company where the coal truck drivers are Negroes and
the oil truck drivers are white. In such institutions as banks,
newspapers, telegraph and telephone companies, Negroes are
never allowed to rise above the position of janitor, elevator
operator, or laborer. In hotels where the waiters, bell boys, and
elevator operators are white, the Negro workers are employed
in the kitchen and as maids and porters. This is the situation
in general where Negroes are employed; but there are numerous
places where Negroes are not considered for any type of employment.

Employers will, of course, give numerous reasons for not
employing Negroes or restricting them to menial jobs. These
"reasons" are, however, simply rationalizations which are more
or less familiar to those acquainted with the influence of race
prejudice in the employment of Negroes. The employment
manager in a bakery which employs Negroes as truck washers
only, said that white people would not like to see Negroes
around. Another employment manager stated quite seriously
that Negroes did not have enough intelligence and imagination
to be carpenters. And still another defended his policy of keeping Negroes in menial occupations on the ground that white
and Negro workers could not work together in the same positions. That these so-called "reasons" are manifestly rationaliza-

in the District of Columbia (Washington: Association for the Study of Negro
Life and History, Inc., n.d.), for an excellent account of the present situation
regarding the employment of Negroes in the District.

tions is shown in the cases of establishments, though relatively few in number, where Negroes hold responsible positions requiring intelligence or where Negroes and whites work together without friction. Or one may find a Negro in a position usually occupied by whites simply because he has worked at the business since its establishment and has been retained for sentimental reasons. Three five-and-ten-cent stores, with an almost 100 per cent colored patronage and located in a Negro neighborhood, provide an exception to the color line in industry by employing Negro sales clerks.

The attitudes of the employers are shared especially by the members of those unions that have a monopoly on certain occupations. For example, the secretary of the bartenders' union would like to see Negro bartenders organized but in separate locals and under the supervision of whites. He feels that this is necessary because Negroes are irresponsible and "they should not be allowed in areas where white bartenders work." The white officer of a large union with white and Negro members felt that the elections should be manipulated in order to keep the superior white minority in control. Such white labor leaders are in the same class with the white employer who punched the clock before his colored workers finished work for the day in order that they might not violate the Wages and Hours Law. It should be noted, however, that the C.I.O. unions are showing a somewhat more democratic attitude toward Negro workers.

In the government there is also a color line, though the caste-like principle is not so rigid as in private employment. At one time a large number of Negroes held the status of clerks, but beginning with the Taft administration and later during the Wilson administration the number was reduced. Since then the great majority of Negro workers have been employed as common laborers or in the "custodial" group including janitors, porters, messengers, and sanitary men. Since the extension of federal activities under the New Deal, a number of separate Negro units have been set up in which Negroes are employed not only in clerical occupations but also in administrative positions. Nevertheless, the old practice of discrimination continues often disguised under the right of administrative officers to select one of three eligible persons on the civil service lists. Some of the more liberal elements in the government unions are making a sincere effort to fight discrimination against Negroes.

Housing and Neighborhood Relations

The majority of Negroes in Washington are the tenants of white landlords. Since the landlord's or real estate agent's interest is primarily economic, he will be courteous to self-respecting tenants of the upper and the middle classes. In dealing with the masses of dependent Negroes, on the other hand, he will not only squeeze as much rent as possible out of them but will address them in southern fashion by their first names. Likewise, in deciding whether he will sell or rent to Negroes, the landlord or real estate agent does not act solely upon the basis of personal prejudices. Of course, in the case of the exclusive white residential areas occupied by the wealthy and the middle-class whites, he will refuse to consider a colored client or tenant, but where neighborhoods are losing their residential character and the whites are moving out, he will readily accept or advertise for colored clients and tenants. In such cases he is governed by impersonal economic and social forces which are turning white neighborhoods over to Negroes and, where rehabilitation is taking place, colored neighborhoods over to whites. In the latter case he will evict his black tenants not so much because they are Negroes but because of profit. The controversies that enter the courts are usually in neighborhoods of indefinite status.

It is difficult to generalize regarding race relations in neighborhoods where whites and Negroes live. The attitudes of the whites range from cordiality to hostility which is more often concealed than open. One may find instances where the parents in a middle-class white family will be cordial toward their colored neighbors and even express preference for them since they may behave better than their former white neighbors, while the children in the family exhibit hostility. On the other hand, the younger children in white families may play with colored children in the streets or on a vacant lot which has been appropriated as a playground. In such spontaneous play groups there are seldom racial difficulties so long as the children are separated from the life of the families of the two races. Of course, in some areas the white parents see to it that their children do not associate at all with colored children. Many of the white families who remain in colored neighborhoods do not have children.

There is scarcely ever any free and open social intercourse between white and colored families in Washington. The so-called white "marooned" families sometimes live as recluses and Negroes do not care for their association. The white and colored men may fraternize outside of their homes in stores or at baseball games, though one would never know this from what whites say of their relations with Negro neighbors. In neighborhoods where the poorer whites and Negroes live, there are associations involving at times clandestine sexual relations despite the seeming hostility between the two groups.

Public Institutions and Discrimination

In the District of Columbia, the federal government in setting up a free public school system accepted the system of separate education that was already in existence.[18] Since the inauguration of a free public school system the federal government has provided for a division of school funds on a proportional basis. Provisions were also made in 1882 for three Negro members of a nine-member board; and although the provision was omitted in 1906, by a "gentlemen's agreement" three members of the board have always been Negroes. There is also a colored first assistant superintendent, who has the colored schools under his supervision. In a survey of the situation during the past fifteen years, it was found that in the elementary schools and more especially in the vocational schools Negro teachers have had a larger

[18] See Howard H. Long, "The Support and Control of Public Education in the District of Columbia," *Journal of Negro Education*, VII (July 1938), 390-99, in which the author gives in addition to the historical facts an answer to the three questions: (1) How have the colored schools fared with reference to the pupil load per teacher as compared with white schools; (2) How have they fared with reference to appropriations; and (3) What has been the general morale of the colored school personnel.

pupil load than white teachers. During ten of the fifteen years, Negro schools have received a smaller percentage of the appropriations to which they were entitled on the basis of enrollment of Negro pupils. In 1927-28 the appropriation was 18.4 per cent less and in 1936-37 it was 14.6 per cent less than was due on this basis. Reductions in recent years have alarmed Negro leaders who have presented intelligent and vigorous protests to Congress because they have felt that these reductions might mean the inauguration of a policy similar to that followed in southern states. Because of recent discriminations against Negro school children, the Interracial Committee of the District of Columbia has issued a pamphlet showing the glaring differences between provisions for white and colored children.[19]

Negroes have free access to museums and other such institutions open to the public. In general, they may get permits to use parks and playgrounds without being assigned to special places. They must use separate swimming pools, however, and are restricted to certain tennis courts and golf courses. In regard to such places as Haines Point, the government has evaded the issue through private concessions.

The local courts and the police reflect more truly the attitudes of a large section of the white community toward Negroes than do the federal agencies. The police courts especially tend to treat all Negroes as buffoons or criminals or members of a subordinate caste. Recently a judge in the traffic court provided amusement over the radio by catechizing a poor, ignorant Negro woman on her amours. Despite the fact that there are colored men and women on the police force, the general treatment of Negroes by white policemen reflects the prejudices of the masses of whites. Although white policemen do not exhibit the same brutalities and discourtesies toward Negroes which are customary in the South, as a rule they do not show the same respect toward Negroes which they show toward white citizens. Recently there have been mass meetings and protests against the shooting

[19] Harlan E. Glazier, *The Color Line in Our Public Schools* (Washington: Interracial Committee of the District of Columbia).

of Negroes by the police. A pamphlet sponsored by the Inter-racial Committee of the District has been published, reporting cases of police brutality and promiscuous killings.[20] The police may show justification for killing Negroes who are dangerous criminals, but the fact cannot be overlooked that since some policemen, at least, believe that Negroes are a subhuman species, they have greater hesitancy about killing a white person. Nothing dramatizes the discriminations against Negroes so much as an unjustified killing of a Negro by the police.

Denial of Civil Rights and Public Opinion

The policy of the white community in regard to the exclusion of Negroes from places of amusement, hotels, and restaurants, or the refusal of drugstores to serve Negroes at soda fountains or of department stores to wait on them are all indications of the present state of public opinion and the mores in regard to race relations. Although Negroes are excluded from the theaters, they were permitted, after a protest in which the white unionists joined, to attend the presentation of the Negro opera "Porgy and Bess." They were even permitted to attend the same theater for two nights during the following week, but on the third night their money was returned and they were politely bowed out of the theater by the usher. When a school teacher refused to leave a theater some years ago, he was ejected by the police. As consolation for this illegal infringement of his rights he was awarded one cent damages. Negroes may attend special luncheon or dinner meetings in the private dining rooms of some of the hotels, but they are fortunate if they are not insulted by a white bellman or elevator boy. Where the Negro is permitted to eat at lunch counters in department stores, some difference in treatment is usually shown. He may be allowed to stand and eat at a lunch counter, but he is barred from a more pretentious lunchroom in the same store. Some of the department stores will show in one way or another that they do not want colored

[20] Harlan E. Glazier, *Brutality Enthroned* (Washington: Interracial Committee of the District of Columbia). It should be pointed out that in at least one case of police brutality a Negro policeman was involved.

patronage. The Negro community was especially incensed when a large department store began requiring colored women to use a special restroom. In vain they held mass meetings, made protests to the management, and inaugurated a boycott. Many of the old Negro settlers recalled that the founder of the store, familiarly known as "Papa," served his numerous Negro customers from a pack on his back. As the policy of discrimination was inaugurated just at the time when Germany was beginning the persecution of Jews, Negroes did not fail to point to the fact that they were being discriminated against by a Jewish establishment which should, in their opinion, have been the last to practice racial discrimination.

The fact that a large number of whites in the District prefer disfranchisement to seeing the Negro with the vote provides a fairly good index to public opinion concerning the place of the Negro in the community. One theater has insisted that Negro entertainers and orchestra leaders appear in menial attire rather than formal dress in order not to offend its white patrons, especially southern Congressmen. The refusal of the Daughters of the American Revolution to permit Marian Anderson to appear in Constitution Hall precipitated an issue which made it possible to get some notion of the state of public opinion on race relations. Although the majority of the letters apparently written by whites were favorable to having Miss Anderson appear in Constitution Hall, there were dissenting voices expressing the traditional notions concerning the social separation of the races and the supremacy of the white race. An editorial in the *News* merely gave a succinct and objective statement of the case under the caption, "A Cultural Note," ending with the statement that Miss Anderson was a Negro. Whatever irony might have been intended by this editorial was certainly lost on the white masses. After the Board of Education refused the use of a white high school auditorium on the grounds that it violated the principle of separate schools, the *Washington Post* published two editorials that not only defended the action of the D.A.R. as a private organization but confused the issue by raising the irrelevant question of the use of school property for pay affairs.[21] Although the Washington newspapers use the terms Mr., Mrs., and Miss in referring to Negroes, especially those of upper-class status, the physicians, interns, and nurses at the Garfield Hospital insist upon addressing all Negroes by their first name. When upper-class Negroes object to this insult, the physicians, interns, and nurses seem to some Negro patients to take a cruel delight in forcing them to accept the insult.[22]

In concluding this section on race relations in Washington, it should be pointed out that there are many informal relations between whites and Negroes which have not been included in the above account. That there are Negroes and whites who associate in crime and vice on terms of equality has embarrassed some sincere churchmen and other respectable white citizens who in sponsoring interracial good will still desire to maintain racial lines. Even in crime, as for example in the "numbers" racket, the white "bankers" have maneuvered control into their hands. There exist also among the stable members of the white and Negro communities informal social relationships which have their basis in mutual attraction and common interests. Such associations are increasing in number and are being fostered by liberal intellectuals and white-collar workers with a labor orientation. The growth of these normal associations is an extremely slow process because the dominant attitudes in the community are opposed to them. The white teachers' local

[21] After a rehearing of the case, the Board of Education consented to permit the use of the auditorium but only upon the agreement that no future requests would be made for the use of white buildings by Negroes. When the Negroes refused to accept this agreement, Miss Anderson sang from the steps of the Lincoln Memorial on Easter Sunday to an open-air gathering, estimated at 75,000 persons. She was introduced by the Secretary of the Interior, the Honorable Harold L. Ickes.

[22] Although Louisville is located in a state with segregation laws, Negroes are not "Jim-Crowed" on the streetcars; and at the railroad station they buy tickets at the window with whites and are not forced to remain in the separate waiting room. On the other hand, white people in Louisville are generally opposed to the use of Mr., Mrs., and Miss in addressing colored people and the newspapers avoid the terms altogether. Likewise in Baltimore in a renowned institution like the Johns Hopkins Hospital the nurses are instructed in their class in Social Ethics not to use Mr., Mrs., and Miss in addressing colored people. A few years ago when the father of a Howard University professor was taken to the Johns Hopkins Hospital and refused to reply when addressed by his first name, the medical authorities informed the professor that his father was apathetic to his environment and was giving negative responses!

still does not care for "fraternal" relations with the colored teachers' local; and since the colored teachers are at the top of the social pyramid in the Negro world, they are not eager to associate with those whom they are wont to classify with "poor whites."

STUDYING THE NEGRO ADOLESCENT IN THE BORDER STATES

It is in the comparatively isolated world of the Negro, described above, that the majority of the 175,000 Negro youth, 84,500 male and 90,500 female, in the border states must find a meaning and purpose in life. Not only must they fit into the social and cultural world of the Negro, but they must also adjust themselves to the pattern of racial relationships which characterizes this area. In adjusting themselves to the white world, upon which the Negro world is dependent economically and from which the Negro world takes over patterns of behavior and ideals, Negro youth are influenced by their family background, their position in the social organization, their group and institutional affiliations, and the social movements and ideologies in the community.

In a study of the effects of minority status upon the personality development of Negro youth all of these variables which must be taken into account emphasize the fact that the experience of a particular youth is of primary importance. Since it would, however, be impossible to make an individual study of all Negro youth in the border states or even to study each of the 9,629 boys and 11,906 girls in Washington, or 3,233 boys and 3,950 girls in Louisville,[23] we have selected boys and girls from the various areas of the Negro community and from the different social strata and associations which comprise its social structure. Though we recognize that each personality has a unique organization and represents a peculiar adjustment to the social world, we have also discovered many similarities within the various classes and groups in the Negro world.

[23] These figures, like the 175,000 cited earlier, are for 1930. In the case of Louisville it was necessary to estimate the number of youths in the age groups 12 to 14 and 20 to 21.

CHAPTER II

THE ROLE OF THE FAMILY

IN THE border states and the District of Columbia the Negro child acquires at birth a certain status. The community decrees through legal regulations and custom that only certain hospitals are open to him; that he be labeled in birth statistics; and that his mother can take him to only certain clinics. However, the child's responses to these limitations upon his participation in the life of the community, and in fact his attitudes toward himself, are not automatically determined but vary according to the personal experiences of the individual. At what age he will become aware of his racial identity and how he will be affected by this awareness are determined in part by the manner in which patterns of discrimination are transmitted to the child. The definitions of his status made in subtle ways by his neighborhood playmates, by his school and church, and by the movies, the radio, and the newspapers are all an important part of the process through which the Negro child learns to know himself in relation to the opportunities and limitations of his social world. This does not mean that the child is merely a passive and plastic organism, played upon by environmental influences. The child is a behaving organism, and his behavior has, of course, physiological bases. Nevertheless the child's behavior, whatever its physiological bases, is influenced in one way or another by the definitions of his cultural environment. Thus differences in the temperament and the intelligence of Negro children become significant in personality organization in somewhat the same way as differences in Negroidness. That is to say, their significance must be examined in terms of the total social experience of the child. The interaction of many forces, physiological and cultural, determines the resultant attitudes; no one factor can be examined alone.

Because of the primary importance of the family in personality organization, it was necessary to obtain as much information as possible on the family relations of the Negro youth included in this study. Although we examined in detail the ways in which the family group had influenced the children's attitudes toward their minority status, it was deemed necessary in order to avoid a biased analysis to secure data on situations and relationships not involving race relations. It was recognized that the personal matters of intimacy, affection, and feelings of security as well as the general culture of the family, though not peculiarly racial in character, would doubtless play some role in the child's response to his status in the outside world. The difficulties which were encountered in obtaining such information on Negro youth were typical of life history investigations. Not only were some individuals better able to recall their experiences, but some were more articulate than others. This latter difficulty was certainly a handicap in dealing with lower-class children, many of whom had reflected as little upon race relations as upon other aspects of the world about them. Even where the youngsters were more articulate and were extremely willing to cooperate with the study, the data obtained were extremely limited from the standpoint of what would be desirable for a thorough exploration of the depths of their personalities. The supplementary information which was supplied in some cases by their parents and other associates did not make up for this deficiency. Notwithstanding these difficulties and obvious gaps in the information, the data which were gathered revealed to a large extent the manner in which the family influences Negro youth in their personal adjustment to their minority status.

The analysis of the role of the family in the personality development of Negro youth which follows is presented in relation to the class structure of the Negro community. This structure though only relatively fixed has proved to be the best frame of reference for understanding the real significance of other factors. The analysis will begin with youth whose parents are employed in domestic and personal service and as common laborers since the vast majority of Negro youth come from lower-class families.[1]

LOWER-CLASS FAMILIES

As indicated by their overt behavior, the youth in lower-class families included in our investigation were, on the whole, accommodated to the inferior status of the Negro in the community. But the outward accommodations often concealed latent conflicts between their wishes and conceptions of themselves on the one hand, and the status assigned them by the white community on the other. These conflicts were revealed in their expressions of resentment toward subordination to whites, in their sporadic outbursts of aggression, and in their sullen and "mean" dispositions, which reflected their humiliations and frustrations.

The attitudes of the youth are undoubtedly influenced by the resentment which their parents, though accommodated to their inferior status, often express within the security of the family. A mother apparently resigned to her inferior status because in her words "white people have all the sway" expresses her resentment at home over the fact that she was compelled to take a dress she tried on in a downtown store. Or take the boy who hears his mother "bawl out" his father because he allowed a white man to address him by his name without using Mr. Or the case of a father who has worked out a technique for getting along with whites at his place of employment but rehearses his resentments to his son and at the same time tells him of the nature of whites with whom he must contend in the outside world.

FOLLOWING IN THE FOOTSTEPS OF THE ELDERS

In some cases of accommodation, these youth had apparently taken over the attitudes of their parents and grandparents who had accepted the unequal status of the races as natural and inevitable. It was in such a situation that a fourteen-year-old brown-skinned boy, the son of a laborer, replied to questions about race relations to the effect that "white people treat colored

[1] Of the 268 youth interviewed in Washington, D.C., and Louisville, Ky., the parents of 154 or about 58 per cent were employed in domestic and personal service and as common laborers.

people all right," and that "Negroes have as good a chance as whites to get jobs" or "as good a chance as they ought to." He added, as if by way of explanation, that "white people have their own shows that they go to and colored folks have their own shows that they go to." However, this youngster, whose parents spend most of their time in church, expressed mildly the wish that he would "like to see them stop lynching colored people in the South."

The attitudes of subordination which have become traditional with the parents in some of the lower-class families rest upon bitter experiences in the South. Even their children have had a taste of the white man's violent resistance to any attempt to get out of "their place." Let us take the case of a twenty-year-old youngster who worked as an assistant cook in a restaurant in Washington. He had never had a fight with a white boy, though significantly enough he had "wanted to many times." He had lived in a small town in North Carolina and as he remarked, "In the South you learn to take a lot of things and just forget it." In the small southern town he had always followed his parents' advice "to keep out of brawls with white loafers," and although "white girls used to make passes" at him and his brother, they ignored such advances. His cautiousness in regard to white people, as well as his acceptance of his parents' instructions, had doubtless been impressed upon him when he was thirteen years old. One day when he went into a garage with his father's Model-T Ford, he started to drink out of a fountain. His story of what happened follows:

> Before I could get a drink a white man yelled across the garage to let me know that "niggers" didn't use that fountain. I was very embarrassed and mad, too, because I was thirsty. I took one swallow of water and the man glared at me and ordered me out of the garage. I didn't go back there anymore.

When he informed his father about the incident, he was told that it was his own fault and that he "should have known better."

A twenty-year-old youngster of fifth-grade education, thick-set with blunt Negroid features and extremely kinky hair, who lived with his uncle, a laborer, had had even more violently impressed upon him, with the approval of his father, the proper behavior of a Negro in relations with whites. When he lived in North Carolina his parents had always taught him and his brothers and sisters

> to do as we were told, be as courteous as possible to white people, don't talk back to them, and do your work as well as possible. They said "niggers" that are liked by white people are those who don't give any trouble and don't ask for much.

This youngster thought his father's advice was good and he had tried to "follow it to the letter." He had not given "white people any trouble" but he had not "bitten his tongue in asking for things." He had found out that "if you can act big enough monkey, you can get almost what you want."

Although this youngster had come to accept his parents' teachings even to the extent that he acted "like a monkey to get things" and did not feel segregated in Washington because here "among his own color" he could have more fun than he has ever had in his life, bitter experiences had doubtless helped to bring about this attitude. When he was quite small he says:

> A white man yanked me off a streetcar because I got on ahead of a white woman. He shook me good and tore my clothes. I walked home crying, knowing that my father would do something about it.

Not only was his childish confidence in his father's power to protect him destroyed when he was told by his father that he "should have known better" and that it was his fault, but he himself became "mad." Later he was to have another humiliating experience when by mistake he went to a theater on the day reserved for whites instead of the following day reserved for Negroes. The white woman at the ticket window told him bluntly, "You ought to know we don't mix 'niggers' and whites in anything in Raleigh." The whites standing about "laughed at me and made fun of me as long as they could make me hear." It is understandable why he says that discrimination in Washington really does not bother him and that he has "no reason to complain," since he has "lots more privileges" than he had in the South.

Many lower-class youth stated that they had not been instructed by their parents concerning how to act toward whites. Typical of such statements is the reply of a laborer's seventeen-year-old, brown-skinned daughter of third year high school standing who lived in a run-down and pauperized neighborhood.

> My father and mother used to live in Northeast in a white neighborhood and I played with white children. They used to come into my house and I used to go into theirs. I never had any trouble. My father and mother never said anything about trouble with whites; in the building where they lived they knew a lot of white people and they never had any trouble with them.

Other cases could be cited. It may be better, however, to consider the objection that may be raised that these youth have forgotten the information about discrimination which was given them by their parents. This may be true in some cases but the very fact of forgetting the instructions of their parents indicates how little attention was given the matter in the family. It is likely that some of the parents had the same attitude as the mother of the thirteen-year-old, dark-skinned boy who wanted to be brown-skinned if born again, though he thought he was not "so handicapped" because he is a Negro. When asked what she told her children concerning the way to behave with whites, she stated that she had never told her children anything because she did not see any reason for such advice. Apparently, to some members of the lower class the existing relations between the races appear so natural and inevitable that it is expected that others will know how to act.

"HEAR AND NOT HEAR"

Usually the parents, even those with a southern background, do not indoctrinate their children with such patently servile attitudes as in some of the above cases. Although as a rule they accept the situation as inevitable, they generally caution their children to avoid trouble with whites. The instructions to the children concerning the avoidance of trouble with whites range from general admonitions about keeping away from "white places because colored aren't allowed" to rather detailed techniques, sometimes accompanied by generalizations on the white man's character. A boy in Louisville was always warned by his mother from childhood to play with his own race. The parents of a boy in Washington cautioned their children to avoid "messy whites" or whites seeking trouble with Negroes. The attitudes which the parents attempt to inculcate are indicated more specifically by what the children are told when they report difficulties with whites. When a girl in Louisville reported to her mother that she and her companions had got into a fight with white girls who attempted to block their passage on the sidewalk, her mother warned her that she should get off the sidewalk to avoid trouble with whites. Nevertheless, this mother, like many mothers and fathers of this class, made the distinction between avoiding trouble over mere words and fighting back when struck by whites. Of course, it needs to be pointed out that some of the parents are of a peaceful disposition and their injunctions to their children against fighting include colored as well as white children.

The conflicts which the children have with whites often arise from being called "nigger." Consistent with their general attitude of accommodation to their status, the parents in lower-class families usually instruct their children to ignore the epithet. However, when young white and colored children who play together become involved in a quarrel, the white children are likely to call the colored children "nigger" and the colored to retaliate with such terms as "peckerwood" or "poor white trash." In many cases the exchange of these epithets only causes a temporary break in their relationship. For example, a girl in Louisville tells how she and her sister slipped the white children back into their yard to play after they had fallen out temporarily with the white children for calling them "niggers." But the mother insisted that they should not play with the white children. In fact, many Negro children do not realize the racial significance of the term, thinking that it refers to "any low-down, dirty person." Their parents may explain the term thus, telling their children that anyone can be a "nigger." When one girl heard the term "nigger," she thought it referred to a white person, and from the manner in which her sisters used the word it sounded "as if they did not like the person." But, generally, colored children soon learn "nigger" is used as a term of contempt for the Negroes.

Although in some lower-class families the parents as well as the children accept the designation of "nigger" with its implied depreciation, or use the term with reference to one another, they resent the term when used by whites. The parents may not show outward resentment and may advise their children against showing resentment, but they seek to salve their self-respect in some manner. A father who "junks around" and whose family lives in one of the "courts" or alleys of Washington, said that when he was called a "nigger," his practice was "to hear and not hear."

"NO 'COAT-TAILING' WHITES LIKE GRANDFATHER"

Despite the accommodation of the parents in lower-class families to their inferior status, the children who live in a different social world are likely to develop suspicion and antagonism toward whites. In some cases the seeds of suspicion have been sown by their parents and grandparents. Take, for example, the case of a freshman college student of athletic prowess in Louisville, who, though smiling and apparently happy, was always on his guard against whites. When a child in the country, he played with white children. But his mother never liked him to play with white children because "white people never did mean colored people any good. When they are in front of your face, they are kindly, but when they are behind your back, they call you 'nigger' and mean you no good." Another college student, twenty-one years of age and from the same city, who said that he had wanted to be white when he was twelve or thirteen because he thought "if you were white, you could get what you wanted," was given similar instruction by his grandmother and older sister. They always told him that "white people don't care anything about Negroes; deep down in their hearts they have no good blood for Negroes." Or let us take the case of a mere thirteen-year-old boy, picked up on the streets of Louisville, whose mother was supporting her eight children by domestic work and the gifts of the man who "goes with her." This boy said that he would still be a Negro if he were light enough to "pass," and was convinced that whites treat Negroes "bad." In relating the following incident he was probably revealing the source of his beliefs and attitudes in regard to whites:

> My little brother was sick and these white people [for whom his mother worked] wanted to lend my mother some money. She wouldn't take it because she said they would own her, make her work like a slave if she didn't pay it back.

Sometimes the youth's hostility toward whites and his proneness to fight back can be traced directly to instructions given him by his parents or grandparents. Very often though the children are cautioned against fighting over epithets, they are told to fight back when attacked by whites. Although the parents of a boy in Louisville constantly warned him against fighting with white boys, his father told him to fight back when struck and his mother added the injunction "to pick up something and try to kill a white person" who struck him. In the lower class, fighting is closely tied up with the idea of manhood. In Washington, an old grandmother, who constantly cautioned her children and grandchildren to avoid trouble with whites, nevertheless told them that if a white person attacked them, they should "stand up and fight like a man."

Lower-class youth in border cities often revolt against the instructions which are given them by their parents and grandparents who have a traditional southern background. Typical of such cases is the attitude of a fourteen-year-old boy who, though he thought that "white people were all right," revolted against the attitude of servility which his grandparents undertook to instill in him. This boy, who was born in Kentucky, had lived and worked with his parents and grandparents on a tobacco farm in North Carolina. The grandfather had taken whatever money he had to his white employer, who in the words of the boy was something like a bank, you know—you could go to him and draw it out when you needed it. I liked to work for this man, too. He and his family were nice to us, and since we lived on his property, we sort of ran things for him on the place. He had a swell big house and my grandfather lived in a log shack.

He added, "We've always gotten along with the white people we lived near or worked with," and stated that trouble started only when "some Negro would get beside himself, and act up and fight, or get fresh with some white girl." He did not, however, accept his grandmother's teaching that "If Negroes stay in their places, they'd get along with white people anywhere." To such advice on race relationships, he objected by saying, "I don't know where that place is. I suppose she means 'coat-tailing' white people. Well, I won't do it!"

SEEING THEMSELVES AS WHITES SEE THEM

Although the boy in the above case tended to revolt against the deferential attitude of his grandparents, he did not fail to take over his father's evaluation of Negroes. In regard to his experience in selling papers in Washington, he said:

I used to have a paper route and only half of them would pay me on time; therefore, I would always be short. But Negroes are like that. They'll buy the world, my father says, if you'll sell it to them on credit.

Efforts to bolster up self-respect through antagonism and suspicion of the white man's motives do not prevent lower-class children from taking over current notions that are derogatory to the Negro. Many of them constantly hear from their parents, as well as outside their homes, of the deficiencies of Negroes. One oft repeated notion is that "Negroes do not stick together." The economic dependence of the Negro upon the white man is laid to this deficiency. One father warned his son who aspired to enter the grocery business that a Negro could not succeed in business because "Negroes do not stick together." The widowed mother of six children, whose recently deceased husband had been a laborer, said that she instructed her children as her mother had instructed her:

> When white folks don't treat you right, don't try to hit back. The Negro is weak—that what he is, and the white man is a power. Vengeance is mine, says the Lord, and we gotta leave to Him to vengeance us. We are the underdog.

The reason the "white man has got the Negro bested," according to this woman, is because "the Negro, he won't stick together. Our folks are just like crabs in a basket, when one tries to reach up and climb out, the others pull him back."

Not only is the general backwardness and dependence of the Negro attributed to some racial defect, but the most trivial things are characterized as such. A girl is indifferent about completing her schooling and is immediately charged with a peculiarly Negro trait of wanting to quit school in seventh or eighth grade, and being content "to end up in somebody's kitchen." The mother of another girl has found that white neighborhoods are noisy and white people have fights, but she stated with disgust, "as to 'niggers'—a colored settlement is all right for those who like it."

"GETTING BY" WITH A VENGEANCE

In some cases, we have seen, lower-class parents have instructed their children that clowning or "acting like a monkey" is a valuable technique for "getting by" or getting what they want from whites. The parents who have used this technique are referring to the method of accommodating themselves in their personal relations to whites, as for example, in the South where relations between the races are often of a personal character. In the city, where relationships become secular and impersonal, a boy or girl convinced that such deception and clowning will enable him to secure what he wants may organize his whole personality about such a conception. This had evidently happened in the case of a very black, twenty-one-year-old boy with kinky hair, whose father was a laborer in a government building in Washington. He boasted of the fact that when he was not cutting school, he was "raising hell while there." He had been a member of a gang that stole and committed rape. His father was constantly getting him out of jail. His parents, he said, told him "many times that the way to get on in the world is to be a man, carry yourself like a gentleman at all times, and to be careful of who you take up with." But, he adds, "if you lived down in Southwest you can't get along with those 'monkeys' and do as they said." He is "trying out" his parents' advice at present, but he does not feel that it is loyal "to walk out on my friends."

Concerning his relations with whites, his father had instructed him as follows:

> To get along with whites let them think at all times that they are better than you are, that the white man is boss, and act as humble as possible.

This youngster had found that his father's advice "worked" and added, "Believe me, I work it often." He had "jived" his way into a number of jobs. In the following statement, he shows with what cynical regard he accepts the role of a "nigger."

> Even as a youngster I was called "nigger" by my friends, and I used the same word when talking to them. From them, I learned what a "nigger" was and also learned the difference between a "nigger" and a white man. I don't know how old I was but I was way down in the grade school. I learned that a "nigger" was a black-skin man, who white people hated and who used them only for servants. My father also helped straighten out the situation for me. Come from other colored kids, I didn't feel badly about it all.

But note that when he is called "nigger" by whites, he will accept it only if the odds are against him. He continues:

> I do hate to be called a "nigger" by a white man, and if the odds aren't too great, he pays for each time he calls me "nigger," because I know he means something entirely different.

> I'm always being told I can't do something because I'm a "nigger." I don't feel badly about it all. I know being a "nigger" there are things I can't do, places I can't go, but I feel that where some tell me something I can't do, somebody will tell me I can do something I want to do. So I don't mind trying and if you know how to flatter and "jive" white people, you can get farther than they expect "niggers" to go. I usually make a big joke of it

and act the part of a clown. I generally get just what I'm after. After all, I think that's all white people want anyway. They just want "niggers" to recognize them as superior, and I'm the man to play their game. I don't care what he says or does as long as he kicks in. One thing sure, he wouldn't call me "nigger" down on Delaware Avenue. Then, too, I usually remember even if he lets you do things, he really doesn't want you to, and you're still a "nigger" to him. I don't feel badly about being told I can't do something because if he lets me hang around long enough, I'll get something out of him.

It is not strange that he regards Elder Michaux and Father Divine as the best leaders of the Negro race and would like to be in their places, since, in his opinion "that so-called religion is nothing but a racket." He sums up his philosophy in the statement: "Jive women and white people, and have enough money to do the things I want to do."

BLACK AND EVIL

Since many lower-class families are of dark complexion, the parents instruct their children concerning *color differences within the Negro group.* In some families they attempt to minimize the importance of color as compared with intelligence or personal achievements. More generally, it appears that the parents build up defenses by the derogation of mixed blood. This derogation often expresses bitterness which has grown out of the slights suffered by them as well as their children in their relations with lighter Negroes. The children often express their envy and bitterness in such statements as "light children think they are cute." A typical example of the parent's derogation of mixed blood is provided in the case of a poor, fifteen-year-old, black girl in Louisville who claimed she was glad that she was black and that if she were born again, she would want to be black, if anything, a little blacker. She said that "yellah is low down, 'cause mama said yellah comes from messin' aroun' uh white man an' any time uh nigger goes to lyin' aroun' 'em it's low an' anythin' that comes from it is low." Yet this same mother had told her daughter that the reason she was so dark was that just before she was born a dark shade was pulled down over her and her mother. Her mother had told her, too, that she would get lighter as she grew older.

Because of the large amount of family disorganization among lower-class Negroes, the child fails to enjoy the security, affectional as well as economic, which children in the middle and upper class enjoy. The child not only sees violence, but is also the object of the violent behavior of his parents. His own behavior will be impulsive, and the family as a socializing agency will have little influence on his conduct. He becomes a person seeking only the satisfaction of individualistic impulses and wishes. But (because of his color) the satisfaction of these impulses and wishes is blocked by whites and often by Negroes of lighter complexion who show the same contempt for him as the whites. He becomes "mean" in the sense that to hurt and to thwart others provides some satisfaction for his own hurts and frustrations. He develops an extreme sensitiveness to imagined slights and impositions and a proneness to fight, reactions which are doubtless expressions of his frustrations and revolt against his lot in the world.

Color differences within the same family may become the basis of invidious distinctions. In those lower-class families where the sense of family solidarity is strong, the parents will attempt to prevent discussions concerning these differences. But in families lacking a feeling of solidarity, color differences may become the source of bitter antagonisms. The child of dark complexion not only may become bitter toward members of his own family but may also constantly engage in aggression toward those in the outside world.

The girl in the case quoted above was the darkest member of a black family of four girls and one boy, the surviving five children in a family of nine. Her father had been dead six years. Between her and her mother, there was bitter antagonism. She liked her brother better than anyone else in her family and was sorry when he married and left home. The only person who was close to her was a girl of her color. She is described as boisterous and is said to "express herself best when cursing." She drinks the cheap whisky which is sold in the neighborhood, carries a knife, and fights the boys with whom she has promiscuous sex relations. Then, too, she has what is described as a "fussy way of talking to you whether she likes or dislikes you." She resents any form of control at home or on the playground and is constantly seeking occasions for conflict. One of the causes of resentment toward her family was the fact that, "them ole niggahs at home make me sick, they're always callin' somebody black." But she would have one believe that she is satisfied with her color and has only contempt for light-colored people. She said:

> Well, I don't care if I am the blackest one—I'm glad I'm black. I wouldn't be yellah for nothin'. If I was born again I'd want to be just as black, if anything, a little blacker. Hell, black is jest as good as any other color. I don't see why niggahs are always hollerin' about somebody bein' black, all niggahs are supposed to be black.

This last notion, as was indicated, was given her by her mother. She constantly expresses her dislike of light-colored people.

> I don't like yellah niggahs, 'cause they think they're so damn cute. Mrs. —— is one of them ole yellah hussies. I hate her; she thinks she's cute because she's got that little ole half white gal over there and she got a little money.

The source of this girl's bitterness toward the lighter upper-class Negroes is revealed in her wishing for clothes and jewelry which the latter can afford and in her admission that a fair girl was cute and had pretty hair.

From the foregoing discussion of the lower class, it is needless to say that this case is not typical of this class. It is presented to indicate in a way the effect upon personality, when, to the burden of family disorganization and ignorance and poverty, the handicap of race and color is added.

FAITH, HOPE, AND CHARITY

The behavior and aspirations of Negroes as well as of other people are not completely differentiated according to class divisions based upon prestige, rank, and social participation. Our classification of lower-class families on the basis of socio-economic status allows for even greater variations in behavior and aspirations. The parents in some of the lower-class families in this study have a sense of personal worth and attempt to prevent their children from developing feelings of inferiority. Their sense of personal dignity is often based upon their religious beliefs concerning the equality of all men "in the sight of God." This attitude is shown in the case of a fourteen-year-old boy in Washington whose father was a laborer. Although his mother "got after him for fighting with white boys," she did not fail to instill in him and his brothers and sister the notion that whites were not better than colored people. According to this boy, his mother always said

> there ain't no white people better than we are. She says for me not ever to think that they are because they ain't. God put us all here and we're just alike. One's just as good as the other to Him. He don't care whether you have a dark skin or a light skin. White people think they are better than colored people because colored people were slaves and they had command over colored people, but we're just as good as they are. They just keep us out of their places to try to make us think that we aren't as good as they.

The same attitude was revealed in the case of a black seventeen-year-old girl in Louisville of senior high school grade, employed in domestic service, who said that her mother told her

> to treat everybody right because we all come from the dust of the earth, even white people, as well off as they think they are. You are going to find good in all people regardless of the color of their face.

Some lower-class parents attempt to give their children a dignified conception of themselves by differentiating the term "nigger" from "Negro" or "colored." A Washington youth of twenty stated:

> I remember as a youngster being called a "nigger" and my mother explained that I was a Negro and that that was what white people meant when they said "nigger" and that they either mispronounced the word or just wanted to insult or be nasty to colored people.

Another Washington youth had always been told by his

mother not to hate anyone and his father had supplemented this with the instruction that he should always be a man no matter "what else he was." From his father, he had also learned that the only chance he had "being black was to be able to do whatever he learned better than the fellow who was white." A widowed woman's sixteen-year-old son who planned to go to college and later enter a law school had received similar instruction. The son knew that his color was a handicap and he would "probably want to be white" if he could be born again; but if he had "to be born a Negro," he would want to be born the same color (dark-brown) but "with a lot more brains." With that change alone he was certain that he "could make accomplishments in spite of color." It is significant that this boy had spent some time in school in New York City, where, according to his report, "he was treated just like white."

MIDDLE-CLASS FAMILIES

For the purposes of this study, families of middle-class social status in the Negro group comprise those families deriving their incomes from skilled and semiskilled occupations. So defined, the middle-class youth are differentiated, on the whole, from those in lower-class families by the fact that they show more sophistication toward their racial status, that they show more consciousness of their social status, and that they are likely to exhibit a greater degree of race consciousness. Their greater self-consciousness and awareness of their status are closely tied up with the fact that these children show more ambition and a greater determination to rise in the world than the lower-class children. The nascent race consciousness of this class is accompanied by a critical attitude toward the deficiencies of the Negro and a deeper resentment of the discriminations practiced by whites.

Although the majority of the middle-class families in our study appeared to be accommodated to their status, they were not so well accommodated as lower-class parents and their children. Although in some middle-class families the children have been told to avoid conflicts with whites and to use such techniques as "jiving" or flattery in order to get along with them, one is likely to find that the children will not accept whole-heartedly such advice. One of the two sons of a janitor, a fifteen-year-old, very dark boy, in the second year high school, was skeptical of his parents' teachings about how to get along with whites. They had told him that he should always "be clean, stop being common, treat them with respect and do as you are told"; but the boy's reaction was, "You can do all these and not get along with them." Another Washington boy, whose father was a skilled artisan, had been told by his father:

> You shouldn't act like you know too much. Treat white people courteous at all times and if necessary, do a little flattering and "coat-tail" kissing.

He felt that since the white people for whom his father worked "thought the world of him," it was probable that his father used these methods. He added that his father took off his hat while talking to white people, called them "Boss" or "Mr. Jim." This boy said that he had always thought "you could get along with anyone if you'd be a real man. But white people don't like Negroes who are men. So I tried my father's method, and, strange enough, it worked. So now I'm 'jiving' and I find I get along swell." "But mind you," this boy confessed, "I hate myself every time I say 'boss' or 'coat-tail' a peckerwood."

"DON'T BE COMMON"

One will note in the first case cited above that the father's instruction to his son included the statement, "Stop being common." In this statement, the father expressed an attitude that often becomes the chief motivating force in the behavior of the youth of middle-class status in their relations to whites. They strive to appear respectable and by so doing belie the statements of whites that Negroes are common. Although the parents of this boy had warned him against fighting, especially with white boys, this warning was not based upon fear of whites or sub-servience. It was based partly upon the rational consideration that a Negro boy is at a disadvantage where the police are concerned, but more especially upon the fact that his father was known in the community and fighting would hurt the reputation of the family.

In fact, many of the warnings which the parents give their children about fighting really mean that they should avoid behaving in a manner which would identify them with the lower class. The mother of one girl had taught her that colored people should not be "resigned to their fate," but should "stand up for their rights." That is the kind of fighting they should do; but entering into physical encounters with whites only tended to "bring the race down." One boy avoided fights with white boys even when they called him "nigger," though he got "pretty angry." He was confident that no white boy would dare "pick on" him. He acted in this way because his mother has warned him to "avoid all fights" if he can, adding that when he got into a fight he became "as low as those who caused it." Of course, in some cases it may be that the parents are attempting to rationalize their attitudes of nonresistance to aggression on the part of the whites and that the children merely take over these rationalizations. But it appears that in most cases these boys and girls are motivated by a desire to maintain a certain respectability in the eyes of Negroes as well as whites.

Since children of these families are conscious of their status and wish to maintain a certain degree of respectability, they resent the fact that "whites put all Negroes in the same class." Moreover, they are indignant over the behavior of lower-class Negroes. A dark-brown, twelve-year-old boy with Negroid features, the son of a bricklayer, who aspires to become a bricklayer like his father and uncle, made the following statement:

> White people treat Negroes pretty bad sometimes and yet I don't blame them sometimes for treating some as they do. It's too bad the good ones have to be treated like the bad ones. I only wish they would treat the bad ones as they deserve and not try to treat us all alike.

Thus, one notes that though these middle-class children are very critical of Negroes, often attributing to them the same characteristics which lower-class children accept as valid, they nevertheless regard these traits as characteristic of the lower class and not of members of their own class. In their behavior and outlook on life, they endeavor to differentiate themselves as much as possible from the lower class. This characteristic is undoubtedly related to the fact that middle-class children are ambitious and seek to rise in the world. It is in this stratum of the Negro population that one finds a conscious struggle to rise above the condition of the masses. For example, one middle-class mother wants her children to get up in the world and said that the "biggest thing" over which she and her mother ever disagreed was the type of school she should enter. As a girl she wanted to enter business school, but her mother "didn't think there was a chance for colored people to do anything in business" and that Negroes only had a chance in the trades. During the course of her story, she remarked significantly, "Lots of older colored folks used to think that." Her mother compelled her to enter a trade school where she took sewing; but she became "awful tired of it," lost interest in school, and got married.

YOU SHOULD HOLD YOUR HEAD UP

The nascent race consciousness which one finds among the middle-class families is even more fundamental in the personality development of Negro youth, so far as their minority status is concerned, than their sophistication about race relations and desire to be respectable. For, as a matter of fact, their desire to maintain respectable standards of behavior is often tied up with race pride. For example, the mother of a fifteen-year-old junior high school girl, when asked what she thought of separate schools and theaters, replied that she thought it was

> just as well to have our own things. There are some white people that are just as disorderly as colored. I think having separate places, you can go and hold your head up and show the white people you are as good as they are.

Where these families have developed some degree of race consciousness, they usually want to ban the discussion of color differences among Negroes. One girl remarked that some of her friends were sensitive about color and talked about it quite a bit; but in her home she was taught that it was "very much out of place for colored people to be talking about color."

In spite of such inhibitions, it is not always possible to keep feelings over color differences from coming to the surface in families of this class. Take the case of a respectable skilled artisan in Louisville who provides a comfortable home and living for his wife and large family and is endeavoring to educate his children. His twenty-year-old son, who thinks that his black father is a "good guy," tells of the following incident which happened when he was only nine. He told this story after he had expressed the opinion that men should be his color (light-brown) and women very fair, but that unfortunately, dark men liked fair women. His father had never had anything to do with his half brother because, so the boy inferred, "it made my father mad because he had a white father and when he married a woman with a white father *that came to see her,* it was just too much for the old man." From the story of the father's outburst, it appears that the resentment originated in the mother's treatment of the two sons.

> I remember when I was nine years old, my mother wanted my uncle and his wife to dinner. My father flew up and started cussing. I never had heard my father cuss before and have never heard him cuss since then. He said, "I don't want them God damned half-white sons of bitches in my house, much less eating my food. He always thought he was better than me and I believe my mother thought so too. My mother, God bless her in her grave, had no business having anything to do with a white man."

According to our informant, his "mother flew back at him" and said,

> My father was a white man and you know it. I'm sick and tired of having you talk about half-white "niggers." They can't help the color they are anymore than you can help the color you are.

The term "nigger" is generally banned by race conscious middle-class families. A girl of middle-class status stated that sometimes she and her sister used the term but they were careful never to let their mother hear them. Then, too, race conscious members of middle-class status think that a self-respecting attitude should prevent people from going where they will be embarrassed. This is not mere rationalization on their part, since they have a sense of personal dignity which they attempt to instill in their children. Children of the middle class are better acquainted with the achievements of Negroes and have more knowledge of outstanding leaders. Their parents seek to cultivate respect for Negroes and the children feel that they should know more. One boy remarked, "I think we ought to know more about our folks, living and dead—what good is it to learn so much about white people and their great men?" Children of this class seem to have two different attitudes toward "passing" for white. In some cases their parents have taught them that it is disloyal to the Negro race to "pass," and in other cases that it is quite all right to "pass" in order to get what you want so long as you are not disloyal to Negroes. Thus loyalty to the Negro becomes a criterion of one's behavior.

"DON'T BE A MONKEY FOR WHITES"

Of course the development of race consciousness and race pride among this class involves at times a deep resentment against whites. Race conscious Negroes especially resent the fact that whites want Negroes to flatter them and to play the role of a clown. One boy said that his parents had told him the way to get along in the world was to act decent and when it came to whites "not to make a monkey out of myself." A boy in a stable and self-respecting family is very bitter because he believes his father, who holds a skilled position in public service, has not been promoted because of his color.

The greater sophistication of this class is indicated often by their insights and reflections upon race relations. One boy observed that white people do not object to using the terms Mr. and Mrs. in addressing Negroes "when they want something." Some of the families have been in the North for a short time and their children, having broadened their outlook, have acquired new notions concerning the relations of whites and Negroes. These children are generally in favor of mixed schools and cite examples of the advantages available where whites and Negroes go to school together.

UPPER-CLASS FAMILIES

We have included in the upper class those families in which the income is derived from professional services, from trade including managers as well as proprietors, and from clerical occupations both in the government and in private industry. Although it is possible to find exceptions to this definition of the upper class, the above socio-economic groups would be represented in any gathering of upper-class Negroes in Washington or Louisville.

The first fact that should be pointed out in regard to the influence of the family on upper-class youth is that their parents never attempt to inculcate attitudes of subordination to white people. Although they may tell their children to avoid conflicts with whites or to ignore such epithets as "nigger," the parents usually accompany their instruction with the explanation that fighting and brawling are unbecoming to a person of their social status or that only "poor whites" use such epithets toward Negroes. Hence many upper-class Negro youth grow up with the false belief that only "poor whites" who lack "culture" are prejudiced against Negroes. It is partly because of such instruction that upper-class youth generally exhibit considerable resentment against lower-class whites and tend to identify themselves with upper-class whites.[2] In this connection it is important to note that upper-class youth who said that they would want to be white if born over generally added that they would not want to be "poor whites."

This is all part of the efforts of upper-class families to protect as far as possible their children not only against the cruder expressions of race prejudice but also from the more subtle forms of racial discrimination. As a rule neither the parents nor

[2] This attitude on the part of upper-class Negroes is widespread. For example, William E. B. DuBois, who was born in Massachusetts, writes concerning his childhood: "I cordially despised the poor Irish and South Germans, who slaved in the mills, and annexed the rich and well-to-do as my natural companions." *Darkwater* (New York: Harcourt, Brace and Howe, 1920), pp. 8-9.

their children are engaged in menial occupations where they would be forced to assume, at least, an attitude of subordination toward whites. Generally, the parents studiously avoid taking their children places where they will be subjected to rebuffs because of race or color. Despite such precautions, parents in upper-class families find it extremely difficult at times to explain, without introducing the fact of their racial status to their children, why they cannot go to various places or eat and drink at certain places.

BLINDERS AGAINST A HOSTILE WORLD

Sometimes the efforts of upper-class parents to protect their children go to fantastic extremes. For example, a teacher would not let anyone use the term "Negro" or "colored" in his home because he did not want his son to acquire the idea of his racial identity and the inferior status involved in the idea. The wife of a professional man described her attempt to keep her son from knowing that he was a Negro in the following way. When he was a small child, she never alluded to race, color, or types in his presence. She brought him to Washington when he was three years old. When she took him with her on shopping trips to Fourteenth Street, and he would want to go to the movies, she would say, "No, dear, mother doesn't think this picture so interesting, we'll go another day or later." She never wanted him to feel he *could not* go. It was always a matter of choice. One day she took him with her to a fashionable bakery and confectionery to get some pecan buns. He was about six years old, and noticing people eating at small tables in the place, piped up, "Mummy, we don't have to go over to the Ten Cent Store to eat. We can have lunch here." Then she had to explain that the hot dogs at the Ten Cent Store were much more appetizing than the lunches served at the confectioner's. The boy continued to believe he could have eaten at these places or gone to any movie until he was about eight years old, when a maid in the home, in spite of strict orders to the contrary, began to talk about white and colored and tell him what the terms meant according to the American setup. Then, too, he had begun to play with X, who also enlightened the boy as to his true race and color. His mother regretted these infringements of her plans, because "we did not want our child to have an inferiority complex. We felt that he would learn soon enough; that his childhood should be free." When asked how she managed to keep him from knowing he went to a colored school, she said nothing at all was mentioned about its being a *colored* school. It was just a matter of going to the *nearest* school. The plan had worked perfectly until the maid referred to began to talk and until the child began to play with the X boy.

But, of course, youth of upper-class status cannot be completely isolated from the white world and its evaluations of Negroes. For example, the youth mentioned above said concerning his mother's efforts to conceal his racial identity:

> I have always understood what "colored" and "white" mean. I don't remember when I didn't know *that*. That's funny, any kid living in Washington—I came here when I was three year old—is bound to know that. I'll bet mother told you she didn't want me to know and all that stuff. I know all right, but it doesn't bother me. I think I can do what I intend to do whether I'm white or colored except that I might have a harder time doing it.

Besides the occasional, though important, firsthand contacts which they must have with whites they are constantly brought into contact with the white world through books, newspapers, magazines, the movies, and the radio. Whenever through these various agencies of communication children of upper-class families hear or read things which are derogatory to the Negro, their parents are quick to combat such influences with ideas of their own and build up a conception of Negroes more suitable to their hearts' desire. Thus, the youth in the upper-class families acquire "ideal" defenses for their egos which become the fabric of their conventional selves. For the investigator it often proves an almost insuperable task to pierce these defenses and discover the real attitudes and feelings of upper-class youth in regard to their status as Negroes. These "ideal" defenses which protect their egos are often responsible for the contradictions between their actual behavior and their verbal explanation of their attitudes.

Thus, while one may say that children of upper-class Negro families are more sophisticated in their attitudes and responses toward their status as Negroes, it should be noted that much of this sophistication represents rationalizations and verbalizations which serve as protective covering for their inner feelings. One upper-class girl, a junior in a northern college, after denying any feeling of difference, inferiority, self-consciousness, or racial consciousness when among her white schoolmates, let slip the remark, "You can ignore being a Negro." When youth in upper-class families thus attempt to "ignore the fact that they are Negroes," they are often assuming the attitude of their parents toward the question of their racial identity. The daughter of a physician said that she had constantly asked her father why the Negro, "though created by the same God" and requiring "the same things for life—food, clothing, shelter—was not treated as the white man's equal"; but that she was always put off with the remark, "Oh, you are young and you will learn."

"BETTER TO REIGN IN HELL THAN TO SERVE IN HEAVEN"

Of course, there are parents in upper-class families who frankly realize the dilemma involved in instructing their children concerning their racial status. One parent remarked:

> I don't think any mothers have yet solved the question altogether satisfactorily. I always try to explain to my children just how it is and in such a way that they won't feel bitter. For instance, there are certain things that Negroes can't go but so far in, so far as occupations are concerned. My boys first seemed to notice the difference when they were about six or seven years old. My experience with my pupils at school has taught me the same thing. We would be downtown and they would say, "Mother, let's go in here." I would tell them concerning some places they wanted to go, "No, you can't go in there. Colored people aren't allowed to go in there." Well, they naturally wanted to know why; then there you were. What could you say!

In their attempt to protect their children from developing feelings of inferiority or insecurity because of their racial identity, upper-class parents are supported in their efforts by their economic security and the status which the family enjoys in the relatively isolated Negro community. It may seem strange to outsiders who view the plight of the Negro generally to learn that when some upper-class children were asked what they desired if they could satisfy only one wish, replied that they found it hard to answer because they had everything they wanted. In the majority of cases upper-class children were interested in things that would bring them greater personal prestige and enjoyment such as wealth and travel. But so far as their status was concerned they were more conscious of their place in the Negro world than their status in the larger world. This seemed to be characteristic of upper-class youth in the border states where the contacts of the upper class are more limited than those of the same class in the metropolitan areas of the North. But as indicated above, upper-class youth are not completely isolated even in the border areas from discrimination on the part of whites. The following statement by an upper-class youth of very fair complexion brings out the conflicting reactions of members of this class to their status as Negroes:

> Sometimes I feel all right—I'd just as well though; I can't change it. At other times, I feel sorry because I am a Negro. There are many classes of us and many in these lower classes do not know how to conduct themselves; yet white people class us all alike. I can't understand that, particularly since there are different classes in their group and they don't fail to make the distinction. I have seen many Negro men who were famous but I realize they had and still have a task to rise above the ever present problem of color. It seems that you just can't get away from it—and you're still classed with the masses and we must be subjected to all racial indignities and are supposed to like it besides.

On another occasion this youth spoke as follows concerning being a Negro:

> I'm proud of the fact that I'm a Negro. Proud of the fact that my family represents the upper stratum of the race which I hope to perpetuate. I am proud of those of my group who have made good despite racial odds and I feel sorry for those stuck in the mire. I realize I can't get through life on my family's or my

father's reputation—that I must make one for myself. However, knowing that there are difficulties that confront us all as Negroes, if I could be born again and had my choice I'd really want to be a white boy—I mean white or my same color, providing I could occupy the same racial and economic level I now enjoy. I am glad I am this color—I'm frequently taken for a foreigner. I wouldn't care to be lighter or darker and be a Negro. I am the darkest one in the family due to my constant outdoor activities. I realize of course that there are places where I can't go despite my family or money just because I happen to be a Negro. With my present education, family background, and so forth, if I was only white I could go places in life. A white face holds supreme over a black one despite its economic and social status. Frankly, it leaves me bewildered. I just don't understand.

In his first statement, this youth indicates that he is conscious of his conflicting feelings. However, in the second statement he seems to be unconscious of his conflicting attitudes toward his racial status. First, there is an assertion of pride in the fact that he is a Negro, but at the same time the confession that if he were born again he would prefer to be white because of the difficulties a Negro must face. Moreover, he is glad that he is not black, though he would not want to be lighter and still be a Negro. To him his color is becoming to his status as an upper-class Negro, but it also has the special value of enabling him to be taken for a foreigner and thereby escaping some discrimination. On the other hand, this youth is proud of his status in the Negro group and feels sorry for lower-class Negroes as those who are "stuck in the mire." Nevertheless, he recognizes his limitations as a Negro despite his family background, money, and social status.

The reactions of this youth are typical in several respects of upper-class persons. Although they are probably the most race conscious elements in the Negro group, their race consciousness has not brought about a transformation of their personalities involving their deepest feelings and aspirations. Usually their pride in their racial identity rests upon feelings of resentment against the treatment received from whites and the ideological defenses and compensations which they have built up as supports to their egos. They do not become identified with racial movements of a nationalistic character. They seek neither in the alien culture of Africa nor in the folk culture of American Negroes a basis for racial identification. But rather they undertake to uphold behind the walls of segregation the same middle-class (in the historic sense) values as white America.

"CAN'T ESCAPE THE SIGN ON ME"

Despite the fact that upper-class youth are able to achieve a relatively stable personality organization, very seldom do they escape entirely the effects of the white world's attitudes about them. A seventeen-year-old college freshman, when asked whether he felt inferior around white people, gave the following bit of frank and incisive self-analysis:

> Off hand, I'd say no, but actually knowing all these things that are thrown up to you about white people being superior—that they look more or less down upon all Negroes—that we have to look to them for everything we get—that they'd rather think of us as mice than men—I don't believe I or any other Negro can help but feel inferior. My father says that it isn't so—that we feel only inferior to those whom we feel are superior. But I don't believe we can feel otherwise. Around white people until I know them a while I feel definitely out of place. Once I played a Ping-pong match with a white boy whose play I know wasn't as good as mine, and boys he managed to beat I beat with ease, but I just couldn't get it out of my mind that I was playing a white boy. Sort of an Indian sign on me, you know.

The statement by this youth is revealing not only because of its frankness but also because it shows the inability of upper-class parents to nullify the influences of the outside world on the youth's feelings and conception of himself as a Negro. The most sheltered youth in the Negro group—those enjoying a high social status and economic security, and protected by the rationalizations and ideologies of their parents—are exposed like the lower classes to the evaluations and discriminations in the larger white world.

SUMMARY

On the basis of the youth studied, the influence of the family upon the personal responses of Negro youth to their minority status may be summarized as follows. First, in many lower-class families the parents undertake to pass on to their children their attitudes of accommodation to an inferior racial status. Their children, however, who have lived in a different social world tend to revolt against such instructions and show considerable hostility toward whites. Even when they take over the techniques of "getting by," which the parents have worked out in their personal relations with whites, these techniques have a different meaning for the children. In some cases the children may organize their whole personalities around such techniques as a means of "getting by" in the world at large. Despite their revolt against the spirit of submission of their parents, lower-class children take over the current stereotypes which are derogatory to the Negro. The darker members of the lower class who have suffered slights from light-colored people (sometimes within their own families) as well as from whites may develop an extreme sensitiveness to slights. They may also develop proneness to aggression because of their frustrations and hurts. A proneness to fighting is encouraged by the large amount of disorganized family life among lower-class Negroes. On the other hand, some parents, despite their poverty and low estate may inspire their children with hope and because of their simple Christian faith may even teach them to have good will toward whites.

Second, parents in middle-class families are less inclined to teach their children to act in a servile manner toward whites. They teach their children to eschew the ways of lower-class Negroes and win the respect of whites by acting according to conventional standards. Their endeavor to avoid lower-class behavior and to appear respectable to whites is closely related to the increasing race pride and race consciousness among this class. The resentment which youth in this class show toward whites is tied up with what they regard as the proper status of Negroes, especially those who have risen above the condition of the masses.

Third, upper-class parents undertake to shield their children against the more subtle as well as the cruder forms of discrimination. They try to accomplish this by concealing from the child his racial identity; by avoiding places and situations where the child would suffer discrimination; and by rationalizations concerning his race and status. In addition, upper-class youth enjoy such concrete advantages as security in the family as well as in the economic relations, and in consequence they are at the top of the social pyramid within the Negro world. It appears that the majority of them would not exchange these advantages for an inferior status within the white world. Yet upper-class youth cannot escape the effects of the derogation of the Negro by the white world. In the next chapter we shall explore some of these affects as they are mediated to Negro youth through neighborhood contacts.

CHAPTER III

NEIGHBORHOOD CONTACTS

In a neighborhood in Southeast Washington, occupied by about the same proportion of families of the two races, a field worker observed white and colored children playing together. The white children apparently had the approval of the parents; for although on several occasions the latter leaned out of the windows to warn their children against swinging on the tree limb, they said nothing to indicate that they objected to their children's colored playmates. The record of the field worker's observation reads as follows:

> Although the white and the colored children were playing together, the white children paid little attention to the colored children except for an occasional grabbing of a colored child to keep him from getting the limb, which was all in fun. The colored children seemed to form a play group within a play group, the white children's talk almost all being addressed to other white children. Moreover, the colored children seemed to hang back and let the white children take the lead during the play. The colored children stood around and watched the white children as if admiring them. However, when the number of colored children increased and the two groups were about equal in numbers, the colored children showed much greater courage in swinging higher and longer on the limb, and much less fear than did the white children.

> When an officer came along one of the colored children was half way down the block by the time the officer spoke and warned them not to play on the limb because they might fall and get hurt. The six white children made no attempt to run. When the policeman came back the second time, all the children ran but one of the colored girls led the group. The white girls were the first to go back to the limb and start swinging on it before the officer was out of sight.

Although it is important to note the difference in the attitudes of the white and the colored children toward the policeman who represented the authority of the larger white community, let us direct our attention to the children. It is apparent from their overt behavior that the colored children hesitated to participate freely in the play group until they had the support of larger numbers of their own race. Even then it appears that they did not participate individually but rather as a group. Their self-consciousness was indicated not only by their initial hesitancy about participating freely in the play but also by their attempt to outstrip the white children. It is in such neighborhood contacts as those described above that some Negro children first become conscious of their racial identity.

As indicated in the chapter on the community, it is difficult to generalize about the relation of white and colored children in the border cities. Although neighborhood contacts range from open hostility to extreme cordiality and good will, our materials lead us to believe that the most frequent type of relationship is similar to that described by a field worker. Her observations concerning the neighborhood in which she had lived for five years were as follows:

> On the south side of the block in which I live there are about eight three- and four-storied apartments occupied by whites, while the Negro families live on the north side of the street. Although there are children on both sides of the street, during the five years that I have lived in an apartment on the colored side I have never seen colored and white children playing together. On the occasion of this study I inquired of all colored children playing on their side if they ever played with the white children, or if they ever had quarrels with them. The answer was no in every case. I never saw any evidences of quarrels or conflicts between the two groups. As far as the white children [and adults] are concerned, the colored children [and adults] do not exist and *vice versa*. In the stores and business places in the neighborhood, members of the two groups never exchange a pleasantry. There may be a veiled hostility beneath the apparent indifference, but it never breaks out.

Contacts between white and colored children are numerous enough, however, in border cities, to affect the colored child's attitude toward his racial status; even where no intercourse exists, as in the above situation, colored children learn to adjust to the attitudes and behavior of whites. Since the type of adjustment is influenced largely by their class position, our analysis of neighborhood contacts will follow, as in the chapter dealing with the family, the class structure in the Negro community.

LOWER-CLASS YOUTH

Since, as we have indicated in the chapter on the family, many lower-class families and children are relatively accommodated to an inferior status, it is not surprising that some of the neighborhood contacts reflect the traditional pattern of race relations. In the following account, told by the fourteen-year-old daughter of a laborer in Southwest Washington, we get a view of lower-class behavior which middle- and upper-class Negroes resent as "being monkeys for whites":

We used to go down to the wharf an' sing an' dance for the white folks down there, an' they'd throw us money. They was real nice. Then, some time the ole police would come an' chase us away. The police did catch us down by the wharf once, an' he beat us good that time, with his hand an' with a switch. He never hit none of us with a club—you see we all livin'. Tell the truth, though, we didn't have no business down there. Police took us home once an' he tell my mother if she don't beat us, he will. Then, my mother she act like she real mad an' she say, "Will I beat 'em? I'll half kill 'em!" Then when police go, she give him a five finger salute and just laugh. She didn't beat us. Some of the white folks down to the wharf is purty nice. Once some of 'em took our pictures. You find it's mostly the poorest class that ain't got nothin' that's the worst.

Usually the relationship of subordination is based upon the economic dependence of the Negro. Among the poorest Negro families the children speak of white neighbors being "nice" because they give their families clothes and food. For example, a twelve-year-old boy in Southeast Washington told the following story:

They [white people] live right across the street there. They're always giving us a lot of things. They don't eat a lot and sometimes they send us leftover food over here. You know white people don't eat much. They give me clothes and shoes. They have a little boy just my size and the other day they gave me a pair of his old pants. They were good ones, too. They paid my sister four dollars a day once just to go down to court and testify for them. My mother was working for them and an old white woman from Georgia that lives up the street about four doors came down and told her to stop hiring colored people. The old white woman didn't like colored people and she didn't want white people to hire colored people. She asked to see my mother and the lady wouldn't let her in the house, so she started tearing off her dress and tore it all off and left her standing there in nothing but her slip and underclothes. I saw it all and she would have had me to testify but I was too young to be in court. She had the old white woman arrested and the case lasted four days. The woman told the judge "naw," she didn't like "niggers" living on her street and what about it. She said she didn't mean to tear the dress off and started crying. She had to pay all the court costs and buy a new dress. The judge ordered her to move off the street and she's gone now.

OLDER PEOPLE KEEP SEGREGATION GOING

In some instances the association between white and colored children may include visits by the latter to the homes of the white children. For example, a ten-year-old boy, the son of a laborer, gives the following revealing account of his feelings when he was invited to a white home:

I only know one white family in this end of town. They live down on X Street. They are very good friends. They treat me fine. They always give me a lot of bottles that I can sell and get money for. They give me about thirty cents worth every week. One time she invited me up to her house to a party she was giving for some children in the neighborhood. I didn't want much to go but I thought I had better go because if I didn't she might not like it and wouldn't invite me to some other things later on that I wanted to go to, so I got dressed and went on to the party. There were only two colored people there. Me and another boy. All the rest were white. I felt ashamed being there with all those white people. I didn't go inside and mix with all the other white kids. I sat out on the porch by myself. I was ashamed and I thought they might get me in there and call me some names so I just stayed out. The other colored boy went on in and played with them just like he was white. They didn't do anything to embarrass him. I went in to get some ice cream and punch. They had a lot of everything. Around here, the white people treat the colored people all right if the colored people act all right towards them.

Usually, it appears from our cases, the contacts which colored children have with white are limited by the existing relations between the adults in the community. This is seen in two cases of lower-class boys. The first is from the account given by a thirteen-year-old boy of his relations with a white playmate.

I come in contact with white people now and then. I know a few white families. My mother works for one white family. They treat me all right. I go over to play with the little boy often. They don't do anything for me. They don't speak to me on the street. I see them on the street lots of times, but they don't speak to me. I don't speak to them neither; I just pass on by and don't say anything to them. If they don't say anything to me, I sure ain't gonna say nothing to them. The little boy always speaks to me and I speak to him but I don't say nothing to the others because they don't say nothing to me. They never have shaken hands with me. They never invite me to their house. The little boy tells me to come over to play with him and I go over and play with him, but they never invite me over. I like to have white friends.

A similar story is told by a sixteen-year-old boy, whose mother worked as a domestic.

I know only one white family and I knew of them through a boy in the family. We played together and his parents even talked to me if we met on the street, but he told me they wouldn't approve of my calling at his home, so to save embarrassment, I never went. He used to come to my home, though, and I didn't object for I don't care to go anywhere I'm not wanted, and I didn't believe it was his fault. It's the older people who keep this thing of segregation going. So I never received any invitations.

Although the boy in the above case is fundamentally right when he says that it is "the older people who keep this thing of segregation going," nevertheless, as white children grow up, they break off their associations with their colored childhood friends. In fact, one reason that Negro children give for not wanting to cultivate friendships with white children is that when the latter grow up they change their attitudes toward their colored playmates. According to a boy in Louisville consciousness of being a Negro first dawned upon him at the age of puberty. He tells the following story:

> I first knew I was a Negro when I was just about the age of fifteen. When I was small I played with white boys and girls, but when I became about fifteen I noticed they had a different feeling toward me; they didn't take up with me as they had in the past. This I believe was because the other white persons would call them and say something to them. There were two white girls I had been playing with ever since I was six years old. A man on the street called them aside and told them not to play with me. They came back and told me what he said. They said, "That man told us not to play with you because you are a Negro." They laughed at that but I felt different. I wondered what was the difference. At fifteen I believe the girls' parents got behind them. We had grown up. Of course the girls speak to me today. Just before school started I saw the oldest one at Fourth and Market. She asked me how I was getting along in school, what grade I was in and told me how she was doing. She had a job as a WPA stenographer.

INTIMACY WITH SELF-CONSCIOUSNESS

Adults undoubtedly influence the behavior of white children, especially at puberty, toward Negro children. But Negro chilren despite the extreme intimacy which sometimes develops between them and white children are conscious of their race. This is shown in the following case from one of the disorganized sections of Washington. A fourteen-year-old girl, who denied at first having had sexual relations with white men, corrected her statement and told the following story:

> Listen, I kinda told you a story there. I take that back. Not exactly a story neither 'cause they wasn't no white men I really had. They was just little boys. We never did live in Georgetown, but my aunt did an' we used ta go over there a lot. Now, see, this is the difference in Georgetown and in Southwest. In Georgetown, white kids an' colored kids play together all the time. The white boys used ta go in an' git their sisters an' we match up an' go from one to the other an' have ourselves a grand time—all mixed up. Tell you the truth, though, I never did think the white boys were as good as the colored boys. I don't know why—somehow they just don't hold you right er

somethin'. We was all about six or seven, or nine or ten. They didn't know nothin' then, though, neither did we. The white kids didn't act no different from the colored. When I was about ten or eleven, I used to go with a little white boy out there, but I never had him, though. He was a German. After I got bigger, that boy used to worry me to death hangin' around; all he knew was, "Mary, please, please." What'd he want? "Some" as all the rest, of course. I never give him nothing, though. I sent him on to some white gal. Let her fix him up. I didn't want him. I ain't played with no white kids since then, though.

The following incident, related by a nineteen-year-old college freshman in Louisville, shows the sensitiveness of Negro children about their racial role even in play relationships:

We used to play movie actresses. We got along all right until one day we played an "Our Gang" picture. They wanted me and Jane to be the little colored children. I didn't think anything about it but Jane said no. We would not play it unless one of them would be a colored child. They said we could play it better than they could because we looked more like colored children than they did. Still Jane wouldn't play. Finally one of the white girls said she would be a little colored child.

Even where colored children play freely with white children in their immediate neighborhood and do not become conscious of their race, other white children may make them race conscious. A girl in Louisville gave the following bit of significant information concerning her childhood relations with whites:

I never thought I was white, but when I was little I never played with anything but white children and I thought I was *it*. When I was a little girl the white children around me never did call me "nigger" but I remember when I was seven or eight the white kids in the next square did. You didn't have to do anything to them. All you had to do was walk down the street.

EXPOSED TO A HOSTILE WORLD

Lower-class youth are constantly exposed from early childhood to the hostility of whites. From their earliest years some of these youth have heard the epithet "nigger" from the mouths of white children. When asked when he first learned he was a Negro, a twelve-year-old boy replied:

When I was real little, a white boy came along and called me "nigger."

When asked how he felt, he added:

It made me mad. I felt like throwing a brick at his head but I was too small to throw one.

A seventeen-year-old girl told this incident to show the attitude of white children in her neighborhood:

Last week my sister and I were going across to our house and we had to pass two white houses. Two little white girls about five years old, yelled at us. "Go back on the other side! This is our house. We don't want niggers crossing on our front. Niggers can't pass here." Their mothers heard them and called them inside. They were sticking out their tongue and saying, "nigger." We didn't say anything to them.

A retarded youth, twenty-one years of age and in the sixth grade, expressed his reaction to the term "nigger" and the treatment he received from whites:

When these things happened I felt embarrassed and angry. Later, I felt like a sick dog. I've only been sorry I was a "nigger" during things like this. I never could understand how or why one man because of his face and position could treat another as I've seen white people treat Negroes. I've felt like I wanted to kill those people who think of you like dogs and who help to make you live like one.

Lower-class girls as well as boys will often fight whites who show hostility toward them. A girl in Louisville tells of her first fight with a white girl:

I had my first fight with a white girl right in here. We were coming down the street. Some white girls hooked arms and wouldn't let us pass. On this particular evening there were only three colored girls along. We made up our minds we weren't going to move and bumped back. One of the white girls bumped back. I shall never forget it. I was really going for her. All the other white girls got scared and ran off and left her. When I was really going good Miss X came down the street in her car. She got out of her car and got me. It was a good thing, too, because the policeman was coming. She took me on home.

In Washington, a fourteen-year-old girl told with much satisfaction of the encounter which her pal had with a white woman:

> Once a white lady rolled a baby carriage right over a girl's feet. This girl, she was one of us. She say [Mary told this with dramatic gestures; she stood up, and put her hands on her hips]: "Lady, you rolled that carriage over my feet." Then the white lady tried to get tight. She say, "Put your feet in your pocket. Why don't you keep your feet out of the way?" Now, that happened down on Sixth and K Street, an' this girl she started beatin' the lady an' the lady grabbed her baby an' started runnin' and yellin'. Girl beat her clear to Sixth and E right on up to the police station. We was runnin' along behind laughin' and yellin'. Purty soon, we say, "Chile, there's the police station. Let's go back." She say, "No, I'm gonna have my white lady." She beat her right on up in front of the station an' then ran back an' we skipped the cops.

The violent behavior which is easily provoked in lower-class youth is, of course, an expression of deep-seated resentment and bitterness toward their lot in life. One girl was known to seek occasions to fight white people.

The most bitter experiences generally occur not in the immediate neighborhood but during contacts with whites in the larger community. A thirteen-year-old girl in Southwest Washington told the following story:

> I used to know one white girl and she was real nice. She's real big now, too, and she still plays with colored children. Most of 'em stop after they git big. She never did call me "nigger." If she did, I'd beat the devil out of her. One day, we were in the dime store and there was a white woman in front of us. Her little boy kept pulling things off the counter. One girl with us said, "If I had a little boy, I wouldn't bring him downtown in a crowd." This woman turned around and said, "Listen, you dirty black nigger, you go to the devil and keep your mouth shut!" The girl wasn't even talkin' to her. If she'd said it to me, I'd a cussed her out. Yesterday a little white boy down near the school spit on me. I chased him, but I couldn't catch him. If I could a caught him, I'd a beat the hell out of him. Some white folks are nice and some aren't. But I don't like none of 'em. Most poor white folks are onery. If I could be born over, I'd like to be a foreigner; I'd rather be a nice brown Hawaiian than anything

else. Gee, they got the prettiest brown skin and the longest black hair. I don't like no light skin. I just don't. It don't look good to me. I'd rather be brown.

A fifteen-year-old boy in the same section tells of an incident in which he suffered embarrassment to the extent that he was sorry that "it fell his luck to be born a Negro":

> When I was a kid, I used to hear folks talking about "colored people," and that dark-skin people were Negroes, so I just concluded I was one too. I don't remember an incident, but I had several experiences of being told I couldn't do things because I was a Negro. I remember one ride on a bus I had to Alexandria where the driver told me I couldn't sit where I wanted to because I happened to be a Negro. It happened before a bus load of white people and they laughed and smiled. I almost cried and I tried to hide in the seat I was in. I felt hurt and embarrassed and was so sorry it fell my luck to be born a Negro.

If space permitted, numerous incidents could be cited in which other youth have had similar experiences, which made them feel like "dropping through the floor," or caused them to "hate themselves," or feel bitter toward whites.

MIDDLE-CLASS YOUTH

One fact that differentiates the neighborhood contacts of middle-class Negro youth from those of lower-class youth is that middle-class children very seldom have neighborhood contacts with the children of their parents' white employers. Thus, in their contacts with white children in the neighborhood the factor of economic dependence upon the whites is generally absent. Then, too, middle-class youth, influenced by such factors as family pride and discipline and a sense of personal dignity, are more likely to be sensitive to the behavior of white youth which follows the traditional pattern of race discrimination than are Negro youth of a lower social position.

To begin our analysis of the neighborhood contacts of middle-class youth, let us consider the case of a thirteen-year-old, chocolate-colored boy whose father was a plumber and whose mother worked for a private family most of the day. Both his father and mother had told him that the best way to get along with white boys was to leave them alone and play with boys of his own race. They had also told him not to fight with white boys but to call a policeman if white boys molested him. This youngster, however, did not think so much of his parents' advice because, as he said, a policeman would not do anything to a white boy. So he had made up his mind that if a white boy bothered him, he was going to defend himself and fight it out with the white boy.

Though this boy admits that sometimes he has wished that he were white in order to enjoy some of the privileges which white people enjoy, he does not believe that white people are superior to colored people. In his words,

> A lot of colored people are better than white people and a lot of white people are better than colored. So that's the way of it. They're all about the same.

But he added that:

> a lots of times colored people act like they aren't as good as white people. When colored people talk to white people they start scratching their head like this and moving back and forth or pulling their hat or doing something. They get nervous; they just can't keep still while they are talking to white people. They act like they are afraid of them. Some of them don't do that but the majority of them do.

This extremely sensitive, middle-class boy plays with white children only occasionally. He has noticed that

> when their mothers see them out playing with colored children they call them in the house and tell them not to play with colored children.

To this statement he added the remark, "White people think they are better than colored people all right."

Concerning his contacts with whites, he told the following story of an incident which had occurred six years previously:

> When I was about nine years old, the white man next door asked me if I wanted to work; I said, "Yes." He was a streetcar conductor and he was giving a big party. He had lots of ice cream and cake and beer and sandwiches and everything. He took me in the house and said go in there. There were a lot of

white people in the room and when I first started in, I was 'shamed to go in. He pushed me on in and the people started saying, "Oh, ain't he a nice little colored boy." My heart was just a beating 'cause I was 'shamed to be in front of all those white people. One of them said, "I bet he can dance good," and another one said, "Go on, Sonny, and dance for us." I was 'shamed to dance and wouldn't do it. One of them reached in his pocket and pulled out a dollar bill and showed it to me. He said, "See this, it's yours if you dance for us." I had my cap in my hands and I was just a pulling at it. I wanted the dollar bill but I didn't want to dance. I looked at the dollar and then I looked at the floor; I moved my feet a little bit and tried to start dancing but I couldn't make myself dance. The man said, "Aw, he ain't gonna dance," and started to put the dollar back in his pocket. I said, "Naw, wait, I'll dance." I didn't want to see him put the dollar back. I started dancing and did something. I don't know what I did but they said, "He can dance good, can't he?" And when I got through, the man gave me the dollar. I ate all the ice cream and cake I wanted because they had plenty of it.

The behavior of this sensitive, thirteen-year-old, middle-class boy presents a marked contrast to that of lower-class children dancing for whites about the wharf. It is also significant that he voluntarily told a long story of having worked for a white woman who always attempted to cheat him out of his pay. The story revealed a certain distrust and hostility toward white people which probably reflected feelings of insecurity. His daydreams seem to support this inference since they generally dealt with situations in which white people were molesting him or he was revenging himself against white people. One of the several daydreams which he recounted was as follows:

I imagined I was working for a white man and he beat me and made me do everything for him, but he paid me my money every week. I imagined that I kept on working for him even though he beat me and treated me so mean. I worked for him a long time and he would always pay me on time and I didn't spend hardly any of the money he paid me. I just kept on saving it and saving it. Then after I had worked for him a long time, I imagined that I got all his money. He had paid me all the money he had for working for him. I was rich and he was poor. I imagined that I bought his house and everything and then hired him to work for me, but I wouldn't pay him but a nickel or a dime and then follow him to the store to see that he spent it so that he wouldn't get rich and I get poor again. I imagined that I made him do all kinds of work. I made him work from "sun-up" till "sun-down." I bought a theater and made him scrub the floors and dust and clean it all over. I would go around behind him and inspect. If I didn't see anything, I would put a little dirt in the corner somewhere and say, "Come back here; here's a little speck that you missed. Come back and get it and see that you don't leave nothing else."

ALOOFNESS AS A PROTECTIVE MECHANISM

Partly because of the conflicts often ensuing from contacts with whites and partly because of the implications of an inferior status when associations with whites occur, middle-class children often remain aloof from white children. A Louisville youth remarked:

> White people have always lived out in our neighborhood, but I never did live next door to any of them and the white people that did live out here, my people didn't consider them as good as we are.

The policy of remaining aloof from white children is due also to the fact that middle-class children learn that when white children reach the age of puberty they are likely to break off their associations. A seventeen-year-old girl in Washington told the following story:

> I played with a white girl who lives next door and my brother played with her brother. She is older than I am. When she went to high school she stopped speaking. I asked mama why she stopped and mama said they all do that. I don't say anything to her. She speaks now only when I go in the store to buy something. She doesn't say much because she knows she will get an answer so short! [Shrug and laugh] This girl's brother called my brother "nigger" once and he beat him up! What would I do if someone called me "nigger"? If it is a grown person, I would probably call them names back which wouldn't do any good. If it is someone my own age, I'd probably chase them down the street! "Nigger" is just a low term for a dark, a black person. It is just a low term for Negro. Some people don't like

to hear the word Negro because people stretch it into nigger; they, and I believe I, too, prefer the word colored.

In their neighborhood contacts, middle-class children are more likely than lower-class children to be protected by their parents against the derogatory implications of the term "nigger" by some rationalization concerning the term. When a girl of five was called "nigger" by a gang of white children, she was told by her mother that anybody could be a "nigger." Frequently, these parents, while telling their children that any "low-down person can be a nigger," add the explanation that they are Negroes.

POLICE ARE INDIFFERENT TO CLASS DISTINCTIONS

Much of the resentment of middle-class Negro youth toward whites is due to the treatment of Negroes by the police. This is illustrated by the following incident recounted by the mother of a middle-class boy:

It's terrible the way these policemen from Number Nine treat colored people. They just beat them up and shoot them and nothing is ever done about it. About three years ago, a colored man and a streetcar conductor got to fighting on the streetcar and there was a fourteen-year-old girl on the streetcar. She was an overgrown girl just like my girl there, and she looked like she was about twenty years old. Being young, she got nervous at seeing the men exchanging blows and she jumped out the window. A policeman who was coming up looked at her and thought she was a woman. He thought she was connected with the fight and started to beating her up. He beat her up so that they had to take her to the hospital. When I heard about it, I was so mad I could boil.

Middle-class youth are especially bitter because of the fact that the police, often indifferent toward or contemptuous of class distinctions among Negroes, treat them like the dangerous criminals usually found among lower-class Negroes.

UPPER-CLASS YOUTH

Although upper-class parents attempt to protect their children from unpleasant experiences because of their race, nevertheless, their children have contacts with whites in the neighborhood which make them race conscious. An upper-class youth, seventeen years of age and of college standing, recounted the following concerning his naive ideas in regard to the meaning of color and how he learned of his racial identity:

> I found out I was something different from folks I had seen when I was quite young by looking in the mirror. I was under the impression at six years old that a colored person was one of different colors or who could change colors. One day up at the corner, I saw a big white man, who while he talked would turn a deep red and then gradually fade back to a pale white. I asked a man if he was a colored man. He told me that wasn't a colored man but a white man and that I was a colored or a Negro boy. I guess I was too young to have any particular feelings in the matter, but it was the first time I discovered I was any different from anyone else.

Sometimes, the fact that many upper-class Negroes are of fair complexion tends to complicate their relations with their white neighbors. This is shown in the story of a mulatto girl in Louisville.

> I remember my cousins used to come to see me. They are light but don't look like white. The white people next door peeped through the fence and said, "Baby's nigger cousins are at her house today." That was a long time ago and I felt rather bad about it. Although they called them "nigger," as soon as we had finished eating they were out there yelling for us to come out. We went out and played with them. They treated my cousins just like they treated me, but I think it really came upon me that I was really colored.

The story of another upper-class boy, of freshman college standing, shows how neighborhood contacts first acquainted him with the term "nigger."

> I used to be much lighter in color than I am now and I wanted to play with white kids out here. When we first moved out on X Street there used to be some white children around. They used to refer to other colored kids as "niggers" and once they called me one. I didn't know just what they meant, so I, in turn, called a colored boy next door a "nigger" in my father's presence. He called me in and told me that there was no such thing

as a "nigger" and if this boy was one, so was I and that we both belonged to the same race.

This boy, who is indifferent to whether he is called colored or a Negro but resents the term "nigger," acknowledges that he would rather be white because of the handicaps Negroes suffer and that he has planned to leave the country some day.

WHITES WITH MONEY DON'T PAY ANY ATTENTION TO NEGROES

Since upper-class families would identify themselves culturally with upper-class whites and often show considerable contempt for "poor whites" and Jews, they do not want their children to associate with lower-class whites, Jews, or immigrants. One fifteen-year-old girl remarked that in her neighborhood there were plenty of Jewish stores. She had never played with any of the children and had no desire to. She saw no advantage in being with Jews or being a Jew. They were discriminated against just as Negroes were, but not as severely and were not liked. They should be friendly with Negroes, but they wanted to be white.

Though upper-class Negroes would like to have their children associate with upper-class white children, upper-class whites do not desire their children to associate with Negro children except when the subordinate status of the latter is clear. This was clearly seen by a twenty-one-year-old college student in Louisville who stated the situation as follows:

Whites were once well off in the neighborhood, friendly, no disturbances. As soon as they moved away disturbances, neighborhood fusses began. People who moved in say "nigger" every once in a while. A little white boy will call a little colored boy "nigger." There is a whole lot of cursing going on. The better class of white people didn't do this. This is the way I think it is throughout the world. The better class of white men have a lot of money and just don't pay any attention to the Negro.

That such is the situation in the border states an upper-class mulatto youth in Washington learned through an experience that left him bitter toward whites. The following incident occurred when he was eight years old:

My brother and I used to play with a couple of white kids of a rather prominent family around the block. That was about eight years ago when we first moved here. All of a sudden the children stopped playing with us, and when we inquired about it, we learned the mother had ordered them to stop playing with us because we were Negroes. We asked mother about it and she tried to explain the situation to us. Personally, I felt pretty badly and for a long time I detested white people and anything white. Gradually that feeling wore off but I still don't trust them. To me, the fact that I was so different from other boys and girls was a distinct shock and it is enough to make a fellow feel inferior and resentful. I don't remember any other occasion other than that of a few weeks ago when some of us went into a drugstore over in Northeast and ordered sodas and when we sat down to drink them, the proprietor informed us the store was due to be closed at that hour, so rushed us without being served. We insisted, of course, upon which he let us know in no uncertain terms that he didn't serve Negroes and that he'd close up the place before he'd do it. We hung around just to see to it that he closed this night ahead of time. What is it about us that makes us so undesirable? Do we contaminate the air in white places? I pride myself on my appearance and looks and feel I could stand beside any Nordic in these respects.

Yet upper-class parents define such behavior on the part of whites as that of ignorant "poor whites" or perhaps of "southern whites." Sometimes they inject into their efforts to neutralize the effect of derogatory terms bitterness and hatred toward whites. Note the mother's instruction to the son in the following case:

I learned I was something different when a group of white boys I used to play with on North Capitol Street where we once lived called me "nigger." My mother told me not to pay any attention, and that they were only white snakes anyway, and that when they called me "nigger," I should call them *snake*. Sometime later, I stopped in a drugstore near Riggs Street where ice cream sodas were being advertised. I ordered one expecting to drink it in the store. The clerk put it in a box and said I couldn't eat it there. I insisted on eating it in the drugstore and the man took me by the arm and put me out. I told my mother about it and she got sore about it but told me the reason I couldn't eat the soda there was because I was a Negro. I did feel pretty badly because I didn't think my being a bit darker than others made such a difference. It was a long time before I wanted to go into any white person's store. I told you of an instance I experienced at a downtown haberdashery, and I have been to several stores in town that didn't want Negro patronage. I'm beginning to hate the fact that I'm a Negro; yet I know I might just as well be satisfied because like a leopard, I couldn't change my spots.

NO ESCAPE FROM THE INSTITUTIONS OF THE COMMUNITY

Of course, there are cases where upper-class colored children are on friendly terms with white children. For example, the son of a professional man gave the following account of his relations with whites:

I know quite a number of white families through church activities. I know a number of them through my mother. I have a number of good friends among the white boys of the community and the church. They have invited me on numerous occasions to their homes. I've been to a few of them and I've had them over to my house. I've had dinner at their homes—one lives on P Street and another on Seventeenth Street. They were very cordial and I had a very agreeable time. The boys had as good a time at my house. I've played basketball for a long time with these fellows, eaten, slept, and played with them. When I meet them on the streetcars or on the streets, they stop and talk. Frequently my mother and me pick up one and drop him off at his house, and on one occasion one of their fathers took me home.

It should not be inferred from the foregoing statement that the white churches receive Negroes or help in the development of friendly relations between white and colored children. In fact, the white churches conform to the customs of the community as is illustrated by the following case:

I learned I was a Negro from my mother. She told me all dark-skinned people were Negroes. I didn't find out just what it meant till I was in the grades in school. I realized then that Negroes had separate theaters, separate churches and schools, and so forth; so there must have been some differences in black and white folks. I felt badly the first time I tried to go to a white church with a white boy I knew, to be told at the church door that colored boys were not allowed. Since then, I've had no use for white people. We are human beings and Christians; yet in churches of all places a difference is made.

Sometimes it is because of the existence of the separate institutions in the larger community that upper-class children especially become keenly conscious of their race. A twelve-year-old son of a government employee gives the following account of how he became aware of his race:

> I found out I was a Negro and different from other boys long ago. After you've gotten eight or nine years old, you begin to notice that you must be different—separate churches, separate schools, separate theaters. But once I went up on Fourteenth Street to a white theater where my brother worked. I thought it would be all right to go see the show. They stopped me at the door and said, "Don't you niggers know you can't come in here?" I felt sort of funny and ashamed. After that I always felt myself not as good as a white person. I know they're no better than I am, but I just always feel that I'm different when I'm around them.

It often happens that where friendly relations have grown up between white and colored children, these relations are spoiled by the customs and practices of the larger community. This is shown in the incident related by the sixteen-year-old son of a government employee:

> I first found out I was a Negro from white children I played with when I was very small. I also heard of people being called black, "nigger," Negro, and colored at home. At first I didn't think anything about it, except as references to my color, but as I grew older I began to feel I was different from other people, and in such a way I wasn't very proud of it. Once I wanted to go with some white children and found I couldn't share the trip because colored people couldn't go. I was pretty young then and felt pretty badly because I didn't think my color should make any difference particularly since for years I had played, eaten, and even slept with the very kids I couldn't take the trip with. I wished the ground would swallow me up, and I felt very ashamed and embarrassed each time I saw my "friends" thereafter. For a while, I hated all white people, but now that I understand, I don't feel so badly any more.

This case is especially interesting because it shows how the child may at first regard his darker skin as a mere physical characteristic; but later is more deeply affected by it because of the manner in which his skin color is socially defined.

Even upper-class youth cannot escape the definition of his racial status either in his neighborhood or in the larger community. In the following case, one can see how an upper-class youth in Washington compensates for his feelings of inferiority by instructing white tourists:

My first experience as far as I can remember happened when I was a very small boy. I used to go around a lot with my father and when we went uptown, I wanted to go in some of the white theaters. Finally, he told me we couldn't go in because they were for white people only. I still couldn't understand why any distinction should be made, but gradually it dawned on me that a white face made a lot of difference. I felt pretty hurt and sort of funny for a while and felt that evidently I wasn't as good as white people but now I don't pay them any mind. Coming home from school, I generally go through the Capitol grounds and I take great pleasure in answering queries of white tourists who stop me.

SUMMARY

Our findings concerning the influence of neighborhood contacts on Negro youth may be summarized with reference to the three classes in the Negro community. Lower-class children are more exposed to the hostility of the white community than either middle- or upper-class children. As a result of the many insults which they suffer, lower-class children are often involved in violent encounters with whites which increase their bitterness in regard to their status. Within their immediate neighborhoods, they may associate on friendly terms with white children but this association is generally limited by the adult members of the community. Consequently, it is not unusual to find that even in their intimate associations with white children, they are conscious of their racial status. Middle-class children who possess, on the whole, a more developed sense of personal dignity, may eschew the association of white children because of the attitude of the adults and also because they know that as the white children reach puberty, they will break off their association with Negro children. Middle-class youth are especially embittered by the tendency on the part of the police to treat all Negroes as lower-class criminals. Upper-class children are insulated as far as possible from the hostility and insults of the white community. Although they have a certain disdain for "poor whites" and would welcome association with middle- and upper-class white children, they do not find whites of either class more disposed to intimate associations than lower-class whites. Despite the protection which is afforded them by their parents, they cannot escape the definitions of racial status which are set up by the institutions of the larger community. Most important of these institutions are the public schools to which we shall turn our attention in the next chapter.

CHAPTER IV

THE SCHOOL

IN OUR American culture the public school embodies in its very conception and at the same time symbolizes as does no other institution the democratic ideal. But actually provisions for the public education of the masses, whites as well as blacks, have been determined by local and regional economic and social forces. In some sections of the South, where a semifeudal system resting upon a decadent plantation economy has tended to nullify the force of the democratic ideal, caste based upon race and color has added complications to the existing class alignments. There a separate school system, which in itself is a denial of the democratic ideal and a concession to the caste principle, has created in many localities inequalities in teaching competence and physical equipment which have made Negro education a mere caricature.

Although in the border states a separate public school system has been a part of the racial mores, the inequalities in equipment and teaching competence have not been so great as in the old South. In Washington, as we have shown in the chapter on the Negro community, provisions for the public education of Negroes have closely paralleled those for whites. Because of this fact, Negroes in Washington have been proud of their schools which have enabled them to share with whites the cultural heritage of America and which at the same time have provided an avenue for the employment of their talents and abilities. Many differences exist, nevertheless, among the public schools of the border states and quite often these variations have been influenced by the classes in the Negro community from which their teachers as well as pupils are drawn. Therefore, in our analysis of the effect of the public schools on Negro youth, we shall again follow the major socio-economic groupings in the Negro community.

LOWER-CLASS YOUTH

That the majority of lower-class youth in Washington believe that they enjoy educational advantages approximately equal to those of whites is indicated by the following typical statements. An eighteen-year-old senior high school student, whose father is a laborer and whose mother works in domestic service, stated:

> As far as schools are concerned, I think we have as good schools and teachers as the whites and each year they are improved. Some of our buildings are very old but buildings don't make the school or turn out better graduates.

A twenty-one-year-old high school graduate expressed a similar opinion when he remarked:

> As far as I know, Negro schools in Washington are as good as the whites. I'd expect to find better buildings, better equipment, better shops, even more courses in the white schools, but despite that, I think our schools and our teachers are just as good. I don't think the white graduates are any better either.

In some cases, at least, these youth think that colored schools are better than the white schools. We may cite the statement of a sixteen-year-old boy who said:

> I think the colored schools are even better than most of the white ones. Whenever a radio contest is given and white and Negro children take part, the Negroes always excel, proving the school has done its part well. I don't think there's a better college in Washington or in the vicinity of Washington than Howard University. They've got everything they need and plenty of well-trained teachers. If I have a chance to go to college, I would like to go out of the city where I could have some fun, but I'd probably go to Howard anyway. Negroes can get all the education they need, probably more than they need in their own schools, so why should they spend more money and worry trying to finish white schools?

The statement of another sixteen-year-old high school boy is in the same vein. He remarked:

> From the point of view of buildings and equipment, the mass of white schools are better than Negroes. I believe, however, that our teachers are better. Standards for Negro teachers have been higher and Negro teachers seem to take more interest in Negro

students than whites would ever take in us. At any rate, I prefer to go to Negro schools and I'd prefer to go to a Negro college.

A nineteen-year-old high school graduate made the following bitter comment:

I think Negro schools are just as good. Looking at some of the silly looking individuals at the white schools, I think our schools are better. I suppose they have better looking schools and more things for the students but we have the best school spirit and I'd rather go to the Negro schools than to the white ones. I think we have a lot more fun, anyway.

COLORED PEOPLE INHERIT OLD WHITE BUILDINGS

In the statements above in which the youth expressed the belief that their schools were as good or better than white schools, there are references to the fact that white children have better school buildings and better equipment. The youth who do not believe that the colored schools are equal to the white institutions generally base their opinions upon this fact as well as the fact that they have inherited the buildings abandoned by whites. When a seventeen-year-old, first-year high school student, the son of a laborer, was asked if he thought colored people had as good schools as the whites, he answered emphatically:

Definitely, no! And I can prove it. In most of the schools, you can't get your mind on your work for watching out for ceilings falling. Half of the ceilings fell in Cardoza just before school closed. This has happened in a number of schools this year, even up at Miner Teachers College, the "junkiest" building I know for a training school for teachers. We always get the buildings after the whites have torn them up, or when they're about to fall to pieces. We get all the out-dated equipment and used stuff. We know the program is different. They have teachers who are more interested in their students than ours. They get all the athletic equipment they want, and have a real schedule of games. Roosevelt, Taft, Eastern, Western, and McKinley High Schools [white] make the Negro schools look like country schools. Compared to our buildings the white high schools look like colleges. Howard looks more like one of those big high schools, and I suppose Howard would compare the same with Harvard.

While the interviewer was taking a fourteen-year-old girl to be interviewed the following conversation took place:

Girl (Pointing to a school building)—Is that Central High School?

Interviewer—Yes, it's a white school.

Girl (Emphatically)—I know it isn't a colored school.

Interviewer—Why not?

Girl—Colored people just don't have schools like that, that's all.

Interviewer—Dunbar is a pretty building.

Girl—Not like Central. Colored people will probably get Central, though, when it starts to break down. Colored people always do.

A similar opinion was expressed by a girl in Louisville, where the inequalities arising from the separate school system are more glaring:

> Negroes have a chance to go to school here nine months. But the schools are not what they should be. When Negroes need a new school they are given one of the old white schools and the whites are given the new building with modern equipment. Negroes don't get the advantage of the equipment until it has gone out of date.

This girl's remarks concerning the nine-month term referred to the shorter terms for colored children in the old South. Since many of the children in the border states come from the lower South, their evaluation of the schools in Washington and Louisville is based upon their experience in the lower South. For example, a twelve-year-old boy in Washington commented as follows:

> I have been in Washington three years. I came from Louise, Virginia. I went to school there, of course, and had lots of fun. Sometimes when we're playing at X School I think of those good old days. We had more time to play and lots of woods near the school to play in. We stopped school in May and had to go back in August. That's one reason I like Washington schools. You learn a whole lot more and I can get all the books I want to read.

SEPARATE OR MIXED SCHOOLS?

When the youth interviewed were asked their opinion of the colored schools in the border cities, they were also given an opportunity to state whether they preferred mixed or separate schools. Although no statistical comparison of the preferences was undertaken, the opinions appeared to be about evenly divided. A boy in Louisville gave the following opinion:

I don't believe I would like any mixed schools. I would like to go to one for about a month but not for a whole term. Negro students that go to mixed schools seem to think they are better than anybody else. I know that from personal experience. I know some boys that live in Indiana—went to high school in Anderson. They seemed to have thought that they had a higher culture than we had—seemed to have thought they mixed with the best people there. On the whole they seemed to have thought they were better than we were. If you are a good athlete in these white schools you just skate along. They thought they could just bring this attitude out to Municipal but they couldn't. One boy lived with me last year. We slept in the same bed. He thought that people should give him money to spend, that he shouldn't have to go to school unless he wanted to—he thought a number of things that were impossible 'cause those people out there don't care anything about anybody. All they want you to do is to do the work.

But another girl in the same city who had been to mixed schools in Chicago spoke as follows:

I went to a white school in Chicago. I think white schools are best because children don't have a chance to become "hinkty" [snobbish]. They are all mixed together and play together. I think white teachers and colored teachers are all the same. I got along just as well with one as I did the other. When I was going to school there I didn't pay any attention to color. I played with white children as much as I played with colored children. I don't remember thinking I was anything but colored, but I have always thought I was just as much as any white person.

In the following statement of a boy in Washington, one can see how contacts with a larger world influence their opinions concerning the desirability of attending mixed schools:

I'm afraid we don't often get all there is to get in our own schools; but I don't believe it's possible to get all the training and education Negroes need in any Negro schools. I had a fellow tell me the other day who is a high school graduate and who visited some schools in Chicago and he said he didn't know till then how little he really knew. You can get a lot more from mixed schools, but I think a few Negroes always get lost in a crowd of white students anywhere.

The same point of view is expressed by another boy in Washington who learned of mixed schools through a friend:

> I've never attended a mixed school. I think I'd like to, though. I know a boy down at school from Boston, and he attended mixed schools until he came here. He says he can't get used to the idea of segregated schools. He speaks beautiful English and I love to hear him talk. A lot of people laugh at the way he talks. He says there's something at a mixed school that makes a Negro excel or drop out. I believe mixed schools are able to knock off rough edges and give you the incentive, the desire to succeed; something that you can't get in Negro schools. Their attitudes are even different.

A few of the youth who indicated a preference for mixed schools were apprehensive of the treatment they would receive, especially from the teachers. An extremely race-conscious girl, twenty-one years of age and of junior college standing, who wished she were darker, stated emphatically:

> I am perfectly satisfied at a colored school. I prefer it. I don't believe a colored pupil can develop properly at a white school. No colored pupil would get the opportunities they get in a colored school. I prefer to make Negro contacts as I will work with the race after I graduate.

Some of the youth who indicated a preference for mixed schools gave as their reason that white teachers were likely to be indifferent to the social status and skin color of Negro children. In voicing such opinions, these youth were expressing the opinion of some lower-class children of dark complexion that their teachers discriminate against them because of their color and social status. Of course, it is difficult to determine to what extent such charges are true.

DO TEACHERS DISCRIMINATE AGAINST THE DARKER PUPILS?

Since the public schools in the past at least have been the chief means by which upper-class Negroes, who are generally of mixed blood, could secure a type of employment consistent

with their training and social position, it is not unlikely that
some teachers have favored fair children, especially those who
come from their own class. However, whether discrimination
exists to the extent indicated by the statements of the youth
interviewed, the fact that the darker children feel that they are
discriminated against is important in studying the development
of their personalities. It should be stated at the outset that some
lower-class children denied that teachers discriminate against
them either on account of their social status or dark color. But
the overwhelming opinion on this point, in Louisville as well
as in Washington, was that the teachers favor the lighter children, especially those of the upper class. Let us, therefore, hear
what the children have to say on this point.

A thirteen-year-old girl asked the interviewer, "Do you know
Miss X at Y School?" and without waiting for a reply continued:

> I hate her. When she gives plays she only puts the real light
> children in them with long pretty hair. She always lets them go
> on her errands, too. An' she don't never let no dark children do
> nothin'. Or, if she does have to use 'em in a play, she always gives
> 'em the shortest, backwardest parts.

Another thirteen-year-old girl stated:

> Over at X School, Miss Z didn't like for dark children to be in
> plays or anything. She liked all the little ole light children better
> than she did the dark ones. She always let the light children do
> things for her. But she never lets the dark ones. She gives light
> children better marks all the time too. Then sometimes she takes
> children round to different rooms and "shows 'em off" to the
> teachers for doing things real good. But she never takes any
> dark ones.

A nineteen-year-old girl in second year high school gave the
following illustrations to prove that some teachers favor lighter
girls who are often of the upper-class status:[1]

---

[1] During an interview with a teacher who denied that any preference was shown
upper-class or lighter children, the interviewer observed that on three occasions
when the teacher wanted a pupil to run errands or do something for her a light
child was selected despite the fact that several dark children eagerly sought the
attention of the teacher when she asked for volunteers to run errands or do whatever was to be done.

I remember once Miss X took up the whole class period explaining something to Mary [an upper-class girl] which she would never have done for the ordinary child. She would have said, "You'll have to see me later. I can't take up the whole period setting you straight." No, indeed, she didn't see you later—she would always get out of it some way or other. Mrs. Y was partial to color, too. She was not liked by most of the kids, light or dark, but she always had her set of pets. They say that Miss Z had her pets, too, hanging around the office, but I never noticed that she picked them from any particular group except that she always had nice looking girls, and girls who usually dressed right well.

Lower-class children in Louisville gave similar testimony on the preference shown fair and upper-class children. A girl reported:

There was a short, light teacher down at X School who was partial to position and color. If your people were big, she gave you a good grade. You could get a good grade too if you were light. She didn't have any time for dark children. She wouldn't even smile at them. When a light child got up to recite she would help them along. If you got up to recite and you were dark and your people weren't big people even if your answer was right you couldn't make an *A*. If you gave the absolutely correct answer, she would add some more on it so she wouldn't have to give you *A*. After she had pumped the answer out of some of her light ones or some big persons' children, she would turn around and say, "Why can't the rest of you do as well?" There was another one at school I just hated. He was a tall brown-skin man. He was partial to position. It didn't make any difference to him what color you were. All he wanted to know was, "Who are your people?" The first class you have under him, he spends asking you who are your people. He asked you where you live and what your parents do for a living. He came out in class one day and said, "Blood will tell." There is one teacher in Y School who is crazy about light girls. He don't say anything to dark girls but he is always fooling with light girls. Everybody knows it, too.

A sixteen-year-old girl of yellow complexion who remarked that she "liked all people darker than I am if they will let me; but most dark people are evil," said that a very dark teacher discriminated against dark children. Her statement follows:

I know some teachers who don't like black children. When I was in Miss X's room she'd always send light children around, sometimes or maybe once and a while she'd send some brown-skinned girl around but she sure wouldn't be black as she is. I liked Miss X myself. Miss Y, she was crazy about light children more than Miss X. Why, when she had somebody to go places for her she'd always send some light person. She like to run me to death when I was in her room.

A fourteen-year-old Washington girl in the seventh grade gave the following story of the origin of her dislike of light-skinned people:

A light teacher slapped me when I was in the third grade. A lot of children were crowding around the teacher's desk and she told us to take our seats. And I was the last child getting to my desk because I stopped to throw some paper in the basket. She came down the aisle and slapped me in my face, and the children laughed. I ain't liked no light people since.

In some cases, the child's teacher may not be guilty of discrimination, but the child's hatred of people of fair complexion can be traced to experiences with other light-skinned Negroes.

In concluding our consideration of the matter of color and class discrimination in the schools, we should point out that the complaints came almost entirely from the girls and that they are directed in most cases against the women teachers.

THE LIGHTER ONES STICK TOGETHER

The comments of the lower-class children concerning ways in which they are discriminated against in the public school include statements concerning the behavior of upper-class children toward them. When a sixteen-year-old Washington girl of dark-brown complexion told the following story, her voice became strained and her eyes filled with tears:

They [the lighter boys and girls] don't want to be around you, and they act "hinkty." They go around with those that look like they do. The lighter ones stick together most of the time. . . . One day I wanted to be with some of them, and they walked away and wouldn't associate with me. . . . One day in the locker room a girl wanted something I had, and I wouldn't give it to her. . . . She said: "Oh, go on away, you old black nigger."

This girl "guessed" that some of the girls "were just 'hinkty' because their parents had good teaching jobs." A light brown-skinned girl of lower-class status (her parents were working in personal service) had a dark girl for a chum. According to her story:

> The kids used to tease her and ask her if she was my servant. She would cry. I told her not to pay them any mind but she worried about it anyhow. She said it was no use for her to go to school. She couldn't get any job worth anything. There was no need in her staying in school because she could get domestic work without finishing school.

Some of the youth in Louisville told stories of fights in school because the darker children were called "black" or "smoky." In one case, a boy said that the teacher whipped the offender. According to his story when he started going to school,

> A boy called another boy black. The teacher told him he had no business calling this other boy black because both were Negroes. She said that there were some light Negroes and some dark Negroes. She gave that boy a whipping.

TEACHERS' INFLUENCE ON PUPILS' CONCEPTION OF NEGRO

The teachers, in fact, influence in a number of ways the pupil's general conception of the Negro. Individually, the teachers give some attention from time to time to achievements of the Negro and the question of race relations. However, it is only during Negro History Week that teachers as a whole present the achievements of the Negro to the pupils. Many of the pupils complained that they never heard of the achievements of Negroes in school except during Negro History Week. One boy said that, "Then we get our fill of the old timers: Booker T. Washington, Paul Laurence Dunbar, Frederick Douglass, and a few others I've forgotten." Another boy remarked that, "There's always a big splurge around Negro History Week but after that passes, the idea of knowing more about Negroes goes with it." He concluded with the cynical statement, "I suppose that is to be expected of books written by and schools run by white people." Another felt that the lack of interest in history on the part of colored pupils was due to the failure to tell of successful colored people. He concluded with the remark, "Who wants to be reading about some white men all the time who probably hated Negroes all his life? I get sick of them."

The teachers' influence on the child's developing conception of the Negro race and of himself as a Negro is not restricted to the formal exercises during Negro History Week or even to what is said in classes in Negro history. They exert a far greater influence through the casual remarks which they make from time to time concerning the Negro. For example, the teachers are naturally concerned with the conduct of their pupils which in some of the tougher sections of the city presents a serious problem of discipline. It seems that some teachers undertake to improve the children's behavior by disparaging remarks concerning the Negro and by holding up to them the supposedly better behavior of white children. In some cases this is probably due to the fact that the teacher, being a member of the upper class, actually has the same attitude toward lower-class Negroes as whites. For example, a freshman college student told the story of his teacher in elementary school and junior high school:

> In junior high and elementary school, she used to always be talking about how much worse colored people were than white people. She said she didn't blame white people for not letting colored people go in their places. She used to say she wouldn't let them come in either if she was white because they were so lame-brained and didn't have sense enough to act right.

One girl stated that the principal told the pupils that Negroes would "never be recognized equally with white people because they don't know how to conduct themselves." Another girl of eighth-grade standing thought that colored people "don't have many privileges because they are noiser than whites." She had learned this from her teacher who had told the pupils that

> colored people always have their mouths stretched from ear to ear. When she, the teacher, is on the streetcar and there are colored and white pupils on the car, the white pupils are talking very nicely, but you can hear the colored ones all over the car. The teacher also told them that they were going to stop colored from riding on the cars or do something about their making so much noise.

Some children, however, do not believe that colored children behave worse than whites or are noisier than white children and resent the aspersions cast upon Negroes. One girl remarked that

she has seen white kids act just as bad as colored ones on the streetcars. They, too, hang out the car windows, sing, attempt to ride free, and so forth. Some of the teachers think that just because these kids are white it isn't so bad. She feels that it is just as bad for them [whites] to act that way as it is for Negroes.

Another girl was emphatic in her statement that

colored children are not noisier than white children. White children make noise the same as all children.

From the statements given by the youth interviewed, the teachers do not attempt to inculcate attitudes of subordination toward whites but undertake to teach the children to avoid conflicts with both white and colored children and to conduct themselves as respectable, law-abiding citizens; that is, as upper-class Negroes and upper-class whites conduct themselves.

MIDDLE-CLASS YOUTH

So far as their opinions of the colored school system are concerned, there is no noticeable difference between middle-class and lower-class youth. A sixteen-year-old boy of first-year high school standing expressed himself as follows:

I think the colored schools are just as good as the white ones and I believe the teachers are just as well trained as the white ones. Some of them even went to the same schools as the whites. I think the high schools are even better. Of course, we don't have all the up-to-date equipment the others have, but for example, X School has the finest photography laboratory in the city schools. My teacher is interested in various things and he has taught me a lot. I like him because he actually knows a lot about everything. You don't find many Negro teachers like that or willing to help no matter how foolish the question.

One of the boys whose conversation was recorded in the introduction gave the following opinions on the relative standing of colored and white schools:

I don't think the colored schools are as fine as the whites because the whites usually get the newest and cleanest buildings with all the newest and best equipment. I don't think white kids learn any more because I don't believe that white teachers as a whole are as well educated and as well prepared as Negro teachers. One of my teachers over at school says that a lot of white Washington teachers don't even have a college degree, and that all Negro teachers must have them to get in. I think they take more interest in us probably because we need it so much more. I wouldn't like to go to a white school. In the first place, I realize I'm much too dark and I just wouldn't want to be thrown with white people that much.

Although this boy expresses a preference for colored schools, this is not the opinion of all middle-class youth. Some middle-class youth expressed their preference for separate schools because they felt colored teachers would show more interest in them. One of these, a girl, added the following statement:

One girl went at one time to mixed schools. She did seem a little strange, but I'm not sure whether it was because she went to mixed schools or was from out of the city. I don't think that white principals—I am sure the principals would be white—of mixed schools would be as interested in the children [colored] as colored principals and colored teachers are. Sometimes I have wished that I lived somewhere else because there are better opportunities for employment in the North. I have heard my father say that.

Some of the middle-class youth who had had experience in mixed schools were in favor of them. A Louisville boy of college standing had spent some time as a child in Chicago. He spoke of his school experiences as follows:

I liked everything about Chicago—wasn't used to going to school with white children, you know. My teacher was white, forty-nine children in the room and wasn't but eleven colored children. I was sitting in the last row in the last seat. In front of me was a white girl and on the side of me was a white girl; the principal's name was Mr. X and teacher's name was Miss X—I will never forget them.

While a Washington girl thought mixed schools would be best, she felt that she would have to get used to them because, as she remarked, "At first I'd look kinda wild; one colored among all those whites."

The sixteen-year-old daughter of a paper hanger, who had definite ambitions and plans for the future, gave the following opinion on the question of attending mixed schools:

> I like all kinds of sports. When I finish X School, I would like to attend Sargent. Then I would like to get my Master's at Columbia University. I became interested in Sargent because all of the physical education teachers are Sargent graduates. Then, too, in all reference books it is listed as the best physical education school. [The interviewer asked how would she like going to a mixed school.] I think I would like it; it would be a change from separate schools. I think everyone should go to a mixed school at least part of the time.

In the matter of what they learn concerning the Negro from their teachers, middle-class youth gave opinions similar to those of lower-class children. They felt first that they did not learn as much as they should about members of their own race. One boy, sixteen, stated with much feeling:

> I've often wondered why we didn't study more about Booker T. Washington than George Washington! No matter how much I try, I can never be a George Washington. What he did, he did for his own people—what Booker T. Washington did, he did for my people. In school, we seldom ever hear about Negroes. If it wasn't for Negro History Week, we'd know a whole lot less. We study white people and white people's history and with all that knowledge, we don't get any whiter and they sure don't treat us like we were becoming whiter.

This deficiency in their instruction, they thought, was only partially made up during Negro History Week when the achievements of the same characters ("those buried and rotted," as one boy put it) are rehearsed. The discussion of the Negro and race relations depends upon the temperament of the teacher and his attitude toward these questions. A few youth complained that one teacher took too much time from the lessons in discussing the race problem. What the pupils resented most, however, was that this teacher was constantly pointing out the deficiencies of Negroes. One middle-class girl said that this made her "boil."

The statements of middle-class girls to the effect that teachers favored pupils of fair complexion differed in two respects from similar statements by lower-class girls. First, they did not include any reference to class differences in connection with differential treatment because of color; and, secondly, there was less apparent bitterness in their remarks. In fact, the middle-class girls in our study appeared to be more sure of their own status and possibilities in the world. In the majority of our cases, middle-class youth denied that discrimination in reference to color was practiced. For example, one girl was confident that it did not exist because, as she remarked, "I know I'm no light-colored child and I have gotten along with the teachers." Another girl of dark-brown complexion gave the following analysis of the situation. Before she went to X High School, she had heard that

> the dark children wouldn't get credit for what they did. I suppose they meant that if you made a certain mark, you weren't apt to receive it, or if you really passed an examination, they may flunk you. But I didn't find X School like that. I think it is the person's personality. Some people can't get along with anybody. There are some light girls who can't get along with anybody. Some people just think it is their color all the time and they will just never get along.

It is true, nevertheless, that in some cases the middle- as well as lower-class children blame their color for their deficiencies and inability to get along with the teachers and other children.

UPPER-CLASS YOUTH

When an upper-class boy was asked who was the most popular student in school, he named another upper-class boy and went on to tell why he was popular:

> He is popular because he dresses well, is a handsome devil, is a star on most of the teams, takes part in almost all the school activities, is an officer of the cadet unit, has a car and money. There are very, very few that could meet all those qualifications. To top it all he is a good student and is well liked by the teachers. His father is a popular professional man and that has a lot to do with it. He has one holdback—he isn't quite light enough for some of the students and teachers, but despite that he "does all right." [That is, he is acceptable for the role.]

It happens that this particular upper-class boy possessed all the qualities which account for the prestige and ascendency of upper-class children in the schools. The slight deficiency in regard to color, a reddish-brown complexion, referred to by our informant, was really no handicap so far as this boy was concerned since he had all the other qualifications. Upper-class boys and girls of darker complexion, though they possess other attributes of upper-class membership, do sometimes encounter discrimination on the part of the teachers and may not be completely accepted into the most intimate circles of upper-class association. For example, an upper-class boy who belonged to an old respected family and whose father held a clerical position in the government felt that he was not fully accepted into the upper class and that he was discriminated against in school because of his dark complexion. He remarked with much bitterness that

> teachers usually set up some dumb-Dora or bum as the best liked and most popular individual. Invariably they're usually some real fair boy or girl from some big shot's family. I've had the color question pushed in my face on many occasions.

CONFLICT BETWEEN CASTE AND CLASS

It is often in the relations among the upper-class youth that the conflict between caste based upon color, and class identification based upon occupation and income, comes to the surface. The following statement is from a girl of lower-class (socio-economic) status who preferred going to another school because of the higher status which she thought her light skin would give her:

> I would be one of the lightest girls in school. They have so many rusty spades at X School that a person my color is fair. The teachers [so one of the boys had told her] at X School want to have some nice-looking children in school.

Upper-class youth of dark complexion speak very frankly concerning color discrimination within the upper class. They are especially bitter because they feel that despite their family background and socio-economic status which should make them eligible for full participation in upper-class activities they are not completely accepted on account of their dark complexion. It is, however, because of their enjoyment of some group participation that they are extremely conscious of discriminations. For example, a very intelligent, medium-brown boy of upper-class status and of college standing made the following statement concerning color discrimination:

> At X School, color discrimination could be noticed in the cadet corps. The officers were usually light boys or light-brown skin. Often, they would bawl out dark boys for the same infraction which they would pass over in a light boy. I look upon this as petty abuse and a copy of white psychology toward all Negroes.

Generally, color discrimination among upper-class youth appears in the more intimate groups such as cliques and clubs. This was apparent in one of the exclusive clubs among high school boys. According to several members of the club, membership is limited to "boys of good character, outstanding achievements, good manners, and a good family background." It is true that the boys who compose the club measured up to these requirements. But there were boys having the same qualifications who said they were excluded because of their dark complexion. A study of the skin color of the members revealed that with one exception they ranged in color from medium-brown to a fair complexion; about an equal number of boys being of medium-brown, light-brown, and fair complexion. The presence of the single member of dark-brown complexion was on the surface a refutation of the statements of dark upper-class boys that dark boys were excluded, but a study of the actual situation indicated that the upper-class dark member of the club owed his membership to the fact that his pretty, light-skinned sisters were sought after by the members of the club. Then, too, it appeared that the fact that this boy had a car helped to overcome whatever objection they might have had to him because of his dark complexion. In spite of these advantages, however, this boy did not participate as freely in the activities of the club as the other members and never assumed leadership in their activities.

An upper-class girl of light-brown complexion whose father was a government employee thought that discrimination on account of color was more noticeable in junior high and high school than in college. In college it is not as obvious, although there may be an undercurrent. She could recall one case which she thought was unusual. In a history class last year, a girl moved from her seat to the one next to her, saying she could not sit by a black girl. Our informant said that she was quite surprised and disgusted and made the girl no answer. The girl who had moved was of fair skin with Negroid features and rather "bad" hair. She thought that as a rule color discrimination breaks down in college because high school groups, composed of girls who have always gone around together [and who somehow seem usually to be around the same color] are broken up upon graduation and new associations are formed.

This girl's observation that color discrimination tends to break down in college points to a general tendency in regard to color caste among Negroes. In the larger Negro world where status is determined by a form of competition in which individual success counts for more than skin color, a light complexion loses much of its significance as a value in determining one's status. In the larger metropolitan areas a fair complexion has less value than in Washington.

"OUR" SCHOOLS ARE EQUAL TO THOSE OF THE WHITES

Upper-class children are, on the whole, satisfied with the colored schools and feel that they are the equal of the white schools. Typical of this attitude is the statement by a girl who said:

I feel that our curriculum and teachers are equal to those of the whites. I have noticed in the past years that those Dunbar or Armstrong graduates who have gone to leading white colleges have done very well as far as scholarship was concerned. I think this does show that our facilities must be on par with the whites. I feel Negroes can get all the education they need here. We have Howard University and Miner Teachers College.

The satisfaction which upper-class youth generally express in regard to the colored schools is due in part to the fact that their parents are alumni of the schools and in many cases teach in these schools. Thus they have come to identify themselves with these institutions which are responsible for their prestige and status in the Negro community. Moreover, many upper-class youth look forward to the time when they, themselves, will find secure and remunerative employment in the public schools.

Although upper-class youth constantly hear the teachers criticizing Negro children for their noisy and uncouth behavior, as a rule they do not object to these talks because they feel that the reprimands are directed to lower-class children who need such talks. For example, a Washington girl states in this regard:

Our school teachers tell us often that Negroes never know how to act. They usually have special reference to the conduct of students on streetcars and in the streets, especially near school. The principal calls assemblies to reprimand the disorderly ones. I am not included because I know I don't cut up on the streetcars nor in the street. To begin with, I ride the cars very seldom. Colored children are more noisy and uncouth than whites. But I don't excuse a white person for his noise just because he is white. I think one is just as bad as the other—noise is noise, whether it is made by a black or white person.

Other upper-class youth spoke in the same vein, always indicating that such talks were needed by lower-class children. Some of them added the remark, as this girl did, that they very seldom rode in streetcars.

Although upper-class youth are, on the whole, satisfied with the public schools, their statements concerning separate and mixed schools do not show a marked preference for separate schools. To some upper-class youth an assertion of preference for separate schools would be an admission of inferiority to whites. In a number of cases their answers to the question of mixed schools included their experiences or those of friends and acquaintances in mixed schools. In the stories of their experiences as well as those of their friends in the white schools, there is little mention of racial discrimination. For example, a girl who attended a white school in the North said:

I had a good time at school at the dances. Colored and white danced together—white girls with colored boys, colored girls with white boys. It didn't attract any attention. A colored girl was one of our class officers and was in the receiving line at our prom. She was a dark girl. She had lovely features and was beautifully dressed. I don't know whether any frat member who started going with a colored student after he got in would be asked out. I never heard of a colored student going to one of their dances. They usually had them downtown at hotels and I don't think any colored student ever went to one. I never heard. The colored and white students at X School were of about the same class—from good types of homes. The school was located sort of between good colored and white sections, though there are not many colored near as Negroes haven't been out that way so long.

A boy who attended a white school admitted that he was lonesome, and that in spite of the disorder of Negro schools he preferred the latter. He said:

I attended a public school in Long Island. I was one of about three colored children there. It was very nice and we were treated like any of the other children. We could do everything the other children did. It was kind of lonesome though and for that reason I'd rather go to an all Negro school. The teachers don't take the kind of interest in you that colored teachers do. I did like it though because in Negro schools the children are always fighting and noisy in and around the school. White children seem a whole lot more considerate.

This boy's statement indicates the ambivalent attitude which upper-class youth show toward the Negro group. Despite their attitude toward the darker lower-class Negroes, they are more outspoken than lower-class youth or even middle-class youth in their dissatisfaction with the meager information given in schools concerning the achievements of the Negro. For example, one of the members of one of the most exclusive boys' clubs remarked with emphasis:

The school system should include a great deal more about Negroes in its curriculum. There's not much use of a Negro becoming famous unless he can stand as an example for others to follow. And to follow such a man, the schools must do their share to keep before Negro children those who have met with success as they've done with Thomas Jefferson, Washington, Lincoln, and others.

SUMMARY

Three important factors must be considered in estimating the effect of public school education in the border states upon the personality development of Negro youth. First, the traditional practice of choosing administrators and teachers from the upper-class has had a profound influence. The schools have reflected the outlook and the interests of the more fortunate social group who enjoy advantages denied to the great mass of Negroes. In some cases the school people have expressed an impatience with Negro youth who have had no cultural background or economic advantages. The effect has been to increase the sense of inferiority and insecurity, particularly among pupils from the lower class.

Second, there are great cultural and economic differences within the Negro community. Social prestige, more so in the past than at present, has been associated with a lightness of complexion. There is definite evidence from the statements of young Negroes to indicate that teachers often discriminate against the darker pupils. Many teachers have expressed strong distaste for the behavior of lower-class Negroes, and they have tried to inspire their pupils with zeal to emulate the upper class. Thus, the great mass of lower-class pupils of dark complexion are made conscious of their inferior status. Only the upper-class pupils appear to experience a full opportunity for success in school adjustments.

Third, although Negro youth must attend separate public schools, in the border states Negro schools have a high degree of efficiency. Graduates who have gone to colleges predominately white have made good scholastic records. The result has been to make Negro youth dissatisfied with an inferior social status. They have demonstrated capacity for academic achievement in schools comparable to those available for white pupils. They realize, therefore, that the Negro is not necessarily condemned to a subordinate position by any innate disability of intellect.

CHAPTER V

THE CHURCH

DESPITE the existence of separate educational
systems in the border states, the public schools mediate to the
vast majority of Negro children patterns of behavior, thoughts,
and ideals common to American culture. Although the character and functioning of the schools are affected by the general
culture of the Negro, the colored public schools in the middle
states are essentially the same as the white institutions. On the
other hand, the Negro church is an institution which the Negro
has made his own. It reflects in its ideologies and practices as
well as in its organization and leadership whatever is unique
and peculiar in the Negro's experience and outlook on life.
Therefore, in seeking to discover how isolation and inferior
social status have affected the personality of Negro youth, one
cannot neglect to study the influence of the church. In studying
this influence, one can best approach the problem, once again,
from the standpoint of the economic and social stratification of
the Negro population.

LOWER-CLASS YOUTH

The majority of lower-class families are affiliated with the
Baptist and Methodist churches. These churches attempt to perpetuate in their services those features which have been traditionally associated with Negro religion. The lower economic
strata of the lower class are attracted to the Holy Rollers and the
Sanctified churches in which the ecstatic form of religious behavior is encouraged. Some of the lower-class youth would
express themselves in the same way as this sixteen-year-old girl
who was a member of a regular Baptist church in Louisville.
One can note in her statement class differences in religious
behavior:

I shout because when you got good religion you shout. Reverend X says you haven't got good religion if you don't shout. He said that these stiff Christians weren't any good, and they didn't have good religion. Most of the people who have good religion sit down in the front of the church but most of the hypocrites sit in the balcony so they can make fun of the way Reverend X talks. They call themselves the "society bunch" of the church; they sit up and laugh at everybody. They make fun of Sis' Mary because she runs all around the church when she gets happy. I don't think that's right, because if that's the way the spirit moves her, they shouldn't laugh. When the spirit comes on you, you feel like hollering and you just holler till the spirit goes down. The spirit dies down when you stop feeling like you want to shout. I like for Reverend X to have revival because he usually gets a preacher who can really preach the gospel. He preaches the gospel when he tells what's in the Bible just like it is. Some preachers are dry, all they do is to stand up and read and talk to you. But the preachers Reverend X brings for the revival are always good. They get the church all stirred up. Sis' Liza Lee sure has got good religion because she sure can shout. Boy! when she starts to shouting I get out of the way because one man can't hold her. I haven't ever seen a woman walk over seats like she does. She really acts when baptizing day comes. When her granddaughter got baptized, she almost walked into the pool. She was sitting on the third seat from the front and she climbed over both pews before the men were able to catch her. But when they finally got her she was climbing up the pulpit trying to get in the pool.

Usually such youths have had the experience of "getting religion." Another girl told the following concerning her experience in "getting religion".

It was in 1931. I had always been taught to pray. In this Baptist revival I sang and prayed. I prayed and people prayed for me. Finally I felt happy. I saw some people shouting; I wanted to shout too, but I couldn't bring myself to it. All I could do was cry. I almost doubted religion when I first got it. I had heard people say that the Lord didn't answer the prayer of sinners. Before I got religion, everything I prayed for I got. Right after I got religion I prayed for something and didn't get it.

Still another girl of this class tells of her activities after "having got religion":

Well, when I got religion I didn't know what it was all about. The superintendent of our Sunday school sent a woman into our neighborhood to gather all the children up and bring them to revival. I went along and got what they call religion. Now I feel different about religion. I believe you should serve the Lord and thank Him for everything you get. Then religion means service. If you belong to a big church and it is getting along fine, you should work in a small church. I belong to the Y Methodist Church, but I work in the Z Methodist Church. It is a small church and needs help. Then Reverend X is the pastor. He is more interested in young people than any colored preacher in town.

In many of the cases studied, lower-class youth had broken away from the church and the religious practices of their parents. They had become "worldly wise" and had come to doubt the sincerity of the ministers and the value of the church. In brief, they reflected in their behavior and attitudes the secularizing influence of the city. Note, for example, the attitude which was expressed in the following statement by a girl in Washington:

I was about fifteen when I joined. I can't say that I felt happy in the sense of getting religion. I felt that I wanted to be a true Christian. I still feel that way. I would say that I like church and I don't like church. I like it well enough to go there one day a week and pay my respects, but I surely don't believe in church like mama does so that her whole life is home and church.

In the following statement by a laborer's son who was in the third year of high school, one can get some notion of the cynical attitude and hostility which some of the lower-class children show toward the church:

I don't like church and never have. I believe most of these so-called church people and ministers are hypocrites. I used to go around to different churches to see friends of mine but I never cared to join any of them. Negro ministers just want your money and personally I think it's just a waste of time and money. It's been a long, long time since I've been at all and I haven't missed a thing.

Another youth, nineteen years of age, who was a high school graduate, expressed himself as follows:

I don't know much about the Bible and nothing of religion. I think it's lots of fun to see Michaux's crowd or Daddy Grace's perform. I don't miss one of their side shows. To me, all religion is about alike. One just a little more dignified than the other, I guess.

Then when asked if he went or belonged to church, he replied:

I used to go around to some of the churches when I was a youngster and didn't know better, but I don't go now, nor do I belong to any. I think it's a waste of time and money to hang around the church. All they want is money, and what do you get? Go to church regularly, listen to dry sermons—and then what have you? I usually spend Sunday with the "numbers" crowd on the corner or go to the show.

Much of the lack of respect for and confidence in the church arises from the fact that some of the ministers who are constantly preaching against dancing and playing cards are guilty of serious moral lapses. A girl in Louisville remarked:

Reverend X is a pretty fair preacher but what I hate about him is that he's always kicking on dancing and playing cards; but let me tell you there ain't a worse set of preachers in town than the Baptist, they do everything—they're big enough—but they're always hollering about dancing, smoking, and drinking and playing cards. They's plenty things worse. I smokes and drinks and plays cards and I don't think it's no sin and nothing he says or does can stop me. I like church but Reverend X just makes me sick talking about dancing and stuff.

IS GOD A WHITE MAN?

These statements do not mean that the church has no influence on the personality of Negro youth. On the contrary, the church contributes a great deal to the self-evaluation of lower-class Negroes. Some of them accept literally the pictures of God and Christ given in Sunday school lessons. Although many are perplexed about whether to picture the Deity as black or white, their responses imply that the idea of white dominance is extended to include even God. When one twenty-one-year-old Washington boy was asked if Christ was a white man or a Negro, he replied:

I've never heard of Him being a Negro, so He must have been

a white man. People would think you were crazy if you told them He was a Negro, especially white people.

Another Washington boy, thirteen, had heard that He was both white and colored, but added:

I'd rather believe He was a white man anyway. White people wouldn't believe in Him if He had been a Negro.

Still another boy, nineteen, admitted that he didn't know, but thought "He was a white man." However, he added:

Negro or white, by the time white people got through, they made Him white, too.

A twenty-year-old youth, who said that he had always been taught that Christ was a white man, laughingly added the following:

Boy! Wouldn't it start a lot of trouble if anybody ever suggested He was anything else. . . . I still say I believe He was a white man.

In contrast to the implied cynicism in the foregoing statement is the remark of a boy:

Pictures I've seen of Him are all white so I just took for granted He was a white man. Had He been a Negro I'd sure heard about it and these Negro preachers would be constantly reminding white people of that fact. As a Jew, He might have been dark, but Jews are supposed to be white, so I guess that makes Him white, too.

On the other hand, a boy, who thought that Christ was white because of the pictures which he had seen, remarked that he did not think it made any difference except that "white people would die first before they'd accept Him as a Negro."

In the statement of a boy who thought "it wouldn't do for Him to have been a Negro," we can detect the derogation of the Negro. He said:

I don't know and I'm afraid I can't answer that one intelligently! But judging by pictures I've seen of Him I believe He was a white man. With his principles of Christianity and Christian living, I don't think it matters what He was. He could have been Chinese all I care. It wouldn't do for Him to have been a Negro. Negroes never follow their own people, and I don't suppose Christ would have had many Negro followers had He been a Negro.

Since these youth think of God and Christ as essentially the same person, their ideas of God are similar to those of Christ. In reply to questions concerning the physical characteristics of God, many of them gave answers like the following:

> The Lord is white. In all the Sunday school books and books I see around with His picture in them, He seems to be white. He always has a straight, narrow nose and long, flowing hair.

> God is a white man, very tall with a long beard.

> The Lord is white. All of the pictures of Him are white.

A laborer's twelve-year-old daughter included in her statement an opinion of Father Divine:

> I am Catholic. I go to St. X. The priest is white, but he is just as nice as he can be to us. What does God look like—I think He looks like the pictures with long hair and long beard and long face. Jesus looks the same. They gave us pictures at church—I have a stack of them, and one was a colored man angel. He was dark, about my color. I never saw any colored women angels. I suppose colored people look the same after they get to heaven. I have heard of Father Divine. He isn't God. He is colored and there aren't any colored Gods . . . at least I never heard of any.

In two instances, the statement was made that the Lord was a mixture of white and colored. A thirteen-year-old boy in Washington stated that the Lord was "brown skin, being half-white and half-colored." Another Washington boy, twelve years of age, thought the Lord was "as much white as He is colored and just as much colored as He is white."

WHAT COLOR ARE NEGROES IN HEAVEN?

These youth also gave opinions on what happened to colored people in heaven both in regard to their color and relations with whites. These opinions may be classified in four groups. First, there were a few opinions stating that all persons will be the same color, but not necessarily white. For example, a Louisville girl spoke as follows:

> I think heaven is a place you go after you die if you have done

what is required here on earth. If you are poor and have done a great deal for the church, you stand more chance of going to heaven than you would if you were rich. Heaven is a place where you will have no worries, no trouble and nothing will ever annoy you. Everybody will be the same color—white or the color Christ is. Christ was a Jew. He wasn't exactly white. He was sorta creamy.

Then, there was a slightly larger number of opinions that Negroes would become white or bright in color. A girl in Louisville stated:

As the Bible says, there won't be any color. Everybody will just be sort of bright. At least I hope so. You may as well stay here if you are going to be the same color.

Another girl thought that everyone would be about her color or lighter! The few remaining opinions were to the effect that Negroes would be white. But the vast majority of opinions held that Negroes would remain the same color but that there would be no racial discrimination. The following opinions are typical of many answers. A Washington boy said:

I think we go to heaven in our same form, shape and color, and to hell the same way. That's one place they don't "Jim-Crow" you—the promised land.

Another Washington boy replied:

I don't think Negroes turn any color to get to heaven. Only in comic strips have I seen Negro angels but we go wherever the whites go and remain black—so without a doubt, we remain the same color in heaven.

According to a girl in Louisville, "The people in heaven will be all colors, because God is not partial." Another Louisville girl spoke in this manner:

I guess they are all colors because God loves everybody. It's a good thing God doesn't pick out people by color because if He did, all the Negroes would be left out.

Although in the following opinions the Washington boys assert that Negroes will not change, what they say concerning the whitening process shows their unconscious bias in regard to whiteness as the standard of excellence and purity. One boy said that any question about Negroes turning white in heaven sounded

> like another phase of segregation and I don't believe of all places that there's any segregation there. I've never heard tell of Negroes having to turn white in heaven, but I don't think they do. If that's the case, there's a lot of white people who would have to turn white to get in.

Another boy spoke cynically:

> I don't think we turn white in heaven, either. If we go to heaven we go in our earthly form and color. If we do a lot of other folks besides Negroes who go will have to go through the same whitening process, for you see few *white* people and they'd have to be purged too!

Such unconscious valuations become even more explicit in the following statement by a Washington boy. He stated:

> I don't think they change any color at all; if Negroes go to heaven, I believe they are still Negroes in heaven. *By that same logic white men would turn black in hell.*

But one boy who did not think that Negroes became white made the following intelligent comment on the origin of such notions:

> We've been taught that things that are pure are white—"White as snow—pure as snow!" So, I suppose if a black man is good and kind, he is considered white in heaven, as a white man is black when his deeds on earth are black. But I don't think Negroes turn white in heaven any more than a white man would turn black in hell—unless it was from burning. [Smiles] All pictures you see of heavenly people are white, too, and perhaps the white man wants to believe we turn white, too, rather than believe Negroes go to the same place as he does after death.

In the last group of opinions, it was frankly asserted that not only would Negroes retain their present complexion but white people would continue to segregate them. Representative of such opinions, which were not numerous, was the statement of a Washington youth who said:

> I've often wondered about "niggers" in heaven, though; I often wonder if they go there at all. I suppose if we all go there together and all these mean white folks are there, there is prob-

ably some part of heaven set aside for them as well as for us. I don't know about that change of color, but I do believe we will live in different parts of heaven. If we can't get along together on earth, we probably wouldn't up there either.

Of course, not all of lower-class youth think of God and heaven in terms of crude physical qualities. For example, a Washington boy replied when asked concerning the color of God: "He isn't any color. He's a spirit." A Louisville girl elaborated her idea of heaven as follows:

I'm not so sure that there is a physical heaven. I think it is a place where everybody will be happy. I am sure some people won't want golden streets nor will they want to sit down all the time. My idea of heaven is a place where I can go to do all things I wasn't able to do on earth because of my limitations. I want to do so many things I know I wouldn't have a life long enough here on earth.

THE CHURCH AND THE PRESENT WORLD

These opinions indicate that Negro youth obtain from the church about the same standard of values in regard to race and color that is current in the dominant white culture. Even Negroes themselves allude to Biblical stories to account for their low social position and for the contempt heaped upon them. A twelve-year-old boy in Washington recalled:

My grandmother told me if Cain hadn't killed Abel there wouldn't be no Negroes. It was wrong for Cain to kill Abel for the Bible says, "We shall not kill" and for doing that we've all got to suffer. I have an uncle down home named Cain and for a long time I thought that my grandmother meant he had killed somebody named Abel, and that was why I was dark and a Negro. I don't believe Cain was a Negro before he killed his brother Abel, but I've heard folks say he was dark after he'd done it, and that from that time on there was a Negro race.

Since the chief concern of the church is with otherworldly matters, it is not surprising that only a few youth reported that they had heard anything in church concerning how to adjust themselves to the white world. One boy remarked that in the South he had heard the minister constantly tell Negroes to be subservient to whites but after coming to Washington, he had never heard anything said about race relations. Some of the Washington youth were, however, disgusted with church because the ministers constantly talked about the shortcomings of the Negro. A twenty-one-year-old high school graduate who lived in Southwest Washington spoke as follows:

> I've never heard any mention of white people at church but they really lay it on these Negroes down here. Most of the talks and sermons are on things a Negro should and shouldn't do— from dancing and gambling to marriage and divorce. If these things didn't give Reverend X subjects to raise hell with, he wouldn't have a thing else to talk about. Negroes should do this and shouldn't do that. That the Bible is against practically everything they do and they should repent, be baptized, and continue to go to church regularly and listen to that tripe. They do say that the Negro could get along better, make more out of himself, and gain more respect from the other group if he conducted himself orderly and tried to be a good citizen. They teach us to clean up our homes and ourselves for the benefit of our health and encourage the young people to go to school and quit loafing around.

This same youth stated that the church which he once attended "turned out to be an institution for the old and feeble and the very young and foolish."

Concerning the value of the church to youth, many of the youth interviewed were severe in their criticism of the church. For example, one Washington boy replied:

> I don't think youth is any more concerned about the church than the church is about them. It is unfortunate because the church could do much for them. But it must have more to offer than it does now. There are too many Negro churches for the good they do. They have too many buildings called churches; too many rascals calling themselves preachers. I go because I haven't anything better to do—and, too, some pretty girls go besides.

Of course, in some of the churches attention is given to the needs of youth. An intelligent, sixteen-year-old high school boy made the following comment concerning his church and minister:

> Our minister, Reverend X, is very interested in youth. He does

give youth a break in the church. His sermons can be understood by all and better still since he has to cater to the old folks in the church yet manages to give a specific sermon on youth and to youth every other week. We are able to ask questions and get a complete understanding of things he teaches. I think the church should have a definite place in our lives, but I don't believe the church can possibly mean as much to youth today as it did to our parents. The lessons of the Bible, if it's to be a living thing, should be made applicable to the new generation. A new interpretation is necessary for the circumstances are bound to be different. My mother is a very religious person and she can't see the necessity of making new changes in the old order of things. The church should consider youth first because the chief problem of the community is youth and the church should be vitally concerned with the adjustment of youngsters today.

MIDDLE-CLASS YOUTH

The middle class, according to our formal classification, occupies in respect to certain types of behavior a marginal position between what is defined as lower- and upper-class behavior. This is especially true in regard to the religious life of this class. The vast majority of middle-class youth come from families which are affiliated either with the Baptist or the Methodist churches or with the other denominations in which the lower classes are found. The more stable elements of the middle class tend to affiliate themselves with the oldest and best established Methodist and Baptist churches. Many of the middle-class young people have broken away from the churches of their parents and attend the churches in which the upper classes worship. The lower strata in the middle class are affiliated with the same churches as the lower class and engage in the same type of ecstatic religious behavior as the latter. Because of these various tendencies, the middle class is a marginal group.

It should also be pointed out that the middle class, that is, those disciplined and regularly employed elements among Negro workers who maintain stable family life and family control and have ambitions for their children, are the backbone of the Negro church. Families in this class give more than liberally of their means for the support of the church and identify them-

selves with the church in a manner in which they are not identified with any other institution in the community. Children in
such families are brought up in the church and the Sunday
school. Although these children feel a certain loyalty and respect for the church, they are influenced by the secularizing
environment of the city. With the foregoing facts in mind, one
is better prepared to understand the divergent responses of
middle-class youth toward questions about religion.

Let us begin with their attitudes toward the church itself.
The statement by a twenty-one-year-old youth who was a member of one of the old Baptist churches is interesting because
it shows that while he does not enjoy the services, he does not
feel satisfied unless he goes to church on Sunday. His statement
was as follows:

> I go to church frequently. I belong to X Baptist Church. I go to
> Sunday school oftener than to church services. Somehow I get
> sick of the same kind of dry sermons and talks. I like church
> though, and somehow feel the day hasn't gone right unless I go
> on Sunday.

Another Washington youth of twenty spoke in a similar vein:

> I belong to the Y Baptist Church. I don't go to church services,
> but I go to Sunday school regularly. I don't care much for those
> long-winded sermons. I don't think it's a waste of time—I just
> can't sit still so long. I think that I'm a Christian and I definitely
> believe in the Bible. I say my prayers every night and I'm such
> a great believer in prayer that I actually cannot sleep unless
> I've said my prayers.

The following statement by a sixteen-year-old youth whose
father was engaged in semiskilled work shows the attitude of
middle-class youth toward the secular activities of his church
and his disgust toward the ecstatic religious behavior of lower-
class Negroes:

> I take church seriously, and I would like to see it as a real place
> of worship; to be able to feel the presence of God. Instead,
> church, mine in particular, is more a place of business with more
> stress on getting money or meddling in other folks' business
> than teaching the scriptures. I think there are too many hypo-
> crites in the church anyway. All the folks who shout and do all

sorts of monkeyshines aren't moved by God. It ought to be a sin for people to do all that useless clowning. To me, it's a disgusting thing. That and knowing how some very religious people of the church act on the outside has made me stay away from church. My mother says the church isn't like it used to be. It must have changed a great deal if it could mean as much as it once did to her.

A seventeen-year-old youth who thinks that the church and religion are important in the lives of Negroes, makes a similar complaint:

I belong to Z Baptist Church. I don't go but about once a month. I guess church is all right but all they want is the money they can get out of you. They get my share all right. I usually give a dime per Sunday and if I don't go but once a month, I give for the four Sundays. I think church and religion are important in the lives of Negroes. It helps to keep them together and besides teaches them things that help them to lead better lives and stay out of trouble. It must be of some value or Negroes wouldn't stick with it, because Negroes seldom stick to anything long unless they're getting something out of it. As I said, I'd rather like church, but I get tired of the same old baloney. I think the church should give an interpretation of the Bible in keeping with modern times. The same sort of tripe that was taught in churches forty years ago is out of date just like schools were forty years ago. The church seems to refuse to become modern.

In the foregoing statement, there is a criticism of the church which is found in the statements of many middle-class youths. A statement of a fifteen-year-old boy reads almost the same as that above:

I'm a church member. I belong to X Baptist Church. My parents belong there, too. The church is very fine and I like to go. I like the music best of all. I go generally just to hear the organ and the choir. I never get much out of the services because the preacher usually talks either above my head, or talks a lot of stuff I don't understand. I don't approve of the type of preaching where people are "shouting" or hollering. And strange enough when he stops, they stop. As I see it, church has no place for young people. We go and listen, but what do we get? I don't get anything. From what I can see, church is only for old people. Since they are the ones who support the church, the minister feels bound to make the church as they want it.

Middle-class youth tell the same story as lower-class youth in regard to what they learn about race relations in the church. Since the churches are concerned with otherworldly matters, they scarcely mention such mundane matters as race relations. A twelve-year-old Washington girl who was a member of a Catholic church recalled that

> once in church the priest got mad with the white people. You see they didn't want to sit by the colored people. So he explained that St. X's is a colored church and if they didn't want to sit by Negroes, they could go to St. Y's Church. [Nearest white church] The white people haven't tried to sit by themselves since. We Sunday school children sit up front and like to feel that we are ahead of the white people anyway. All the kids I know don't bother much about religion.

The last sentence in this girl's statement is significant. Another Washington girl of sixteen, who attended the Methodist church, was uncertain whether she heard the minister of her church speak on race relations:

> I attend the X Methodist Church. I believe last Sunday the minister spoke of everyone being the same, white and colored, and no one being better than the other. Perhaps, I am getting him mixed with someone else.

From the following, it appears that some ministers occasionally invent rationalizations to take the sting from the epithet used toward the Negro:

> Reverend X and Reverend Y have always tried to tell us there were classes of people and not colors; he says there are some "niggers" but all of them aren't black or colored people. They say there are white "niggers" and colored "niggers." Reverend X said if we are going to fight somebody about the word "nigger," we should fight colored people, too, when they call us "niggers."

The ideas which these youth have concerning the physical character of Jesus, as in the case of lower-class youth, show the influence of pictures used in Sunday school and elsewhere. Without exception, they are sure that Christ was white. Of course, they are usually acquainted with the historical conception that Jesus was of Jewish parentage. A statement by a Washington boy is typical of most responses:

> I've never given it a thought; though I suppose He was a white man—all the pictures we see of Him make Him a white man. Then, too, He was said to be a Jew and unless there are really Negro Jews, then He was a white man. If white people thought He wasn't white, they'd drop Him like a "hot potato."

The imagery which they have of God is that He, too, is white, but without exception they believe that Negroes remain the same color in heaven and that there is no segregation. However, in the following statement by a twenty-one-year-old Washington youth, one can see how whiteness is unconsciously assumed to be the standard of purity:

> I don't think Negroes turn white in heaven. If they're black on earth, they are black in heaven. White men with black hearts don't go either, so I suppose Negroes' hearts turn white or are whitened to get into heaven. I don't believe there would be any segregation there if Christ's word is to be believed.

Naturally, some of the youths have outgrown their own crude notions of God and heaven, as the seventeen-year-old daughter of a skilled Washington worker indicates in her statement:

> How do I think of God? Now, you have me mixed up! . . . but I see, I think of Him more as a spirit. I used to think of Him as a man like the picture of Him. Not as a colored man. Now, since I have grown I think of Him more as a spirit and Jesus as being the human one. There is a God or something because the trees couldn't just grow or all the insects and lowly creatures just come; even us as human beings couldn't have just appeared so that there must be a God. I never did believe people became angels. I believe that there is a place you go to be punished and that there is a place you go when you are good, but I don't believe that there are angels.

But, of course, some middle-class youth feel about heaven and hell as the Louisville boy who said:

> Everybody in my family has got religion. I've had it since I was twelve years old. I didn't know much what I was doing but mama said after a child was twelve, he had to answer for his own sins and I got religion. Since I have been, say, about fif-

teen, I ain't believed in hell and the devil. I believe when you die you are just like a dog or a pig; you just ain't no more.

UPPER-CLASS YOUTH

When we come to consider the influence of the church on the personality of upper-class youth, we must bear in mind what has been said concerning the general outlook of this class. There are, of course, some upper-class families who do not have church connections or are indifferent to church. To them the church is one of the institutions through which they maintain contacts with friends. Generally, they feel that it has a salutary influence on the young. One upper-class youth, a Washington boy, seventeen years of age and a junior in a northern college, spoke of his relation and attitude to the church as follows:

Since I was quite small, I have been attending X Methodist Church. I think I go more or less because it is one of the things to do and most likely shall continue to go on that basis or from habit. I don't believe regular attendance is necessary or highly desirable for character formation. Formal church services have always seemed to me to be a kind of exhibitionism anyway, emotionalism at its height with the protection of morality. I never did understand Sunday school. There was no interpretation or analysis—nothing was clear. My parents did not insist on my going either to church or Sunday school. Both go when they feel like it. They stay home with good grace when they feel like it.

Another Washington boy, only ten years of age, said bluntly:

I go to church all the time. I just go because I haven't anything else to do and my mother makes me go.

A boy in Louisville spoke likewise, but added:

I see people there that otherwise I might not see over a certain period of time.

ATTITUDES TOWARD THE CHURCH

Although some upper-class youth are forced to go to church, they state frankly that they are not benefited by it. For example, a seventeen-year-old boy said:

Frankly, I don't get anything out of church, because there's little to get. I go from force of habit because the whole family goes every Sunday. My father is pretty strict about many things —and church in particular, so nobody complains any time. Everybody just goes; then we don't have to hear great arguments from him.

Another seventeen-year-old boy, a freshman college student, elaborated his objections to the church in the following statement:

To tell the truth, I get absolutely nothing. The minister is about as useless a creature as could possibly be found. His sermons are lacking in intelligence and half the time you can't tell what he's talking about. I hate anyone to try to appeal to my emotions. I don't mind having my intellect challenged! Instead of giving a concise interpretation of the Bible itself and applying it to its practical counterpart in life of today, he just picks a verse of the Good Book for a text and rambles till he's tired and I'm tired. The services, like a lot of Negro churches, certainly don't appeal to you. I'd just as soon stay home—and I generally do, now that I'm not made to go by my parents. I'm probably the only boy my size and age who has remained in the service of the church at all. Some months ago I was asked to take a Sunday school class and I go each Sunday morning to do that job. I enjoy it tremendously and we are able to do much more constructive thinking and to my mind give more practical presentations—presentations that don't have to deal in personalities, as the minister does. I feel I have religion, so I must do my part in the work of the church.

His statement concerning his objection to the emotional appeal is characteristic of the upper class, who always emphasize the fact that they enjoy sermons "that appeal to the intellect." That is the reason they often give for attending the Congregational, Presbyterian, and Catholic churches. An eighteen-year-old high school boy stated his attitude thus:

I don't belong to any church here yet but I am a Presbyterian and I usually go to the Presbyterian church. I like to go to church, not Sunday school. I think I've outgrown Sunday school now. I like the services and I find most ministers of the Presbyterian church give practical, intelligible, and interesting as well as "understandable" sermons. That's one reason I prefer the Presbyterians to the Baptists. In the Baptist church the minister himself seldom knows what he is talking about. Reverend X is a good man and I like him. He seems like a man who tries to practice what he preaches. To be honest I go to church because I just feel better because I go. Sunday seems kind of wrong when I stay away. Of course, I enjoy the service after I get there, and I like to learn about Bible history, and so forth, but I always feel better because I've gone.

The reference to antics in church in the following statement by the sixteen-year-old son of a physician who concedes that the influence of the church is on the whole good, refers to lower-class religious behavior:

I think the church plays an important part in every man's life —white or black. Despite the fact that we do have too many churches, I think they're all doing their best to elevate the race and save most of us from destruction; I don't approve of many of the antics in the church—shouting, constant wrangling over money, but despite it all, I still think we're getting something out of it.

A fifteen-year-old youth, the son of a school teacher, who belongs to a Baptist church expressed his disgust at lower-class religious behavior and indicated that he was about to join the Episcopal or Catholic church:

The church offers less than any place I know. Most of us go because we want to see and be seen. I belong to X Baptist Church. The minister there is a pretty well educated and intelligent person. He talks very slowly and pauses so often you almost drop off to sleep before he starts to speak again. But even he is preferred to some of the visiting preachers. [Then came a vivid dramatization of the poses struck by these "gospel slingers," with their fervent gestures and efforts to "shout" the people.] I do believe they pay the sisters and brothers to put on the shout act. We have one of those big stoves in the church auditorium and one Sunday a sister got happy and backed on the stove. She sure came to life and wasted no time flying out of church. . . . They are so concerned about money over there that they don't do much else. I get sick of long services, begging for money, and you don't learn nothing, so I've just about given up church. I've thought of joining up with the Episcopalians or Catholics. I like those people; they seem fair and square, and willing to do everything to help you. I like their services, too. Well, I still go to Sunday school and gosh, you learn less there. Do you know how Sunday school lessons are conducted? Well, say there are ten of us in a class. There possibly would be twenty

—or twenty-five paragraphs in the lesson. Each of us is given a paragraph to read in turn and that's all. I thought Sunday school teachers taught you something in Sunday school! I could take the book home and read it there for all the good it does. I'm beginning to think the church is a lot of hooey and the ministry instead of a profession, it's a racket. When the minister is dumb and the people dumber, the church is in a bad spot. No wonder children don't care to go to church and the old people sleep. I haven't heard a sermon yet I understood, and I've never heard any advice given on how Negroes should treat white people, and that sort of thing!

Some of these youths are frankly skeptical in their attitudes toward religion. As one youth who belonged to the Congregational church stated: "I think I believe in the Bible—with certain reservations." Likewise, the statement of a thirteen-year-old boy who belonged to the Catholic church reveals the growing skepticism of these youth:

We have to give so much money to the church. The priest says the money is for God's work, when we all know it's to keep the priest and the church going. Who is the priest that we must confess our sins to? He's a man like the rest of us and probably sins like us. I think such a faith can make one awful narrow and small—but I was brought up in it and I try to see the good in it. Religion is all right and probably very necessary to some people, but some people carry it too far. There's no sense in letting religion take all your interests. My mother does and she thinks I should.

The last sentence in the above statement shows the conflict between the attitude and outlook of the younger and older generation. A seventeen-year-old college freshman who had drifted away from the church felt that the minister's sermons were for the "old heads."

WAS JESUS A WHITE MAN?

So far as their ideas of Jesus and their mental imagery of God are concerned, upper-class youth cannot be distinguished on the whole from middle- and lower-class youth. This is evidently due to the fact that they have received their notions from the same sources as the latter. However, upper-class youth have a clearer conception of Jesus as a human personality and do not confuse him with God. A ten-year-old boy made this clear reply:

> Jesus was white, at least he ought to be if he isn't. His parents were white. The Bible says his mother and father, Joseph and Mary, were Jews; so he must have been too.

In some of their replies they reveal their cynical attitude toward whites. Another Washington boy, seventeen years of age and in the first year of college, spoke as follows:

> I've truly often wondered. I understand he was a Jew—as such, I suppose he was a white man. White men paint all the pictures of Him—so black or white in life, He is made white in reproductions of His likeness.

One finds the same attitude in the reply of another seventeen-year-old Washington youth of freshman college standing:

> It's the consensus of opinion that Jesus was a white man. I've never given it a thought but I presume He was. All the pictures I've seen, He was a white man. If by any chance He was anything else, the white people have taken great pains to make Him a white man throughout these many, many years.

The reply of another Washington youth of third-year high school standing not only reveals a certain cynicism toward whites but an unfavorable evaluation of Negroes. He stated:

> I don't know, but I'm almost certain He was a white man. Because had He been a Negro, white people would never admit it; Negroes would never have followed Him; and He probably wouldn't have been the light of the world in the first place.

Another third-year high school boy gave the following sober statement:

> Because Christ was a Jew, He must have been a white man. I'd rather think of Him as a *man,* not as a white man or a Negro. One tries to make Him superior and the other would lessen His greatness. I've always seen pictures of Him as a white man. All pictures of angels are made white, too. If Negroes go to heaven as angels, I firmly believe they remain the same color and do not change to white. Since we go to heaven as spirits, I should say there would be no color anyway.

Although this boy is evidently uncertain or confused concerning the color of Negroes in heaven, other youth had definite opinions. A Louisville youth thought that

> everybody will be the same color because heaven is an ideal place and God would certainly see to it that the same antagonism that befalls man here on earth would not beset heaven.

A Louisville girl thought that "people will be equal" and that

> if they are equal they will be the same color. I imagine everybody will be about Christ's color—about an olive or a light brown.

A Washington youth who thought that Negroes did not change color, nevertheless, in his reply unconsciously made whiteness the standard of purity. He concluded his statement with the following:

> Our hearts change from black to white—they'd have to, to get into heaven, but I'm sure faces and bodies would remain the same as on earth.

In closing our discussion of the influence of the church on upper-class youth, it should be made clear that these youth have not deserted the church altogether and that many of them feel the need of religion. The seventeen-year-old boy who said that he got absolutely nothing out of the church, nevertheless claimed that he had "got religion" and went on to explain as follows:

> I don't know exactly and probably no one knows. But I believe it's the result that you get when you profess love and belief in God, try to live the life the Bible teaches, and have a profound desire to do something worth while for others as well as for yourself. That is something fine for which you don't expect remuneration, but do for humanitarian reasons alone. But with the many conflicting interpretations I get of the Bible and its teachings, I'm almost afraid to think for myself for fear I lose this one ideal.

Although this youth is afraid to think at present, the problems which he will face in life as a Negro will force him to think and he may lose his "one ideal" as many upper-class Negroes have done.

SUMMARY

Our discussion of the role of the church in the adjustment of Negro youth to their minority status points to certain fairly definite conclusions. First, it is clear that despite the fact the Negro church is on the whole an institution created, supported, and controlled by Negroes, there is nothing in its ideology to cause Negro youth to have greater respect for themselves as Negroes. The majority of Negro youth of all classes believe that God is white. To lower-class youth, He resembles a kindly, paternalistic, upper-class white man. They believe that because of His goodness and justice, colored people will not suffer discrimination in the other world. Second, because of its otherworldly outlook, the Negro church practically ignores the problem of the status of the Negro in this world. The present status of the Negro is taken for granted and the Negro is taught to look forward to the other world for more equitable relations between men. The lower classes, especially the most illiterate and the most impoverished, find in the ecstatic form of religious services an outlet for their pent up emotions and frustrations. Third, partly because of the church's otherworldly outlook and concern with orthodoxy and partly because of the secularization of life in the city, Negro youth are very critical of the church and in many cases scoff at its pretensions as a way to salvation. Fourth, in those relatively few cases where churches show some intelligent understanding of the outlook and problems of Negro youth and set up organizations to this end, the response on their part is, on the whole, favorable.

CHAPTER VI

SEEKING EMPLOYMENT

NEGRO youth in common with youth of other races are concerned with the prospects if not the problems of a career and making a living. When some youth, mostly of lower-class status, were asked their opinions concerning the schools, we have already seen how they expressed misgivings concerning the value of education for Negroes, since so many avenues of employment were closed to them. Now when they are asked what changes they would like to see in the relations between whites and Negroes, their real concern for future employment becomes even more apparent. This concern proved to be particularly true of lower-class youth, who in almost every case placed the wish for an equal chance for employment first among the changes desired in race relations.

LOWER-CLASS YOUTH

Our analysis of the concern which lower-class youth express in regard to the prospects for employment may begin with the statement of the eighteen-year-old daughter of a laborer in the third year of college. She stated:

> It's getting so now that they are giving the whites a lot of jobs that whites never used to accept. Take street cleaning. White people never used to do that; they are doing it now.

A Washington youth, twenty-one, expressed his desire for change in the following words:

> Well, I'd like to see Negroes given better jobs; permitted to live in better homes and better looking neighborhoods. I'd like to see any difference shown be based on other things than color. I mean on ability or knowledge or training. A man's color shouldn't be any indication that he can't do a job as well as a fellow with some other color. I'd like to see white people treat Negroes with as much respect as they expect of us.

To another laborer's son, a better chance to compete with whites for jobs was the "only real change" he would like.

> The only real change I'd like to see would be a better chance to compete with whites for jobs; more jobs available for Negroes and better salaries for those who get them. I'd like to see whites quit shoving Negroes around. I'd also like to see more sports between whites and Negroes. Otherwise, I'm perfectly satisfied.

Even a retarded twenty-year-old youth in the fifth grade, who "didn't know any particular things" he would like altered, expressed the same desire concerning changes in race relations:

> I don't know any particular things I could say I'd like to see changed yet in Washington—but I'd like to see white people give "niggers" a better chance for decent jobs and pay them decently when they get them. I get tired of seeing "niggers" pushed around wherever they are.

Although an eighteen-year-old youth of senior high school standing enumerated a number of barriers which he would like to see eradicated, he did not fail to include as one the present discrimination in employment in Washington. He said,

> I'd like to see all segregation wiped out. I'd like to be able to go where I please and do the things I want. I'd like to be able to go to white schools as well as colored. I'd like to see whites make more jobs available for Negroes and give them an even break to get them. I'd like to see white people treat Negroes as they deserve to be treated, those who are rough, treat roughly, and those who are well-trained and educated, treat them as educated people.

We have the same desire expressed by a laborer's twenty-one-year-old son who has only attended high school for a short period. To his desire for an equal chance with whites for employment is added his resentment against the brutality of policemen, whose victims are generally defenseless lower-class Negroes:

> I'd like to see white people give Negroes an equal chance on merit; and give reward where it's due; to give jobs not on color but on experience and willingness to work. I should have just

as good a chance for an office job or an elevator job as any white boy with as little education as I have. White people don't treat us fairly and even white policemen seem to get a great kick out of beating up Negroes, not only because of the things they do, but because they happen to be Negroes and can't fight back.

Negro youth are especially resentful when well-qualified individuals within their own number are deprived of advancement and forced to work under less well-trained white supervisors. Typical of such opinions is the statement of a twenty-one-year-old high school graduate who said:

Negroes can do anything and any job that any other man can do. I've been on laboring jobs where laboring Negroes like me could do better supervisory and trade work than the whites over them. I've seen them help out those dumb blokes that the WPA put over us. Wherever there's a job, there's a Negro somewhere that could handle it. Too bad the government doesn't take a gambling chance and try.

He went on to give his opinions concerning employment with the government:

Anybody who knew the setup in the city of Washington would know that Negroes never have equal chances for jobs with white people. When a flock of Negroes are taken in the government you can just bet a larger number of whites went in at the same time as clerks, typists, and so forth. It isn't fair because there are many of us who can do the same jobs. All we need is the chance; I've worked several times for the U.S. Government on part-time and as a laborer and I know what they do. A Negro's best bet is with the government and they see to it that deserving Negroes get good breaks when they do get in.

A statement by a twenty-year-old youth who had completed high school indicated that job discrimination caused him to become discouraged about going to school and created in him a feeling of inferiority to whites. His statement was:

Our chances aren't as good by any means as the white man's and never will be unless the white man's attitude changes and Negroes make adjustments in their training and study. It's a situation like that makes fellows like me not want to waste years studying to do what? I know that there's no difference

between the white man and me, but I can't help feeling he is
better than I am when he is trained to do his work and then
has all the chances of doing it.

A youth in Louisville spoke as follows:

Negroes don't have half the chance whites do. There are some
jobs Negroes can't get at all. There are some executive jobs with
big concerns for which some Negroes are qualified but can't
get them. In some places Negroes don't even have the chance
to qualify. They don't have the opportunity to go through the
Naval Training School. They don't have the opportunity to
learn to fly like the whites. To qualify for some jobs you have
to have money and Negroes don't have the necessary money.
Whites think Negroes are not supposed to do nothing but laboring work. Here of late, whites are trying to take this away from
them. There used to be a time when a white man didn't want a
job on the garbage truck or as porter. Now, they're trying to
take these jobs away from Negroes. Out there where my brothers
work nearly all the help used to be colored. Every time a colored
man kicks the bucket or leaves he is replaced by a white man.
Now they have it so that there aren't but three colored out there.

The very question whether Negroes had the same chance as
whites was a source of amusement to another youth:

Don't make me laugh! You know "niggers" don't have the
chance white people have anywhere and I don't care what anyone says, Washington's no exception. You have a worse chance
if you happen to be a stranger and don't know white people
here. "Niggers" have never had the chance I think they ought
to have. It isn't our fault I don't think, it's just that white people won't give us a chance.

Another youth, nineteen, thought that the interviewer should
"know better than to ask such a question." However, he went on
to answer:

You know as well as I do that whites always have a better chance
at jobs, especially fairly good ones, and if they're pushed, they'll
take over the measly ones. I've tried for a long time to get on
WPA, NYA, and in the playground work. Always the same
story—"no openings," and whites walking in getting jobs every
day. Then, too, they make it tough on Negroes anyway. They
know how few of us get a chance to go to college, so they require a degree and so much experience. Usually, where a Negro

has one, he lacks the other. Those who are lucky enough to have both still are not working. But such is life for Negroes. If you ain't white, you just ain't right!

The last part of his statement in regard to formal educational preparation was similar to the statements of other youth. One described the situation as follows:

Negroes don't have as good a chance to get jobs as white people, now or ever. There are only a few jobs open to Negroes and whites alike and there are usually so many candidates for the jobs that few get them anyway. Segregation plays a big part in this and the lack of educated, well-trained Negroes does the rest.

Likewise in the following statement a youth expressed the feeling of a small number that Negroes are qualified for certain types of jobs. This statement also betrays the type of criticism of the Negro which lower-class youth often express:

I think Negroes could do more important work than they do now if they had the chance. On the other hand, they have many chances for jobs that they aren't prepared to do. Public offices, congressmen, and so forth, are jobs that only a few Negroes are trained to do. For most of them the hardest job is getting the necessary preparation. Most "niggers" don't want to work for jobs. They take a degree in something and expect jobs of all fields to fall to them, knowing that they aren't prepared. Hence, a few qualify.

At least one youth, who was eighteen and in the senior high school, felt that Negroes had the same chances for employment as whites. But he based his opinion on the personal experience of his father. He said:

Washington may be a southern town, but I don't think there's much segregation when it comes to jobs. I feel that I can compete with a fellow and have just as good a chance as he has. For instance, when my father went for the job he has at X's, a white man applied at the same time. My father had a better record and education than the white man, so he got the job. So I feel that if you know your stuff and have a good education, your chances are as good as anybody's. So if I apply for a job and a white fellow or another "nigger" gets it—it wouldn't be because of my color but my references and preparation for the work that would count. White people who hire other people don't base preference around here on color! I've seen it happen time and time again when I applied at different places for jobs. They took me on regardless of who else applied. And there's certainly no mistaking that I'm a Negro! I really think that Negroes have as good a chance for most jobs as white people.

In the majority of the relatively small number of cases in which the opinion was expressed that Negroes had equal chances with whites, there was the qualifying statement that it was true only in respect to certain types of jobs. The following statement was made by a retarded youth, twenty-one and in the sixth grade:

For hard, laboring jobs, Negroes have as good a chance as white men—sometimes better, but for half-way decent jobs and those that pay something and don't work you to death, the white man's chances are always better. We expect to see him get the breaks; when a white man isn't given the break and a Negro is hired, you can bet there's something wrong with the job or he wouldn't have it.

SHOULD NEGROES "PASS" IN ORDER TO GET JOBS?

Although the vast majority of lower-class youth do not think that Negroes have equal chances with whites in securing employment, they were quite divided in their opinions concerning whether fair Negroes should "pass" for white in order to get a job. There were some who gave an unqualified affirmative answer as the fourteen-year-old son of a laborer. His reply was:

I'd say if you could pass for any purposes, I think it would be all right! By all means, for a job, and I'd go to white theaters, dances, hotels and live in a white neighborhood if I could.

A retarded twenty-year-old youth spoke likewise:

Sure, I think it is all right. If I could pass I sure would. And for any other reason if I found it to my advantage, as school, I'd go to a white school for sure.

A ten-year-old boy gave the following reply which indicated his feeling in general concerning the relations of Negroes to whites:

Sure, it's all right to pass if you can. If I was light enough to pass, I sure would. I don't see anything wrong with it. White people ain't no better than colored people and if some colored people can pass for white and get a good job or something, they ought to go on and do it.

Some of the youth thought that "passing" for white was justifiable only where it was a matter of securing a job. A seventeen-year-old senior high school boy remarked:

With that exception, I say "yes." There certainly could be ways of getting around a situation like that but for a job, I don't think it's any harm to pass.

Other youth thought that passing involved too great a risk. As a nineteen-year-old high school graduate remarked:

Listen, I think it's all right to pass for any reason if you can get away with it, for a job, to a theater, or any place else. Negroes who do though take an awful chance. I should think if you're found out, it would be better to not ever have tried.

Another nineteen-year-old high school boy was practically of the same opinion. He stated:

I guess that's all right if he has to do that to get a job, and if he doesn't lose his head because he was successful. Trouble is, he takes a big risk because usually he's found out in the end— and the job goes bye-bye! A lot of Negroes get to really believe that because they look like they're white, that they actually are. Most of them I know look like white, but still act like "niggers."

The remark in the last statement, "if he doesn't lose his head," is characteristic of some of the objections or qualifications which these youth make in regard to "passing." The following statement by a twenty-one-year-old lad who had spent some time in high school, not only contains the above mentioned qualification, but also shows antagonism toward the lighter and upper-class Negroes. His statement was as follows:

I don't say it's all right, but I do say if it is necessary to get a job, I'd say O.K., providing the "nigger" could remain a "nigger" to his friends and those who know him. You run a big risk anyway, and sooner or later you're found out and put back in your place; and if you do as most "niggers" do who can pass, you ain't got no place when you come back. There used to be quite a number of girls and fellers over at school who could pass for white and they make you sick. And then the teachers made matters worse by thinking them cute and making over them.

The statement of a seventeen-year-old high school youth indicates the same attitude toward the lighter Negroes who can "pass":

I guess that's O.K. I'd probably do it if I could, but most Negroes who can pass take it much farther than that. They try to convince other Negroes and themselves as well that they are not Negroes. I always say if they were supposed to be white God would have made them so. I'll bet any white person who can pass for a Negro wouldn't be trying so hard to do it.

The twenty-one-year-old son of a laborer shows a similar attitude, but he probes more deeply into the matter of "passing." He stated:

Sure, for those who look and feel like they're white, I'd say it's O.K. As for me, I'd probably look white and feel the same as I do now. And somehow I don't think that would work. I'm afraid most Negroes who can "pass" let it go to their heads and they don't come down to earth until some white person gives them a jolt or the cold shoulder. Then they come sneaking back to their own people. Sooner or later, you're found out— then where are you? I don't enjoy being a "nigger," but I'd enjoy being a white one a lot less.

This youth's statement about feeling "like you're white" raises the important fact of being conscious of one's race. To another youth, a twenty-year-old son of a laborer, this seems to be as important as getting a job:

I think it's all right to pass for any purpose unless it's just to be white when you know and he or she knows they aren't. If I could get a job that way, I would—and I think any person who had the opportunity and wouldn't, is a fool.

Some of the objections to "passing" involve the question of loyalty to one's race and one's self-respect. A twenty-one-year-old youth of sixth grade standing stated his attitude as follows:

I don't think there's any excuse for a Negro to try to "pass" for white to get a job. If he gets it, he won't have it long, so I don't think it's worth all the trouble and the risk you take. Once they find out you try to put a thing like that over them, they'll sure make things miserable for you. I think Negroes who look like white are pretty dumb to leave their own people to go over to those who don't want them.

Although the objection by a fourteen-year-old boy was supposedly based upon the matter of self-respect, it also betrayed a certain animus toward those who are able to "pass." In fact, it should be kept in mind that these responses are from lower-class Negroes who are unable to "pass" for white. His statement was:

No, I wouldn't want to be able to pass for white. And I don't think it's all right to pass for any purpose. After all, there are other jobs, though they might not pay as much, but you could keep your self-respect and besides you wouldn't be taking the risks of getting put out of a good job when they found out you were a Negro. Negroes who try to pass for white are "messy" anyway. They usually think they're so much better than other people.

A sixteen-year-old girl of third-year high school standing insisted that Negroes "should be what they are and not try to fool anyone." Likewise, another girl, nineteen, thought that Negroes "should stick to their own people in their own class." And still another girl expressed her emphatic disapproval in the following words: "You know you are colored and that they don't want you."

"I NEVER WORKED FOR WHAT THEY CALL GOOD WHITE PEOPLE"

Some of the youth in our study had had some experience not only in seeking employment but also actually working at different jobs. Such experiences had brought them into contact with whites. One fourteen-year-old boy who had "worked a little bit" gave the following account of his experiences:

I worked a little bit. I worked in a grocery store a little while and I do a lot of work around the house. Yes, sir, I worked for a white man in the grocery store. I got along all right with him. I wasn't doing nothing but cleaning up. One day a little white boy came around and asked for a job and he fired me and gave the job to the white boy. Later on, I saw him and he asked me if I wanted the job back, but I said, "no." He wasn't paying nothing much anyway and I didn't care if he did give the job to the white boy. I guess the white boy must not of been any good.

Many of the youth had had paper routes which brought them into contact with whites. One boy speaking of his paper route offered the following remarks concerning whites and Negroes:

> I used to deliver papers in a Negro neighborhood and "niggers" and "poor whites" are alike. You deliver them papers and they have you come around a dozen times to collect.

A nineteen-year-old high school graduate who had vainly sought work was especially incensed because of the practice of sending Negro applicants to some Negro "leader" who had been chosen to "look after" colored applicants. He asked sarcastically: "Do I think colored people have as good a chance to get a job as white people?" And answered as follows:

> Ain't that some question to ask! I should say I don't! As many times as I've been downtown trying to get a job that I could have gotten if I hadn't been colored I ought to know the answer to that question. I go down there to see a man about getting a job and what does he do? He sends me over to see X. He tells me to go over and see my representative and see what he can do. Well, goddam, he ain't my representative no more than he is a Jew's representative or a white man's representative. I'm a citizen of the United States, born in the United States, just like any white person and why should I have a special representative when I want to get a job. If a white man goes down to some office to get a job they don't send him to a white man who they say is a special representative. Hell, no, they just give him an application blank and tell him to fill it out and consider it on how good he is. But, if I go down there or you go down there, they won't give you a blank, they'll send you to X, and what will he do for you? Not a damn thing. He's doing just what he's getting paid for doing. Sitting down there giving you the run around and keeping you from getting a job.

He then told of going to see the Negro leader. His statement not only shows the divergent class interests within the Negro group, but also reveals the frequent distrust and bitterness which lower-class Negroes show toward those of the upper class who have been placed in positions of authority. He reported:

> I go to see X and after I sit around there for about a week trying to see him, he will look around and send me back to the same office I was at first. I'll spend another week or two trying to see him again and then when I do see him he'll say there's nothing open just now and that maybe it would be a good idea to go back and see X. But X's just like most of the colored leaders. They betray their own race to keep a good job for themselves. He's sitting down there drawing six thousand a year as special representative of the Negroes to keep the Negroes from getting jobs; as long as he's drawing his salary he don't give a damn whether any Negro ever gets a job or not.

This same youth related his experience with white people:

> I never have worked for what some people call good white people. But I've worked for some bad ones. I worked for one old white woman who was prejudiced as hell. When I started working for her I hadn't ever thought about colored people being any different than white people, but she did everything she could to let me know that white people were better than colored people. She made me hate her. When she came around I just naturally started to looking all mean and evil. I was always expecting her to make some crack. She didn't have nothing much, but times was pretty good then and everybody had a little something. She paid me $10 a week. That was just before the depression. I didn't have any arguments with her. It wouldn't do me any good to argue with her. She was the boss.

Many of the lower-class girls had done some work in domestic service. One eighteen-year-old high school girl in Washington made the following comparison between whites in Virginia and Washington:

> I have worked for white people in Washington and Virginia. Sometimes now different people I have worked for during the summer will call me and I will go out and serve a dinner. There isn't much difference between the white people in Virginia and Washington except I make more money here and I have more privileges. Now, here when I worked for white, I had a definite time to rest and the woman told me I could use the family tub and toilet. In Virginia, I couldn't use the family tub.

Negro youth in the border cities often come in contact with

whites from the lower South who are accustomed to treat Negroes differently from the manner in which they are generally treated in the border cities. This is especially true of Louisville, which is closer to the old South. A youth who was employed as a porter in one of the terminals in Louisville gave the following account of his contacts with whites from the lower South:

I'll tell you about those southern white people that come in off those southeastern lines because I hate them. They come in and call you "black," call you "nigger." They want to act like they're a great deal better than you are. They throw paper all over the floor and tell you where they came from they didn't allow any colored people. Some tell you how they treat colored people in their home town. You may find a good one from down there once in a while but they'll all call you out of your name. One told me that he was a Mississippi "peckerwood" and had ten "niggers" down there working for him but he liked them all. I felt like saying something to him but I didn't. He gave me a quarter; that's the reason I didn't bawl him out.

Some of the older youth had been on WPA jobs. A twenty-one-year-old high school graduate who had had a laborer's job on the WPA spoke of his experience as follows:

On this last job we had an Irishman from Georgia who used to be boss of a chain gang and he tried to run the labor gang the same way. He was a dumb brute and knew nothing about the work, and a white supervisor had to tell him what to do and how to get along with the men. He didn't dare get sassy with us though and I believe he hated a lot of us because he couldn't treat us as he'd like to. Well, the gang was digging ditches. A lot of the men were getting 60 cents an hour and the rest of us 40 cents. So I got sick of that and I didn't like ditch digging anyway. So I came out of the hole and worked on top. We used to kid and talk as we worked and the "peck" couldn't stand that. So he ordered me in the hole. I told him I felt we all should get the same pay, doing identically the same work. Several others agreed, so three days later he handed each of us a white slip saying there were too many men on the job and we had to go. I had no idea he'd gotten a notion like that; anyway, we're off.

Some youth desperately seek any kind of employment, and after they have hunted in vain become greatly discouraged. This was the case with a twenty-one-year-old youth in Washington who explained:

> I can do anything, mostly any kind of laboring work. I've got good references, too, from the Jew up the street who lets me work around the store on Saturday and a white man on a bread truck I used to work with. I've done almost every kind of laboring work and I don't care how hard it is. I've worked on coal trucks, with a huckster, and even housework. I was registered with WPA and the U.S. Employment Office, but I'm dropped off WPA rolls until I've had another interview and one of those so-called investigations. The Employment Office didn't find anything for me, so I just gave up and I haven't been down there to register for a long time. They were all very nice to me, though —but I suppose that's the least they could do since they wouldn't find me a job. I wouldn't mind digging ditches or anything else.

The last sentence in the above statement reveals an attitude which many of these youth exhibit in regard to making a living. For example, a fifteen-year-old girl stated simply:

> I don't care what kind of work I do, just so I get paid for it.

And a mere ten-year-old boy spoke likewise. He said:

> It doesn't make any difference to me what people think about the type of work I'm doing, just so I'm making a lot of money.

A twenty-one-year-old youth expressed a typical criticism of Negroes and a certain cynical resignation to his status when he remarked:

> If I could earn enough to live on, I wouldn't care what I did. I don't think people should be so particular, especially "niggers." They'd be better off if they didn't try to pick and choose jobs. After all somebody must do the unpleasant work. I've done my share—the only kick I made was that I didn't think I was being paid fairly for it. It seems usually that the harder, most unpleasant work usually falls to "niggers" and they get paid least for it. I suppose if they paid more for it, they'd probably find somebody else for the job and the chances are that would be some white people.

Another twenty-one-year-old Washington boy who had attended high school spoke as follows:

Whatever you do for a living is important, but I don't think the job itself is important. If you have a white-collar job and make no money at it, I don't think it's as important as a job of less importance if it pays more. I don't care what the job is, as long as a decent wage is paid, I'll take it and it's important to me until another job shows up that pays more. It doesn't matter what a man does as long as he earns a living. I guess we all would like to have jobs where you sit around looking important and dressed well, but most jobs like that don't pay a damn thing. Furthermore, white people are more apt to help you anyway if you look shabby, and the few clothes I have I've got to wear when I'm off from work.

The remark which this youth added is typical of the techniques which the lower class feel are necessary to adjust themselves to whites. The nineteen-year-old high school graduate who made the following statement feels as many youth that money is the important item:

I don't think the job is so important. To hell with a job if I could make more money doing something else. It doesn't matter what you do as long as it's honest work you're doing. If I could earn a living as a street cleaner or a garbage collector, I'd prefer that to being a school teacher without a job. I'm not particular as long as I can find work. I'd like to be able to earn more than it takes to live on but I'd be satisfied until I could make more. After all, you can't have everything.

But some of these youth look upon the job itself as an important consideration. This is apparent in the remark of a Louisville boy who denies it at the beginning of his statement:

It doesn't make so much difference with me as long as it's not too tiresome and not too long. It does matter if a person is a gambler or a racketeer. A gambler is likely to end up with nothing. There's considerable risk he takes, too. I imagine he is discontented because he always fears the law will catch up with him.

A girl in Louisville made the following observation:

A person's job is really important because it really determines the status of a person. If a man is gainfully employed it gets him by in many cases where money talks but sooner or later the front built up by his income falls and there you are to face the world.

The eighteen-year-old daughter of a laborer in Washington sized up the situation of the poorer lower-class Negroes as follows:

Anything is good as long as you can have a little money after the bills are paid. It's so hard to get any money these days for what you do. Housework don't pay very much, and you have to work hard to get it. Some people go into rackets to get money. Those who couldn't get money any other way do. Some of them try to get jobs and they can't so they go into a racket. The only trouble is that most of them are taking money from the poorer people in these rackets. If you can't get enough money on the job to pay the bills, you've got to get it from somewhere. People play the numbers. I think it's all right.

LOOKING FORWARD TO THE FUTURE

The ambition which these youth have for the future reflects their beliefs concerning the Negroes' chances for employment and the valuations which they place upon the importance of certain types of employment. Generally speaking, those who are ambitious to rise above their present status spoke of the type of profession they hoped to be in ten years from now. Approximately a fifth of this group hoped to become doctors, lawyers, teachers, and social workers—professions in which Negroes have been successful. Some of these lower-class youth are stimulated to rise above their present position not only by contacts outside the home, such as in the school, but also by the advice of their parents. A seventeen-year-old second-year high school girl who thinks that "a decent job is teaching school, a stenographer, working around an office, nothing that has to do with scrubbing," said that her mother

has told us we should stay in school and get as much education as we can so we won't have to work in white folks' kitchens. She said she didn't have the advantages that we have and we should take advantage of the school. My sister has gone back to learn typewriting so she can get a decent job.

Generally those who hoped to rise no higher than skilled and unskilled labor spoke of being married and having a job ten years hence. A twenty-one-year-old high school graduate wanted to be able to give his children the type of education which he had been unable to secure for himself. He stated:

> I expect to have a job, earning enough money to provide a home for the family and to help the other youngsters go on to schools as I'd hoped to do. I'd like to go in some business of my own. That's the only chance a Negro has to be independent of white people.

When a Louisville youth was asked if he could have one wish, what it would be, he replied:

> I would wish I had some things I need now—a good job. I'm working extra now. Things are in a rush. When things slow up
>
> I will be out of a job. I wish I had a permanent job making about twenty or twenty-five dollars a week.

And when he was asked what he wanted to be doing ten years hence, his answer was as follows:

> Ten years from today I would like to own my own home, have two children, me and my wife be in good health and have a good job making about twenty or twenty-five dollars a week.

Some of those who do not aspire to enter the professional class believe that the Negro's salvation is to be found in mechanical employment. A nineteen-year-old Washington high school graduate who held such opinions revealed his prejudice against upper-class Negroes in the following statement:

> I always wanted to be a mechanic. I haven't had any training in mechanics but I'm interested in mechanical things. I didn't take mechanics in school but I did spend a lot of time in the shops. I believe the Negro's best chance in life is work with his hands. These so-called successful Negroes aren't doing a thing but "jibing." They get by with a lot of mouth, the kind of pull you can get with rackets, and paying your way through. I don't have any such friends and my folks don't have the money. So, like a lot of other fellows, we could be more successful in business where the use of the hands is more important than the head. I know a lot of Negroes who have made good as printers, sign painters, paper hangers, mechanics, and bricklayers. I'm sorry I didn't take up mechanics in school. Perhaps I'll be able to pick it up somewhere.

But he is not so hopeful of succeeding for he remarked:

> I doubt it now. I did want to be a mechanic and I could prob-
> ably become one if I could find a good instructor without work-
> ing myself to death learning. But it doesn't matter much now
> just so I can get a good job. I took the Civil Service exam this
> morning for a messenger and maybe I can get that.

Some of these youth have given little thought to the future
and confess that they care little about the type of employment
they enter. As one twenty-one-year-old youth remarked:

> I don't know and I don't particularly care how I would like
> to earn my living. However, I can drive a car well and I know
> a little about mechanics and I'd like to have a real good chauf-
> feur's job. I'd sure like to be driving somebody's fine big car.

When asked if he thought he would be able to do this, his
reply was:

> I don't know. I only said I wish I could get such a job. Jobs like
> that are scarce and only a few Negroes get them anyway. I guess
> I don't dress well enough, have enough schooling, or know
> enough important people to get a job like that.

Then, there are a few youth who talk as the twenty-one-year-
old son of a laborer did when asked if he had any objective in
life:

> Nothing in particular! I just want that job and a chance to earn
> good money. Any job will do that will provide that. I want to
> have a home of my own and, if possible, go into some business
> or racket. Liquor, numbers, or women, all the same to me. You
> know, I used to be known as a bad egg around these parts and
> I've got a reputation to live up to. I've got to do something!

ARE WHITE OR COLORED EMPLOYERS PREFERABLE?

Before concluding our discussion of the ambitions and hopes
of these youth, we should say a word about their preferences
concerning white and colored employers. The preferences fall
into three classes. First, there are those lower-class youth who
say frankly that they prefer working for whites, and, in justifying
their preference, they indicate their acceptance of the stereotypes concerning Negroes as well as their accommodation to
their inferior status. Since space will permit only a single quo-

tation from each group, we cite this statement by a twenty-year-old Washington youth:

I'd rather work for white people any day than Negroes. In the first place, a "nigger" hasn't anything. If a white man hires you, he asks what your price is. If he's willing to take you at that price, O.K.; if not, he'll tell you he can't use you. Then at the end of the performance your money's waiting for you. And you don't have to wait all night to get it. We used to be on a theater circuit and we had a white manager. But when you deal with a Negro, he's going to Jew you down—"Is that the lowest you can come for?"—then when the show is over you get "The crowd is small tonight and I didn't make my money. Can't you take this much and come back later in the week for the rest?" Then you'll probably have to wait half the night to get any of it. "Niggers" aren't businessmen at all. I always use that word "nigger." I don't mind white people saying it or colored people either. I don't think they mean any harm by it. Furthermore, we call each other that all the time, so we shouldn't mind.

Second, there are some youth who say that they are indifferent about the race of their employer. For this group we shall let a seventeen-year-old youth of third-year high school standing speak:

It really wouldn't matter to me, so long as either one paid me regularly and well. I can get along equally well with Negroes and whites. I've been looking for jobs now for quite some time but those I'd be able to get would require me quitting school and I know I can't do that. Jobs for Negro boys around here sure are scarce!

Third, there are those youth who state that they prefer working for colored people. One boy who said he preferred to work for colored people added the significant statement: "I would be proud to see a colored person in position to hire someone." A nineteen-year-old youth who had finished high school expressed his preference as follows:

I've worked for whites as well as colored. I've washed an old Jew's car several times and worked on Saturdays in a Jew store. They treated me all right, but they don't pay nothing. I've worked for Negroes, too. I'd rather work for Negroes; they're much more considerate and don't usually hang around watching you work. They'd just as soon pay you one day as any other, but those I've worked for paid eventually. I've cleaned up some doctors' and dentists' offices and worked a little on their cars and yards, and they treat you like human beings.

In this last statement we have an attitude that is more characteristic of middle-class youth to whom we shall now turn our attention.

MIDDLE-CLASS YOUTH

The vast majority of middle-class youth who were interviewed expressed preference for Negro employers, although to some the race of their employer did not matter. The following may be taken as characteristic of the majority of statements from middle-class youth. This opinion was expressed by a twenty-year-old youth who had completed junior high school:

I'd rather work for Negroes anytime. I've had two or three little jobs working with white people, but I don't think they're so hot. I worked at a white drugstore for a while—holding that job at night and the garage job in the day. But my hours on the latter job were changed to night so I had to give up the store job. The one at the filling station paid me more and I had less work to do. I like to work for Negroes better because they don't "holler" at you or call you "nigger." At the filling station, the man tells you what to do or what he wants done, then goes off and lets you do it. I didn't pay any attention to the white people calling me "nigger." I did hate it, but just shut my mouth and went on. When I did start working for a colored man, I began to feel that I was a human being. It was just like somebody had lifted a big burden off me—I sort of felt free. Eventually, I know I'll probably be working for some white person, that can't be helped I suppose, for we all have to look to white men for jobs, food, and clothing. The only way I see to avoid it is more business places run by Negroes hiring more Negroes.

An inclusive wish for change in the employment situation was expressed by a middle-class youth as follows:

I'd like to see white people treat Negroes like men and women and not like servants or somebody beneath them. I'd like to see white people give Negroes a fair break at jobs, good salaries. I'd like to see white people willing to share all phases of life, recreation, education, and so forth, with Negroes. I'd like to see white people stop segregating us and treat us like human beings as they do in other places.

Likewise, in regard to chances with whites for employment, middle-class youth are practically unanimous in the opinion that whites have better chances than Negroes. To a twenty-one-year-old college freshman, it was a known fact that

Negroes don't have the chance that whites have, but I haven't experienced such segregation for jobs. I don't think my color has had anything to do with it. I just never found a job open to compete for. Color, I know, plays an important part in getting jobs. Without a doubt, a white man prefers to hire one of his own before he'll take a Negro. I suppose if we controlled jobs, we'd do the same thing. At least, we would if we had race consciousness as white people do. We ought to have the same chances that anybody else has if we can do the work. Up around New York, things are far different in this respect. You can get a job regardless of color or race if you can do the job. I think Negroes can do any job white men can do and I think our greatest mistake is not getting the preparation in all the things white men have jobs for. Ordinarily, Negroes are all satisfied to become doctors, dentists, lawyers, or teachers. There are hundreds of other fields where Negroes might be used if they knew the work.

Freddie, the fifteen-year-old boy referred to in the introduction, spoke as follows:

I think my chances for an education are as good if not better than the average white boy. I say better because white boys knowing they have better chances for jobs don't feel it necessary to get all the education I want to get, to even get the same break for the same job. Given a chance to compete with a white boy from the standpoint of brains and general knowledge, I think my chances are as good as a white boy's. But if white men have anything to do with giving out jobs, I know the white boy's chances are far better than mine even if I am better prepared than he is. It's too bad we have to depend almost wholly on white people to give us jobs. Maybe the only real break will come when we can get our own people to give us jobs. Our chances should be far greater. We can do any job as well as a white man and our color as well as our conduct keeps us from getting those jobs. We can't change our color, but we can change our conduct. White people think we're all alike and we who try to behave ourselves get treated like those who don't. That's unfair to begin with for among all people there are bad ones as well as good ones. At that rate, they couldn't even hire a white man. There certainly are enough bad ones. We fight too much, drink too much, carry on too much foolishness.

Warren, whose personality we shall attempt to explore in Part II, gave the following opinion:

Negroes don't get as good chances for jobs as white people. Most jobs prefer a white face to experience. That shouldn't be, of course, but the white man is in a position to choose what he wants. I think a Negro could do any job as well if not better than any white man. Somewhere in this country there is a Negro who could even handle the job of President, and do a good job of it. I think we'd have a far better chance when more of our people get an education. In the South, where thousands of Negroes live, the white man is still able to boss them around, and they are perfectly satisfied. Our schools are getting better and bigger every day, and I guess more of us are going to them.

The eighteen-year-old son of a skilled workman was emphatic in his opinion that Negroes do not have as good a chance at employment as whites. His use of the term "nigger" was to emphasize the white man's contempt rather than his acceptance of the term as a proper designation for Negroes:

I don't believe a "nigger" has as good a chance to get anything as white people have! They see to it that our chances are always few and far between. They ought to have many more opportunities than they have now and even if in time they can get them—"nigger's" chances will still not be equal to the whites'. Manhood, ability, and education come in colors—white to black, and a "nigger" is never considered equal to a white man no matter how good a man he is or what his ability and training is.

This same youth, when asked if he thought it was all right for Negroes of fair complexion to "pass" in order to get a job, answered

I guess it's all right in a case like that, but it shouldn't be necessary, and I wouldn't want to take the chance. But the Negroes I know wouldn't stop at that. It makes me hot to see the girls up the street grin at every white man they see, and I get hotter when I see them easing out of the company of Negroes when they see a white person coming around.

One can note in the above statement a certain hostility toward whites, which in the present case may be accentuated because of the sexual factor, but there is also an element of race pride in which a self-respecting attitude toward whites is involved. This becomes more apparent in the statement of a seventeen-year-old youth of third-year high school standing. His objection to "passing" in order to get a job was stated in the following words:

No, I believe there are jobs that light-skin Negroes could get without trying to horn in on people that don't want them or who wouldn't hesitate to deny them jobs if it was known they were Negroes, or to throw them out when they did find out. Every man should be honest with himself and I can't see how Negroes can try to make other people as well as themselves think they're white and be honest first with themselves.

Of course, since this statement was made by a very black boy, it may involve a certain hostility or envy toward Negroes of fair complexion. It may also reflect the compensations which he has erected to protect his ego. Or it may express a highly developed race conscious attitude in which loyalty to one's inner feelings regarding racial identification is of paramount importance.

Some of the middle-class youth who have worked at odd jobs after school or during the summer vacations reported on the racial factor in their work experiences. A twelve-year-old boy in the eighth grade told the following story:

I used to know an old white man who ran a grocery store right across the street there. When I was nine years old, he had me work for him all day once. I moved bottles and stacked up cans and put away sugar and worked all day long for him. When I got through, he only gave me ten cents. My father went over to see him about it and he told my father I didn't do much work.

Another boy, thirteen and in the seventh grade, said that he used to work for "some white lady" who

would cheat you out of your money, if she could. She would tell you she was going to pay you the next day and she never would pay you.

The statement of a sixteen-year-old high school boy indicates the resentment of some youth in this class toward taking orders from whites. He said concerning his work experiences:

> Sure, I've worked. I used to work in a store for a colored man, and I cut lawns for a white woman. I was treated all right in both cases, but I'd much rather work for colored people than for white anyway. They don't pay you as much but they don't try to *run all over you* and know so much as white people do. I used to deliver papers, too, but gave it up because of poor paying customers.

Middle-class youth are generally ambitious to rise in the world and they are spurred in their ambitions by their parents. Freddie, whom we have met in the introduction, said:

> No, I don't care to work now, that is unless I can find something to do in the summers or after school hours. I've seen too many fellows who quit school early and then turn out to be sorry for it. My father says as long as he can work and keep us in school, that we should go. He tells us of his little education and how he wished he had had the opportunity to get more. He vowed that his boys should get all he could possibly give. All of us like school so he won't have much trouble keeping us there. The weeks I was out on account of my mother's illness and my father's injury caused me to get left once, the first time I ever failed to make the next higher grade. It took me some time, but I've caught up now!

The majority of middle-class youth have ambitions to rise above the skilled and semiskilled occupations in which their parents are engaged. For example, Freddie said:

> I want to be a physical education teacher. I want to play on the football and basketball teams and learn enough about all sports to be able to teach them. I've made up my mind to do just that and nothing's going to stop me. Out of a graduating class of 124, only about ten are going to college. Most of the boys are going to CCC camps. I don't see why they don't go on with their school work but I suppose it's the best place for them. As for me, I'd better not look like even wanting to quit school. My father is determined that we'll stay in school. I even hope to be an officer next year. I love military training. I haven't got a uniform yet, but my father promises to get me one this year.

In some cases, of course, the parents want their children to pursue the skilled occupations in which they are engaged. A sixteen-year-old high school youth, whose father was a mechanic, said of the conflict between his father's ambition for him and his own desires for the future:

> I'd like most to earn my living as a commercial artist. If I can possibly get the training, I'll have a business of my own. I think a person's job is most important. I don't know any duller way to earn a living than becoming an automobile mechanic as my father insists, even if I did make more money with cars. Money isn't everything and it certainly can't take the place of a thing as creative as art work. I don't think a person really "lives" unless he is following work of his own choice and in which he is best fitted. I suppose you make the least money in jobs we choose, but I wouldn't get much satisfaction substituting something else.

On the other hand, the father may desire his son to enter a "higher" occupation although the son prefers to follow his father's trade. This was the case with a twelve-year-old boy whose mother attempted to resolve the conflict. He said:

> I want to work in the post office or be a paper hanger. My father doesn't want me to be a paper hanger; he wants me to work in the post office, but my mother says that maybe I could make a business out of paper hanging and make good money out of it if I like to do that type of work.

Naturally, some of the middle-class youth hope to follow in the footsteps of their parents. In the following statement by a twelve-year-old boy, one can see how the family has influenced his choice of an occupation:

> I'd like to be a bricklayer when I grow up. My father and uncle are bricklayers and work under a white contractor. They both make good money, too. I know I can learn to lay bricks some day at school, but my father says that would be a waste of time because he can teach me how to do it. I think I can do it pretty well now. My father showed me how and I've helped him do it. And I think a person's job is very important 'specially if he's doing something he always wanted to do. I'd rather do what I wanted to do even if I got less money than I could get doing something else.

In such cases family traditions have developed to the point that they influence the child's ambitions and outlook on life. The influence of family traditions will become more apparent as we consider the upper-class youth.

UPPER-CLASS YOUTH

Although upper-class youth share with the other classes some concern about equal chances with whites for employment, the emphasis of their objections to present race relations was, generally speaking, on the denial of social and civil rights. This difference in emphasis was undoubtedly due chiefly to two causes: upper-class youth enjoy greater economic security, and their ambitions are directed, on the whole, to the professional and business fields in which Negroes have found a place behind the walls of segregation. A seventeen-year-old high school youth, whose father was a government employee, spoke as follows:

> I'd like to see whites give us a chance to do the things we want to. Not that I want to be on a social level with any of them. I'd just like the opportunities of doing the everyday things human beings like to do. I'd like to see them give Negroes a better chance at jobs. I'd like to see better schools, preferably mixed ones, for Negroes. We'd get a lot more out of life that way. We'd all be happier and make better lives for us all.

Another seventeen-year-old youth spoke in a vein more characteristic of the upperclass:

> I think it [segregation] is all quite unnecessary. There are Negroes I don't want to associate with and white people who would associate with me wouldn't necessarily have to associate with those I, too, thought were undesirable. "Jim-Crow" practices don't help anyone—just creates hard feelings and causes much inconvenience. I'm not particular about associating with white people. All I want to do is to go any place my money will pay for and my desires require. I want an equal break at schools and jobs. I don't want any part of their girls and women—I have little enough to do with my own. There are as many if not more whites ready at all times to exploit Negroes as there are Negroes who want to exploit the whites.

In the following statement, an eighteen-year-old youth shows an appreciation for the more fundamental disabilities under which Negroes live:

> I'd like to see white people give us a decent break. Last year the Negroes had the highest death rate for tuberculosis. Why? Because there aren't decent hospitals or places for them to be taken care of, and poor, dirty, cold houses to go back to. Better care of our health, better homes, and better jobs so we can have the things we need, that's what I'd like to see. Take this infantile paralysis drive, for instance. That isn't for Negroes. With all those millions of dimes, just as many Negroes will die from the disease. That's white man's justice. What chance have we with thumbs down on us all the time? It sure is a trial to be a Negro, I don't care what anyone says.

"NO MATTER HOW GOOD I AM, MY CHANCES WITH WHITES ARE NEVER AS GOOD"

It is in respect to the Negro's chances with whites for employment that youth of the lower, middle, and upper class are in essential agreement. Since, as we have seen, upper-class youth are often not only protected from the cruder forms of prejudice but also are actually kept in ignorance of discriminations, it is not unnatural that some of them have grown up with the notion that competence and efficiency would be recognized whatever the color of the person possessing these qualities. But they learn, like the seventeen-year-old college youth who expressed his disillusionment as follows:

> I used to feel if I knew my work and could do it better than white or black, my chances would be as good. From observation, I've noted that no matter how good I am, my chances with whites are never as good. It is quite obvious in Washington that Negroes do not have the chances for the jobs that whites have. That should not be, of course, and there should be hundreds of jobs available for trained Negroes. There certainly isn't much inducement to work or study knowing that in competition with a white fellow your chances are slim. It's enough to discourage the best of us.

A sixteen-year-old high school girl, whose father was engaged in business, gave her opinion as follows:

> I don't think Negroes have equal opportunities for jobs. They are limited to teaching and professions with some openings in

the government service. I do think that many Negroes are prepared to hold more important jobs than they are given the opportunity. Some Negroes don't take advantage of the chances they get, but those who would make the best workers don't always get the best jobs.

One seventeen-year-old youth, the son of a government employee, attempted to estimate the chances of a white youth in comparison with those of a colored youth. He said:

About one hundred to one are the odds against me in favor of the white boy. It doesn't matter how smart I am, what kind of family I'm from, what I know, or what I can do, my chances are always slim compared with a boy with a white face. Negroes don't have the chances they ought to have—whites take care of that. That's one group that looks out for themselves.

Another boy, the thirteen-year-old son of a government employee, spoke from the experience of his father:

Negroes don't have chances like white people for jobs. Not that they can't do the job but just because of color. They should have them and maybe some day they will. Many Negroes are prepared for all sorts of jobs but the white man keeps the jobs for his own people and usually *gives* Negroes what's left. And until Negroes *fight* for what they want, demand the jobs or make jobs for their own people, they will always get just what's left. Negroes can do any job any white man can do. Give us a chance at any job, and we'll do just as good as the rest. There are many jobs in the government my father says that Negroes should have —I mean office work—and a lot of white men have come since he started doing the same work he's doing at the X Department and have been promoted over him. It isn't fair. The least white people could do would be to give you a fair chance. But that's the last thing they think of doing, and I think they enjoy keeping away the chances we should have.

One youth was especially incensed because the denial of chances to compete with whites was countenanced "right in the nation's capital." He remarked:

We are well aware of the fact that the white boy's chances are always better than a Negro's for work. Your chances are seldom as good as five to one. Experience doesn't count so much these days—darn it, it's the color of your face that matters. Take, for instance, the Negro football player from B—— University who had to sit it out on the bench at Griffith Stadium last Saturday because W—— University refused to play the game if the Negro played. He was their star player, too. Probably W—— University knew that, too. It was a shame, and more so that it should happen right here in the nation's capital.

A freshman college youth, seventeen, expressed himself as follows:

I don't think Negroes have equal chances with whites in any work or in any profession. White physicians for example get all sorts of breaks in the government—army and navy, and in big hospitals and clinics. Negro doctors have to be satisfied in a great measure with a small practice and once in a while work in Negro hospitals.

This youth's experiences had been so unpleasant that he had quit his job with the determination to "go after jobs" in which he "had as good a chance as anyone else." He asserted:

My experience has been that Negroes' chances for jobs aren't as good as whites' in Washington. I suppose much of it is due to the fact that too many whites—Virginians live and work in Washington. Negroes' chances are always slim where whites are involved for jobs. My father helped me to get a job in the X Department cafeteria and had he not gone to influential white men in the building I wouldn't have gotten on at all. Such is life, I suppose—my father says it's just a Negro's lot. They resented my being there so much I stood it about as long as I could and quit. I used to feel pretty badly over the fact being thrown in my face that I was a "nigger" and I decided from then on to go after jobs, if I could be independent of mere jobs —jobs that color didn't mean so much—jobs that I had as good a chance as anyone else.

Upper-class youth, especially the girls, seldom work before completing their secondary education. A freshman college youth, the son of a professional man, told of the opposition of his family when he tried to get jobs. He said:

I have done a few odd jobs and even sold papers. I haven't worked for white people at all. I guess I could get along with them, though. Anybody who could get along with Negroes can get along with anybody else. I've tried to get jobs as I told you but I always meet opposition because of my family. Nobody seems to think I should work or even want to work.

The sixteen-year-old son of a physician spoke in a similar vein:

I've never worked. I've always wanted to work but my parents insisted that I finish school first and then think about working. I'd have no preference—I'd just as soon work for Negroes as whites. I can get along with anyone and as long as my employer, whoever he might be, pays me promptly and well, nothing else matters.

Of course, some of the youth have had paper routes. One seventeen-year-old freshman college youth said:

I've never had a real job. The only one I had was a paper delivery route. I had very little to do with the whites I came in contact with, but got along with them swell. I've always wanted a job, but my parents insisted that I finish school first, and that I'd have plenty of time to work.

Some of the upper-class parents want their children to do some form of work in order to develop in them a spirit of independence. This was the case with the seventeen-year-old son of a government clerk. His statement was:

I've never had a job, though my father has encouraged me to get one. He wants me to feel more independent of my parents. He tried to get me a job at the X Department this past summer, but was unsuccessful. Up to this point, I haven't been looking for work and no job has come my way. I have no objections to working; but I don't seem to have the knack of getting jobs like some fellows. It makes no difference whether I work for white or colored as long as it's a job.

One seventeen-year-old college freshman spoke as follows concerning his work experience:

I've had a couple of jobs in my life. I worked for a Jew in a grocery store as a clerk; I've worked in the kitchen of a hotel and I've held an elevator operator's relief job. All of these were for white people. I got along swell and rather liked to work for them as individuals. The Jew had me from 9 to 4 P.M., in the store, seven days a week, at $6 a week, so I didn't keep that long. I didn't have any time to myself. The others were O.K. I noticed though that in these "hot spots" the whites got all the soft jobs, while the Negroes did all the actual work; the white fellows getting $15 a week and the Negroes, $10. It wasn't fair and I never could understand such inequality. Even color shouldn't make such a difference.

Since the upper class is composed largely of mixed bloods and there are among them many who can "pass" for white, one would expect them to have on the whole a different attitude toward "passing" from that which prevails in the lower and middle class. The answers of upper-class youth seem to confirm this assumption. A boy, just eleven years old, the son of a physician, spoke as follows:

> I think it's all right to "pass" for anything. As long as a Negro can make white people respect him by looking white, I think it's all right to do it. Then, maybe white people realize we're not beneath them after all. We must have the same blood to have the same looks, same color and hair. Those of us who can pass see an easier time, anyhow, and I'd say to all such Negroes, "Go ahead." The Negroes who usually object are the ones who nobody would mistake to be anything else but Negroes. Most of them say if I can't do the things you can do—you won't either.

His statement concerning those who are unable to "pass" is true in some cases. A young college woman who was unable to "pass" stated that she thought colored people should not "pass," but admitted that she wished that she could "pass" in order to "fool" white people. Her objection to "passing" on the part of colored people was that the Negro owed "a certain amount of loyalty to his own race." A seventeen-year-old high school boy said:

> By all means if you think you can get by. I would if I could— but you run risks of getting caught and embarrassed. I wouldn't like that. It would be lots of fun to do business with white people who think they know Negroes to have one in their midst and they not know it. [Loud laugh]

A boy, only ten years old, who said that it would be "unloyal to the colored race for the colored people to pass for white when they don't have to," nevertheless, thought it "would be simple [crazy] to starve rather than take work because you had to pass for white." A seventeen-year-old youth who was a member of an exclusive boys' club stated his opinion as follows:

> I think "passing" is all right so long as others don't have to pay a price for their good fortune in being able to go over to the other side. If I could pass, I'd aspire to better jobs than I could get being just a Negro. So I can't say it's wrong for others to do it. But once a Negro can make white people think he is white, he then wants all Negroes to think so, too. To keep a job among white people as a white person, he has to divorce himself from his Negro friends and acquaintances. Most Negroes I know who can "pass" don't like to do that because I suppose they never know when they'll have to come back to the same old friends.

His statement about the "good fortune in being able to go over to the other side" is significant. Upper-class youth, like their parents, generally regard the ability to "pass" as a piece of good fortune. When a fourteen-year-old girl was asked about "passing," she answered:

> I suppose I already do a bit of that. That is, if you mean going downtown to the theaters. I attend those shows because they give a little more for one's money than is given on U Street or at the Howard. I see no harm in "passing" if one gets enjoyment out of it or gets something that he otherwise would not have. I am referring to holding a job which you are supposed to be white to have.

She then went on as follows to discuss the question of the attendance of Negroes at white theaters and her opinion of the behavior of Negroes:

> I disagree with whites coming to our theaters and not extending the same courtesy to us. I think if they let Negroes attend the white shows the novelty would soon wear off because of the lack of variety in theaters. These theaters here are not like those in New York where you can see any type of show. Negroes would crowd the theaters at the beginning and in the end just the *better class* would keep up attendance. In a way I don't blame the whites for prohibiting some Negroes. I get so disgusted when I see colored people putting their feet on the chairs or making undue noises. They seem to have no self-respect. [The interviewer asked if some whites did not do this.] I suppose so, but I haven't seen as much of it downtown as I have witnessed on U Street. I speak to my friends about it and they only laugh,

saying that I try to be so "hinkty." I don't care what they say, but I know how to act when out in public. I feel sorry for them [lower-class Negroes] and wonder if they will ever learn any better.

This girl's attitude is typical of many upper-class Negroes who would escape from the limitations of the color line as well as the disagreeable association with lower-class Negroes.

"BE SOMEBODY EVERYBODY LOOKS UP TO"

When upper-class youth were asked concerning their ambitions for the future, they showed that they had definite ambitions and were confident that they could achieve their aims in life. A thirteen-year-old boy, the son of a government clerk, stated with assurance:

Well, anyway, I'm going to be a doctor when I grow up. I think doctors are important people. They make a lot of money, have fine homes and cars, so why shouldn't I get them the same way and besides be somebody everybody looks up to. I don't know what it will cost but my folks will help me and I can always work.

A seventeen-year-old youth, both of whose parents were employed in professional occupations, made the following observation on his ambition to become a physician:

My chief interest is chemistry. I plan to be a physician. I want to take my medical work at McGill. I haven't quite decided yet. I prefer McGill because of its standing and fairness, and because I believe that Negroes should get as varied experience as they can. One of the greatest dreams of my life is to specialize in health in slum areas, to work on slum clearance and new housing from the standpoint of health. I think there is still a great deal to be done in the matter of health for Negroes. I don't know where I'd like to practice; perhaps here or some place in the West where Negroes have congregated. My parents have never tried to influence me in any specific interest. They have exposed me to the best experiences within their means and I have been free to form my judgments for myself. They have given advice with reasons for their attitudes.

An eleven-year-old son of a physician is determined to become an aviator, no matter what white people do. Concerning what he hoped to be doing ten years hence, he said:

I hope either to be almost through college or in some military school. I want to be studying aviation even if they ground me like they did that fellow Davis. I intend to fly some day at any cost. I'd like to go to Tuskegee and study under that fellow who flew for Haile Selassie in Ethiopia. That's the kind of life I like.

Although upper-class youth plan to enter a variety of professional and other higher occupations, the vast majority hope to become physicians, dentists, teachers, and social workers; occupations in which the upper class has found an outlet for their talent and training.

SUMMARY

To sum up this chapter, certain conclusions may be stated concerning the data which have been presented. Lower-class, middle-class, and, in some cases, upper-class youth place an equal chance with whites for jobs first among the changes which they would like to see in race relations. Because of the competition with whites for jobs, and because of general unemployment, lower- and middle-class youth are concerned about the narrowing opportunities for work even in those occupations in which Negroes have heretofore made a living. Negro youth of all classes are agreed that Negroes do not have equal chances with whites for jobs, whatever their qualifications. Lower- and middle-class youth have had considerable working experience which has brought them into contact with whites. Although youth of both classes (though middle-class youth to a lesser degree) are partially accommodated to their inferior status, their experiences with whites have bred distrust and animosity. In order to survive, many of them are convinced that they must adopt various techniques in order to conceal their real feelings and thereby propitiate the white man. The majority of lower-class youth look forward to employment in unskilled and laboring occupations, though a minority hope to rise above their present condition. But because of the lack of opportunities for employment, many lower-class youth are becoming convinced that illegal and antisocial means of making a living must be resorted to and are justified.

Many of the middle-class youth are ambitious and hope to

rise above their present status and enter upper-class occupations. Upper-class youth are, on the whole, self-confident about the future. The majority of them plan to enter the occupations in which upper-class Negroes have found employment and an outlet for their talents behind the walls of segregation. Upper-class youth do not feel that they have to use the same techniques as lower- and middle-class youth in order to survive. But, nevertheless, they are resentful of the many limitations under which they work and, where their fair complexion will permit, they sometimes use it as a means of breaking through the color line. Although it is not evident in our data, the lack of opportunity to compete with whites and assume adult responsibilities undoubtedly prevents Negro youth from maturing as they should under normal conditions.

CHAPTER VII

SOCIAL MOVEMENTS AND IDEOLOGIES

In THIS chapter we shall attempt to analyze
the ways in which Negro youth are influenced in their conceptions of themselves as Negroes, in their attitudes toward
whites, and in their aspirations and outlook on life by various
social movements and ideas that are current in the Negro community. In regard to social movements it is necessary to consult
Appendix B in which social movements and ideologies in
Washington, D.C., are discussed. There it is pointed out that
Negro communities in border cities, in contrast to those in the
metropolitan areas in the North, are seldom stirred by those
unorganized forms of unrest motivated by the Negro's hope for
a new way of life or an escape from his difficulties. Consequently,
our discussion will not deal with what are, strictly speaking,
social movements, but with various established organizations
which aim to improve the social and economic conditions of
Negroes. The same might be said concerning these communities
in regard to ideologies, if we restricted our use of the term to
consciously formulated doctrines concerning the liberation of
the Negro from his poverty and low social status. But here we
are using the term to designate ways of thinking which are characteristic of different classes in the community and are communicated to youth through the family, the church, the school, and
the press. So defined, the ideologies which are current in border
cities, though not so rich and varied as in northern urban areas,
nevertheless influence the attitudes and behavior of youth in
their role as Negroes.

LOWER-CLASS YOUTH

Since many of the lower-class families originated in the South,
they have the outlook of the Negro folk whose ideas and beliefs
have been modified by contacts with the secular life of the city.

Although the parents continue in many cases to view the world more or less from the standpoint of their folk background, the outlook of their children is influenced by the school, the newspaper, the cinema, and other devices of civilization. Because of the fact, however, that lower-class youth are more or less isolated by their poverty and lower level of culture, they are influenced less by movements and ideas than are the other classes in the community. Even in mass meetings which are called to protest against some injustice against Negroes, scarcely a sprinkling of lower-class youth may be found. Such meetings generally attract the educated and more sophisticated members of the community, even though the lower-class Negroes may have been more directly affected by the injustice.

In the border cities, nothing arouses so much resentment among Negroes against discrimination as cases of police brutality. This situation evidently arises from a number of factors. Many lower-class youth have had such unpleasant experiences with the police that their hostility has finally been aroused. They especially resent the naive stereotypes concerning the race by which some police justify their treatment of Negroes as inferior or inhuman. Moreover, since the police are recruited from the poorer classes of whites who often regard the Negro as a competitor and too close to them in social status, they are particularly anxious to "keep the Negro in his place." Let us take as an example of such an attitude on the part of the police the experience of a Negro youth:

I was down at the public library and got to playing and running around with some white and colored boys. The police chased us off but said, "You kids can't play here, and you there, you black so-and-so 'nigger,' stay up in the section and don't play down here." I felt pretty badly about the whole affair and particularly after what the officer said to me. And worst of all, he seemed to single me out to hurt my feelings. I thought of reporting the incident, but thought better of the uselessness of it all. The white boys scattered and came back and started all over again. I felt awful funny at that time and for the first time I felt embarrassed and as if suddenly I had waked up and found myself different from other people.

Despite the fact that many lower-class youth harbor resentment against the police, they do not crowd the mass meetings protesting police brutality. They rely on their ability to avoid the police as much as possible and in rare cases resort to individual acts of violence.

When one considers such organized efforts as the National Association for the Advancement of Colored People, he finds that the majority never heard of the organization or have no idea of its aims and program. The local Urban League, which was only organized during the past twelve months, is practically unknown among lower-class Negroes. A twenty-one-year-old girl, whose parents were engaged in domestic and personal service, made the following reply when she was asked if she knew what N.A.A.C.P. stood for:

> Its the National Association for the Advancement of Colored People, but I haven't heard of them in ages. I don't know any young people who belong.

A nineteen-year-old boy, whose father was a laborer, replied when asked if he knew anything about the N.A.A.C.P.:

> I have read a little around here at the "Y" about the N.A.A.C.P. That's the club that was interested in the Scottsboro case, isn't it? If its like other Negro organizations, it won't last long—at least no longer than some smart Negro or white man can get hold of the money in it.

These replies are typical of what little knowledge lower-class youth had concerning this organization. Moreover, the latter part of the last statement is indicative of their cynical distrust of organizations designed to improve their status and well-being. A college girl said that both the N.A.A.C.P. and the Urban League were comprised of doctors, lawyers, and teachers and were not interested in the problems of the masses. Lower-class youth in Louisville made similar statements. All of this shows how little lower-class youth, because of their isolation and their lack of incentives, are affected by these organizations in border cities.

Perhaps no movement, if we may speak of it as a movement, has secured as much publicity and stirred the lowest layers of the Negro community as the campaign of the New Negro Alliance to force the Peoples Drug Store in Washington through picketing to employ Negro clerks. By handbills and publicity in Negro newspapers and mass meetings the efforts of this organization were communicated to the masses of Negroes. A girl who did not even know what the "N" in N.A.A.C.P. stood for knew, however, about the New Negro Alliance and stated that it had "more young people." The masses were impressed by the sight of Negroes and whites parading before the very stores which they frequented. The movement was, of course, one in which there was a conflict of interests; on the one hand, there was the desire not so much for employment as for status symbolized by the employment of Negroes in white-collar jobs; and, on the other hand, the desire to purchase the cheap goods available in these chain drugstores. In fact, one eighteen-year-old girl of junior college rank stated frankly that the economic factor caused her to circumvent the picket line by going to another of the chain stores. She said:

> I don't go to the one at U or Seventh and M Streets. But I go to Logan Circle. My brother goes on through and of course they don't have nothing to say to him. If I went, they would have a lot of talk. But I find that the Peoples Drug Store charges 50 cents for medicine I pay 75 cents for elsewhere. Again, I have saved as much as 27 cents. I have bought an article for 98 cents that cost $1.25 elsewhere. I disapprove of this picketing, it is communistic. Let them [Negroes] open a drugstore where the prices will be cheap. But why try to tell people where to spend their money. They are making monkeys out of themselves.

This girl was one of the small minority who oppose the picketing. By way of explanation, it should be noted that although her father is a laborer, her brother, who through his profession and his Reserve Officer's commission has achieved upper-class status, has undoubtedly influenced her to regard picketing as "communistic." The other youth who are opposed to the picketing exhibit a lower-class point of view which accepts the customary disparagement and dependence of the Negro. For example, a seventeen-year-old youth, the daughter of a laborer, made the following statement:

Then, too, if they put colored clerks in there, something is bound to go wrong. There would be some stealing sure as you're born. Negroes just can't help doing wrong. You know how things stand around in the Peoples Drug Stores. I don't say all of them would steal, but the race always has to suffer for what one does. . . . I don't think it is right to risk the jobs of all those people, two hundred and some, for one job. If these white people get mad, they will turn off all those men they have now.

The overwhelming majority of lower-class youth are in favor of the picketing. In some cases, to be sure, they are confused; especially since the drug company has replied to the picketing with counter-propaganda concerning the number of Negroes employed and the possibility of their losing their jobs. For example, a high school graduate spoke as follows:

I would rather work for colored if I could get enough money from them. I think they treat you better. Then, I like the idea of being around my own people. I have gotten so interested in the N.N.A. campaign to put a Negro clerk in the Peoples Drug Stores at Seventh and M Streets and at Fourteenth and U since I've been working for Mrs. X. Her brother is in charge of the picketing. I was all in favor of it at first, but now I am confused. I hate to think 228 men may be losing their jobs for the sake of one or two clerks. I don't know what to think, but I still wouldn't go pass the picket line.

One will note in the above remark that the girl was influenced in her attitude by an upper-class Negro. In spite of such confusion in attitudes, the picketing campaign has aroused, and to some extent given an opportunity for, expression of the latent militancy among Negroes. A twenty-one-year-old youth of college standing, whose parents are in personal and domestic service, remarked that Negroes would not get their rights until they started to work for them and cited the picketing in confirmation of her opinion. She said:

They won't know until they start *working* that they're going to get anything—like picketing the Peoples Drug Stores. Now, that is something worth while. I give them credit. I wouldn't pass that line for anything. I think Mr. X made a mistake but I don't think the school would be picketed. He is too popular with the students in spite of the fact that they might not agree with him. They wouldn't lose him for anything. They really like him. I know I do. I think it's just a matter of him being so old now. You know how it is; older people just think different from young people.

A seventeen-year-old son of a laborer, of third-year high school standing, felt that the campaign would have been successful by now if it had been waged in New York where Negroes are more militant and more cooperative, and explained:

Color and race are the factors that keep Negroes out. We have no way to demand and get the things we want. If the Peoples Drug Stores concerned were picketed in New York as they are here for Negro clerks, Negroes would have gotten what they demanded or closed up the places if they happen to be located in Negro neighborhoods. It would work here, too, if Negroes could and would stick together. There are Negroes in this country with as brilliant minds as there are white ones. And I think the white people know that, too, so they keep us all out.

"NEGROES DON'T STICK TOGETHER"

The statement of this youth concerning Negroes "sticking together" expresses a notion that has wide currency in Negro communities. Negro newspapers and public speakers constantly speak of the fact that Negroes do not "stick together." This idea circulates and influences the thinking of youth despite the fact that thousands of Negroes do "stick together" in church organizations and lodges. Very often the Negro newspapers as well as public speakers and leaders say that if the Negroes "stuck together" like the Jews they would be able to improve their status.[1] This idea was echoed in the statement of a Louisville youth who cited an example:

Negroes don't work together. A colored man had a grocery over at Twentieth and Chestnut. It was a very nice grocery. He had to buy fixtures for the grocery but he said Negroes didn't patronize him so he had to turn them back. If the Negroes would work together like the Jews we would have a race. I think we would get some place if we would just work together. One reason I think they don't work together is because they

[1] The author does not know to what extent such thinking is typical of minority groups. He has noted on numerous occasions that Jews have asserted that if Jews "stuck together" as Negroes do, they would be able to achieve great things.

are afraid of the white man. They are afraid that if they work against the white man they won't get enough to live off of because most Negroes don't have money. If the white man wanted to hold back their money the Negroes would die of starvation. Mostly what the Negro thinks about is eating—eating and sleeping.

The son of a laborer in Louisville who thought that the greatest problem of Negroes was "sticking together," remarked:

You know the greatest problem the Negro has is sticking together. They could keep white people from lynching if every time the white people got a crowd to lynch a colored man, they would get a crowd just as large and keep them from doing it. Some of them may get killed but I betcha if they did this about five or six times they would stop lynching them.

Another youth in Louisville spoke in a similar vein and attempted to prove that Negroes did not "stick together" as white people do. He said:

I learned that they [whites] are not better than nobody else and that they will do anything for money—anything. White people cooperate better than colored people. For example, if there's a group of colored people working together and one is the leader they get jealous and find faults with the leader and never are satisfied with nothing the leader does. But white people always pull together and cooperate with their leaders unless it's politics. Get that because a whole lot of guys will say, "Look how they pull against President Roosevelt," but you see that's politics and he is compelled to have enemies because one side is Democrats and the other Republicans. If there is a leader in the white group where politics is not concerned they will all work as one with their leader. If they have a baseball team, for example, and the coach doesn't start the first nine that they think he should start, they still have the spirit and fight to win; but colored people—if a coach starts nine that they think he shouldn't start—will have more long faces, no spirit, no team— will have no teamwork at all.

A girl in Louisville thought that "Negroes come into the world just like white people but white people cooperate more and have more." A Washington boy when asked what changes he would like to see in the treatment of Negroes began by saying that he "would like to see Negroes change" and learn to "stick together." He went on:

> If they would stick together, act right, and not take so much stuff off white people, they'd treat Negroes as they have to treat them in other places. Around New York, Negroes don't just sit or go around begging white people to give them breaks on jobs. They're in a position by cooperativeness to demand justice, equal rights, and jobs.

Although the lack of the ability of Negroes to "stick together" is spoken of as a generalized characteristic of Negroes, usually "sticking together" as a way of racial salvation has a very definite and concrete reference. Since the upper class in the Negro community have a middle-class outlook (in the historic sense) and since they are the most articulate members of the Negro community, "sticking together" generally refers to a type of economic cooperation in which they are especially interested. Despite the objective conditions which make impossible the creation of a segregated economy, Negro "leaders," public speakers, and Negro newspapers continue to spread the idea that the Negro's economic improvement can be achieved through the development of Negro business. These ideas are communicated to Negro youth and many of them feel vaguely if Negroes would only cooperate or had the capacity to "stick together" for business purposes their employment difficulties would be solved. Typical of their opinions in this regard is the statement of a sixteen-year-old high school boy whose mother works in domestic service. His mother has told him that as the "races continue to intermingle and intermarry" the problems of the Negro will disappear. He thinks that they "probably will, but it will take many generations to do it for a new crop of Negro-haters spring up daily." But his belief is that the only hope for the Negro

> lies in the further development of Negro business—a development sufficient to make use of thousands of educated Negro men and women now employed by whites and among the ranks of the unemployed. Negro development for Negroes! We'll never get far if we have to depend wholly on the white man.

Success in business enterprise is very often symbolized in the community by certain people who are looked upon as "leaders."

Some of the lower-class youth expressed a desire to be like certain people—for example, like a businessman, usually one who had achieved success as an undertaker and who was able to ride around in a fine car and enjoy leisure.

WHAT THEY THINK OF NEGRO LEADERS

So far as personalities in the larger Negro community were concerned, there were only about four outstanding "leaders" who seemingly had any great influence on the personality of lower-class youth. Actually, lower-class youth know very little about or have never heard of such men as W. E. B. DuBois, James Weldon Johnson, Walter White, Carter G. Woodson, or even Robert R. Moton. The majority of them did know about Booker T. Washington and, what was more important to them, that he had overcome ignorance and poverty, disadvantages similar to their own. One seventeen-year-old youth of second-year high school standing stated his attitude thus:

> I'd like to be a leader among Negroes, and have the training and the position necessary to help them. I'd like to be a real man, and above all, an independent man. As long as you've always got to be guarding against your job, you can never say or do much. That's what hurts us most. We have to depend too much on the white man and the sooner we can stand alone the better off we'll be. I'd like to be like Booker Washington. He believed that a Negro was best fitted to work with his hands and that a large number of us would always depend on the soil for a living. That's why I'd like to do something to make the mass of Negroes make their work on the farm more profitable. I'd probably never get as far as he did or make the contributions to the race he did but I'll do my best. I like farming and agriculture work and I'd like to know more about it. I've often wanted to be like other people, Joe Louis, for instance, because of the publicity, the pleasure there must be at knocking hell out of a white man who thinks he is your superior, and for the money in the boxing game.

Among living leaders who have not only captured the imagination of lower-class youth but whom they would emulate, Professor George Carver of Tuskegee is one of the three most important. A sixteen-year-old ninth-grade boy stated his opinion as follows:

If I had to choose one individual to be like, I'd like to be like Dr. Carver. It's encouraging to poor boys that he came from poor surroundings and by hard work finally became one of the country's leading scientists. If he can do it, so can others. So can I. I want to be myself always and I don't want education or opportunity to go to my head.

A nineteen-year-old youth expressed his desire to be like Carver in the following words:

As I said, Dr. Carver is the one I'm most interested in and I think he is the greatest living Negro. People extol others who have been dead a long time but I prefer to pick my guiding star among the living. I think he has done more to prove the real worth of Negroes, contributed more to science and his successes have done more to perpetuate the race than any other man. I'd like to be like him—a real man, and a scientist. I don't think he is a good businessman, but you can't expect everything from one individual.

Although it is quite likely that a movie showing the life of Carver was responsible for his popularity as a model, it appears that there were other factors responsible since some of these youth had not seen the picture. It is very likely, as some actually stated, that Carver symbolized the success of a poor black boy who had achieved distinction in the world, and that they identified their own lot and struggles with him. It is probably for the same reason that Mrs. Mary McLeod Bethune, the director of the division of Negro affairs of the National Youth Administration, has become the idol of lower-class youth. One dark eighteen-year-old youth of freshman college standing said that he had "heard of a few colored people who are nationally famous," but he couldn't "think of any of them now except Mrs. Bethune." When a lower-class girl in Louisville was asked to name outstanding Negroes in the United States, she placed Mrs. Bethune at the head of the list with the remark:

She is a Negro woman who has worked up and has got everything by herself. Most colored people work for self-benefit, but hers has all been for the benefit of the Negroes as a whole.

When this same girl was asked which of the leaders she would rather be, she answered:

I would prefer being Mrs. Bethune because she is the most out-standing and has worked harder than any of them to get what she wanted.

Another Louisville youth in naming Mrs. Bethune first among Negro leaders said that she was "a very outstanding lady," and added the significant statement: "When she first began her career she was very handicapped. In spite of this, she has made a success." A twenty-one-year-old Washington girl, a high school graduate in domestic service, who had thought "for a long time" that NYA stood for Negro Youth Administration, knew that Mrs. Bethune was head of a government agency that helped poor Negro children to go through school. A fourteen-year-old girl of ninth-grade standing recalled that she felt proud of Mrs. Bethune as she spoke at her school. This girl volunteered the statement that she read in a paper that Mrs. Bethune had gone to the White House and had dinner with Mrs. Roosevelt.

To many of these lower-class children, Mrs. Bethune, both because of her decidedly Negroid features and her early struggles, is a symbol of hope. They have seen other Negroes achieve distinction but they were generally of mixed blood; but here was a woman who looked like themselves and had struggled with poverty as they are now struggling. Nevertheless, she had achieved distinction and was accepted by whites.

Some of the boys who said that they wanted to be like Professor Carver or Booker T. Washington named Joe Louis as their second choice. For example, one Washington youth, twenty years of age and in the second year of high school, remarked:

> Well, since I can't get the education to do work of a man like Booker T. Washington, I'd prefer as a second choice to be like Joe Louis. I like him because he is a real man, earns good money, is good to his mother, and doesn't put on airs because of his wealth or position.

To many lower-class youth Joe Louis is important and worthy of emulation for other reasons. An eighteen-year-old Washington youth of senior high school standing spoke as follows:

> Well, for years whites have kicked Negroes about and I'm

happy somebody came along who could kick the stuffings out of the toughest "hombres" the whites could put up against him. Fighting Joe Louis is just a short method of violent suicide. I think he's important for Negroes to feel that one of their kind who could excel even with or against the best white competition. I think he's important because without an education he rose from nothing at all to the top—from poverty to riches— from an unknown to a world-famous man. Other men who have become important had greater advantages to begin with than he had. Despite all odds he succeeded. That's the test of a man's ability and courage.

Thus Joe Louis enables many lower-class youth (in fact, many Negro youth and adults in all classes) to inflict vicariously the aggressions which they would like to carry out against whites for the discriminations and insults which they have suffered. A nineteen-year-old Washington youth, a high school graduate, said:

I've tried to follow in Louis' footsteps, but I'm not big enough. I've heard all of his fights and seen him several times here in Washington. I've thrilled at every damned "peck" he knocked over and helped raise hell in the U Street celebrations after each one. When he lost, I felt pretty bad, though I'll ever feel something was wrong—crooked. He sure proved something was wrong the way he beat up Schmeling the second time.

Another Washington youth, seventeen and in the third year of high school, who would rather be Joe Louis than any Negro in the entire country, made the significant remark: "That's one Negro white men respect." The twenty-one-year-old son of a laborer declared that the "whole Southwest is for Joe and we had wild celebrations after every fight." He continued:

The night he lost was a sad one for we had planned big doings. I'll always believe he was doped. Something was wrong but in my mind he was still champion! You can't beat a Negro doing anything if you give him an equal break. And white people know it, that's why they keep us out of so many things right here in Washington. Joe Louis is sure a credit to his race and I'm proud of him. People like him help to make you forget you're just a Negro. And we sure need a lot more like him. We'd be a lot better off!

Likewise, a ten-year-old son of a laborer would rather be Joe Louis than any other Negro in the country because he "would get a lot of fun going in the ring and beating up somebody." He added, "Joe Louis has done a lot to make the colored race recognized."

THE IDEAL OF BROWN AMERICA

Joe Louis, the "Brown Bomber" as he is known in the white as well as in the Negro world, is a symbol of the conquest of the white man by the Negro. Although Joe Louis is as a matter of fact brown in complexion, the very designation brown is not without significance as far as the Negro is concerned. This is true despite the fact that a fair or white complexion has considerable prestige in the Negro community. Many lower-class youth say frankly that if they were born again they would prefer to be white,[2] and it is true that Negro newspapers both

[2] Because of current uncritical notions concerning the desire on the part of Negroes to be white, certain facts should be pointed out in regard to the statements of these youth to the effect that they preferred or wanted to be white. We may dismiss as irrelevant to the point at issue here the frequent assertion, which may or may not be true, that Negroes do not want to be white but want to enjoy what whites enjoy. Our interest here is in what these youth actually want or wish. It should be stated that in the majority of cases we do not have sufficient data to arrive at conclusions concerning their wishes in this regard. What is important, however, is that one should distinguish between mere verbal responses which were given after the youth reflected or thought about the question and arrived at an abstract conclusion; and the response which represented more truly his feelings, attitudes, and imaginings in regard to being white. For example, one girl remarked: "I said I didn't want to be white but I don't know why I said so. I guess we say a lot of things *without thinking*. We are always trying to get white. That looks like we want to be white no matter what we say. When you stop to *think*, they [whites] have every advantage—the best of everything. After all, a colored person who says he doesn't want to be white must be kinda off. I guess I was myself when I said I didn't want to be. If I had my life to live over again, I'm sure I would want to be born white—even looking like white is not the same thing. I would pass if I could; I don't blame people who can." On the other hand, a ten-year-old boy described his attitude as follows: "Sometimes I have wished I was a white boy, but I don't guess I really do want to be a white boy. I get along all right being colored. If I could be born over again, I would want to be just a little darker than I am now. I'm not glad that I'm light and I'm not sorry. I feel satisfied." The majority of these youth, so far as the interviews disclosed, appeared to "accept themselves" or thought of themselves in the various roles which they played in their group relations. To be sure, there were cases where they imagined themselves white and wanted to become other "selves." Only when they felt frustrated in their wishes and impulses because of their racial identity and imagined

create and reflect this attitude through their numerous advertisements of products to whiten or bleach the skin. But in spite of this tendency the majority of youth covered in this study reported that they preferred to have a brown complexion, preferred a mate of brown complexion and children of the same color. When a black Louisville girl was asked what color she would like to be if she were born again, she answered: "I would like to be a high brown like X so I could wear any color clothes I'd want to." Then when the interviewer asked: "What color are you?" she replied: "Black." Then, giggling, she added: "No, I'm chocolate brown." In her humorous reply, she attempts to describe her complexion according to what is taken to be the ideal. When one Louisville girl was asked what kind of colored woman she thought was pretty, she answered:

My ideal woman is brown, not dark brown, has dreamy eyes, small nose, a head that isn't too large, long thin eyebrows, a chin not too long nor too short. She should weigh about one hundred and twenty-five pounds, have a nice shape and coarse black hair. My ideal man should be tall and handsome, reddish tan, feet not too large, small eyes, thin nose, not too long, high cheek bones, hair so-so, dress pretty nice, head not too large and not too small and a small chin not too long nor too short.

Youth of brown complexion generally wanted to remain their same complexion. A girl in Louisville remarked:

If I were to be born over again I would like to be the same brown color I am now. This color appeals to me simply because I have associated it with myself all these years and therefore I am quite content. Then, too, from careful observation I have concluded that color is not an asset in regard to worth-while achievements.

A Washington girl described her "boy friend" and described the type of husband she would prefer.

He is a good height, medium brown with pretty hair—doesn't seem to be stuck on himself. I hate a person who is self-conceited. I think it is the worst thing in the world. I would like a hus-

---

themselves carrying out their wishes and desires as white persons and participating in the white world could we legitimately say that they really wished that they were white.

band who would be from medium brown to light. I hate to say I wouldn't marry a dark boy, but dark people have such a hard time; dark girls especially. You read the ads for the most ordinary domestic job and they want a light brown or light girl. Even that old Jew wanted to know what color I was. I think it is awful.

It appears from the answers of these youth that the Negroes are gradually developing a conception of themselves as brown people rather than black people. Undoubtedly idealized pictures of Negroes are helping them to identify themselves as brown people.[3]

MIDDLE-CLASS YOUTH

So far as the influence of social movements and ideologies on Negro youth is concerned, it is difficult to distinguish middle-class from lower-class youth. Middle-class youth are scarcely better acquainted with such organizations as the N.A.A.C.P. and the Urban League than lower-class persons. One middle-class youth did not know whether the NYA and the N.A.A.C.P. were the same organization and added that she heard at school "what the N.A.A.C.P. stands for" but she had forgotten. She knew that it had "something to do with the advancement of colored people."

Middle-class youth were divided in their opinions concerning the picketing of the Peoples Drug Stores. Some of them felt that Negroes should establish their own businesses and provide employment opportunities. For example, two sisters who approved the picketing, spoke thus:

First Sister—There should be as many colored working in the stores as whites. There should be more colored drugstores.

Second Sister—Of course, you can't blame everything on the white people. Colored people will naturally employ colored people; therefore white people will naturally employ whites. So colored people in power should have businesses and employ colored.

First Sister—That's what I say, there should be more colored drugstores. There is only one colored drugstore in Southeast.

[3] Edwin R. Embree, *Brown America* (New York: Viking Press, 1931).

The same four Negroes—Booker T. Washington, Mrs. Mary M. Bethune, Professor George Carver, and Joe Louis—who were considered outstanding and worthy of emulation by lower-class Negroes were also so regarded by middle-class youth. A youth in Louisville thought that if Negroes had only followed Booker T. Washington, they would have been better off, and added: "He taught Negroes to be unselfish. George Carver is an exact replica of him. When Edison offered him ten thousand dollars to work in his plant, he refused because he knew all his work would belong to Edison and he wouldn't get any recognition as a black man. That shows his unselfishness." In this statement is echoed the general belief that Negroes will not "stick together." This same youth stated: "Being a Negro is bad but it wouldn't be so bad if they would just stick together instead of each one looking out just for himself." Mrs. Bethune is admired by the youth of this class because, as one girl said, "she has educated herself and wants to educate others, and is doing something for youth."

Naturally, all of the middle-class youth know of Joe Louis. Although not many said that they would want to be like him, practically all of them admired him and wished that they had his money. One Washington junior high school youth spoke thus:

> I think Joe Louis is an important Negro. He has money and prestige. He has put his money to good use and his championship makes him an outstanding Negro. I've heard most of his fights either here or at the filling station and he has always been a great hero to me. I felt pretty badly when he lost a fight and always will think there was something funny about the one he lost to Schmeling. I just love to hear him beat the daylights out of so-called good white men.

The feeling expressed in the above statement is similar to that of lower-class youth for whom Joe Louis provides a means by which they may carry out vicariously their aggressions against whites. But in the following statement by the twenty-year-old son of a semiskilled worker, Joe Louis' money was of primary consideration:

> Of all the men we mentioned who I thought were important,

I think I'd like to be like Joe Louis. Why? Well, chiefly because of his money. I heard the other day that he got $4.23 for his first fight. And to tell the truth, I could even use that amount. Oh, boy! What I couldn't do with some of the money he has made. Money isn't everything, but it can certainly get most anything. A man, whether black or white, can't get very far without money and there's really not much use in trying. I'd like to have money no matter what I had to do to get it. It looks as though I'm not going to get much by working for it. My father worked hard all his life and we don't even own our home. My clothes are pretty ragged as you see and there's little I can do to earn money to buy more, and my father says if I want them, I'll have to get out and get the money to buy them.

A brown complexion, with variations of course, seems to be the ideal color for middle-class youth. Because of the various shades of skin coloring among Negroes, some of these youth have worked out singular notions about color values. The daughter of a skilled worker spoke as follows:

What do I think the prettiest color?—a brown. If you notice a light-colored person is prettier than a white person and a child of a dark and a light person is prettier than its parents. I think people should mix up, but not marry white people because you lose the respect of white and colored people. I'm for staying in the race. But I wouldn't marry a man as dark as I am. If I married someone my own color, I wouldn't see any sense to it. If two dark people marry, they may as well stay single. Well, I want to have some children, not so many, but a few and I think you should marry someone a different color. If you notice, you most always see a couple of different colors. When two people marry of the same color, their children are usually funny looking. Some people talk about marrying their own color but that is foolishness!

Let us take the case of a twelve-year-old girl of eighth-grade standing whose father is a skilled worker. This girl is of a tawny-brown complexion and has soft, silky, brown hair. She said that she had "never thought about being colored, one way or another," and that it did not matter to her and added: "I'm having a good time." Then she continued with the following comment:

I don't want to be white. I'd just like to pass sometimes, like I told you when I want to go downtown. I hated to wait so long for "Snow White." Some of the kids who can pass went down to see it. There is no other time that I've wanted to be white. I'm satisfied with my color. I wouldn't want to be lighter or darker. People have told me I'm a pretty color, but that isn't why I'm satisfied. I'm satisfied because I don't believe you should be wishing yourself this or that, but go and get along with what you have. Some girls have more clothes and things than I have, but I don't worry about that. I know I have more than lots of other people. I wouldn't mind being lighter, but I surely wouldn't want to be any darker. [Smiled and shook her head] Dark people have a hard time.

Although some of the middle-class youth said that if they were born again, they would prefer to be white, the majority wanted to be the same complexion. As one Louisville girl put it:

If I was born over again, I would want to be about the same color I am now. I can't find anything wrong with it. If I could make myself over, I would. I wouldn't be so tall. I'd have long hair, a small mouth, a keen nose, pretty black eyes, and a good form. I would like most to be a light-brown skin. I am medium-brown skin.

From the statements of these youth concerning color preferences, it appears that the black or darker lower-class youth regard a brown skin as the ideal complexion or the complexion which they would like to be. But when middle-class youth state that they are satisfied with their brown complexion, it appears that they are expressing their feeling of racial identification.

UPPER-CLASS YOUTH

Since upper-class youth come from families with a middle-class outlook (in the historic sense), it is not surprising to find some of them thinking like the seventeen-year-old senior high youth, the son of a government clerk, who said:

The hearts of white man can't be changed, so the only solution is better and bigger business by Negroes which will hire Negro youth to conduct it. Since whites won't hire us, it's up to us to hire and give jobs to our own people. That means that Negroes must patronize their own business enterprises, to build them to proportions where large numbers of Negroes can be hired. The attitude of Negroes must be changed, for too many of them think only of themselves, don't give honest values and try to beat each other out of their "eye teeth."

This youth is so firmly convinced that the Negro should build a separate economy that he is opposed to the picketing of the drugstore. He remarked:

Take the Peoples Drug Store picketing. I don't think that's going to be of great benefit to Negroes. It probably will only cause those who are working to be fired. Picketing for one or two Negro clerks won't be of great financial benefit to the race. What should be done would be to use the money now spent for picketing to build a first class drugstore, advertise it widely, and patronize it. That would do more good than letting our businesses suffer while we tried to stifle somebody else's. I'm not in favor of such measures. To me, they only make us look ridiculous.

A twelve-year-old girl of eighth-grade standing did not know whether she approved of picketing or not. Her attitude toward picketing could be summed up as follows: There were some disadvantages in being colored, but she didn't think she would feel them until she was grown. She did not know whether she approved of the picketing or not. She understood the purpose all right. She would go into the store if there was anything in there that she wanted on sale. She would pay no attention to the signs. She would get articles where they were cheapest. She had never seen colored clerks except in colored drugstores. Negroes should stick to their own race—try to get work in colored drugstores.

The attitude of some of these youth toward the picketing of the white chain drugstore is influenced by their beliefs in separate business enterprises for Negroes. For example, a sixteen-year-old senior high school girl, whose father is a successful businessman, spoke as follows:

I have often wondered why we as a race cannot succeed in business as the white race advances. You take this picketing of the Peoples Drug Store. I am in favor of the idea, but I think their method of attack is wrong. The Negroes should build a worthwhile drugstore like the Peoples so that when they decide to

demand better jobs for Negroes, their people will have an alter-
native to turn to immediately. I know I went all the way down
to X's Drug Store to get some things. Of course, they didn't have
everything I wanted, but I got those which he had. Now, where
am I going to get these other things on my list? I suppose I will
just have to wait until I can get downtown. Why hasn't Dr. Y
expanded? Why couldn't Dr. Z have made good? I tell you why
—as soon as a colored man gets a little bit of money he buys a
large car, fine clothes, a big house, he lives above his means. He
thinks too much of the social side of life. I'm not the "old dyed-
in-the-wool" type of person, but I feel that people should use
some sense and should be able to distinguish between business
and pleasure. I smoke and drink occasionally, but I certainly
don't let these things interfere with business. Well, I didn't mean
to get all worked up like this, but I like to express my opinion
on the matter in hopes that others will benefit by my experience.

This same girl, who evidently has considerable race pride,
brought in the matter of picketing again when talking about
family pride:

Our race is not the only one guilty of striving to know the
right people, but that still doesn't make it right in my mind.
I wouldn't like to be white. I'm satisfied with my color and have
never thought of being otherwise. I am not sorry that I cannot
pass. I believe one should try to uphold his race as much as
possible. You take, for instance, the picketing that is going on
against the Peoples Drug Stores. I wouldn't have the nerve to
walk in there while our people are attempting to get better jobs
for Negroes. I think Mr. X, who is supposed to be an educator
and leader of his race, should be "tarred and feathered" for
going in there. Some Negroes have no race pride whatsoever.

Some of these upper-class youth are, nevertheless, definitely
in favor of the picketing. A nineteen-year-old girl of third-year
college standing expressed herself as follows:

I have just become interested in the New Negro Alliance since
they have been picketing the Peoples Drug Stores at Fourteenth
and U and at Seventh and M. They want to get employment
for Negroes. I wouldn't go past the picket line. I think they
are perfectly right to picket. I'd carry a sign. I'd think any young
person interested in getting a job of any kind would be more
than willing to carry a sign. My parents hope it will mean that

Negroes can stick together on some point. They feel that Negroes will weaken before it's over, but I don't. I'm praying for them to hold out.

The following statement from a sixteen-year-old senior college student, whose father has been a leader in militant movements among Negroes, reflects the racial militancy of a certain section of the upper class. She stated with emphasis:

I am in favor of fighting for one's rights, and I do believe that Negroes should be hired as clerks. After all, there are Negroes who are prepared to hold such jobs. The white people feel that they can monopolize everything. I would never have the nerve to go in any of the stores while the campaign is going on. I believe in supporting your race until the end—win or lose. I think Mr. X should be shot for going in the store and for making the statement that he did. And, he is supposed to be a leader of Negroes. At least, you would expect him to be such. [Because of his position] He is no example for those under him at all. [The interviewer asked her if she would picket.] To be truthful, I don't think I would. I believe I can give my support in other ways. I think those who carry the signs should be dressed more neatly. It would take away that wild, radical look that most people have who participate in such events. No, I don't think I would be willing to carry the sign, but I wouldn't go in the store for anything.

It is interesting to note in the latter part of her statement that she thinks that those carrying signs should be "dressed more neatly," since they would not then have the "wild radical look that most people have who participate in such events." She expresses a typical upper-class attitude; namely, that Negroes should be respectable and conform to the behavior of upper-class or cultured whites.

The sixteen-year-old daughter of a professional man made the following statement concerning the picketing:

According to the financial reports the sales have gone down greatly—especially the store at Seventh and M Streets where the Negro population is extremely large. I would like to see more Negroes interested in this type of work. The Negro should fight for his social and civic rights because, after all, all men are supposed to be created equal. I am a member of the N.A.A.C.P. but I regret to say that I know little about the organization. I know that it attempts to get justice for Negroes especially in cases of lynchings. Walter White is an important leader in this organization and in the Negro race. I don't know much about those Negroes who are considered leaders. I realize my education on the subject is very limited.

RACIAL MILITANCY

The above statement not only expresses the spirit of racial militancy which characterizes some sections of the upper class, but also shows that although such organizations as the N.A.A.C.P. are an expression of upper-class protest against present racial relations, the majority of upper-class youth have little interest in them or any real understanding of their aims. Naturally, the more articulate and race conscious upper-class Negroes endeavor to enlist the support of their colleagues as well as of the lower-class masses, but their success even within their own class is limited. Such leaders are especially concerned with the failure of Negroes to "stick together," which means a failure to patronize business enterprises which are under upper-class leadership.

The influence exerted by the personalities of Negro leaders of national repute on upper-class youth appears from their statements to be different from that exerted on the more naive middle- and lower-class youth. The upper-class youth seem to be more aware of the philosophy of race relations represented by these leaders. For example, an eighteen-year-old youth, a junior in a northern college, made the following statement:

I am not an admirer of Booker T. Washington. He founded Tuskegee Institute, but I do not agree with his policy of teaching the Negro only manual arts or trades. I get so angry when a person, especially white, refers to him as a great Negro leader. He might have been a leader during his time, but that has passed long ago. I had an argument with a white girl at school about this very thing. She mentioned his name as an outstanding Negro. I stopped her in the middle of her sentence and said, "Now, listen, if you want to discuss this point with me, please omit his name because I do not agree with his belief of social inequality. He believed in working only with the hands. Negroes have the ability to do mental work just as any white person."

Many of the upper-class youth did, nevertheless, name Booker T. Washington among the important leaders in the country, although few said that they wanted to be like him. Professor Carver proved to be the most popular model for these upper-class youth. Typical of such statements was that of a seventeen-year-old senior high school youth who stated:

> I think I'd like to be like Dr. Carver. I'd like to be a scientist like him. I admire him for his unselfishness and his willingness to serve humanity without reward. I'd like to see him make it possible for many Negroes to profit commercially and financially by his discoveries. But he came from poor surroundings and has made good. With a better home life than he had and opportunities available for work and education, I should be able to make some contributions some day.

Although not many upper-class youth wanted to be like Joe Louis, they admired him. To youth in the upper class as in the two lower classes, Joe Louis is both a symbol and a person with whom they can identify themselves in his conquests of whites. A seventeen-year-old college freshman spoke of Joe Louis' fights as follows:

> I was hitting every blow with him and taking with him those he got. And when he lost, I really felt sick. Somehow I didn't even want to go on the street the next day. One thing he's done, he's certainly made the so-called white fighters have a wholesome respect for his fists. I suppose symbolically that's the only way white people can be made to respect Negroes in other walks of life.

The majority of these youth do not actually want to be like Joe Louis because of the implications of the status of a prize fighter. Note, for example, the remark of a senior college youth, a young woman, who said:

> Outside of fighting, I think he is a laughing stock. It is too bad he is so ignorant. I listen to his fights. When he lost I cried, I felt so bad about it, but there was so much to that Schmeling fight. After his last fight, we went down on U Street; it didn't look disorderly to me. Then it seemed as if the people were having a good time. I read later of them destroying property. I did all my yelling right here in this house and on my own front. Of course, if I had been out in the street listening to the fight, I

might have joined in the cheering. I think the people who went around beating up white people are just ignorant—that doesn't help a bit.

It is also important to note that Mrs. Bethune was not the heroine among upper-class youth that she was among the lower class. She was noted by some upper-class youth as a distinguished person, though actually criticized in one instance. Perhaps many of them felt like the Louisville girl who said: "I would like to be like Mrs. Bethune on account of her work. I would like to sing like Marian Anderson, and I would like to look like Olivia de Havilland." On the other hand, many upper-class youth, being very individualistic, undoubtedly felt like the seventeen-year-old son of a professional man in Washington, who said:

> I don't think I'd like to be like any of them, and that includes my father. I just want to be myself and I'm following no pattern. I'll make one for myself. If I had to make a choice though, I'd want to be like Judge Hastie—brilliant, successful as a lawyer, and generally well-liked—with money and position.

DO THEY WANT TO BE WHITE?

Because of the large proportion of persons among the upper class with a fair complexion, and because of the value which is often attached to such a complexion, it is not surprising that a brown skin is not the ideal in this class as it is in the two lower groups. Many of the upper-class youth say frankly that they would prefer to be white if born again. Then, there are those of brown complexion who prefer to be lighter. It seems that so far as ideas about themselves as a race are concerned, they prefer to be regarded as a light-brown race. Then, too, it seems that since there is no possibility of changing their complexion, some of them simply accept what they have. One seventeen-year-old Washingtonian stated his attitude as follows:

> No, I'm not proud of the fact that I'm a "nigger"! I haven't seen any reason why I should be proud. I am well satisfied with my present color, though I'm aware of the advantages of being white. For that reason alone, I'd like to be white. A lot of my relatives can pass for white, but seldom try it. I can understand that. It saves a lot of possible embarrassment. I know a lot of Negroes who do pass, and I don't blame them. I would too if I

could. It won't be long before we will be so intermixed, no distinction can be made as to color.

It is more probable that the majority of upper-class youth who are determined to achieve anything in the world feel like the seventeen-year-old youth who dramatically related his change in attitude toward his racial identity as follows:

I tell you, I used to regret that I was colored, but I don't any more. I did regret it until about four years ago when I was at high school. A speaker was at assembly once who really changed my opinion. I don't remember his name, but he was very good. He told us that Negroes should look upon their race as a challenge to them to jump all hurdles, to do the job in spite of all obstacles, that there wasn't anything a white man did that a colored man couldn't do if only he would not feel licked from the start. Right then, I made up my mind that I would not waste any time regretting I was colored, but that I would be a man as other men and give the best within me. It would be necessary, I knew, as the speaker said, to throw off my fears and get to work. I don't know whether that speaker influenced any-one else or not. I didn't discuss it with any of the children. I did mention it at home and was encouraged by my parents in my new views. Before this time, I had the picture fixed in my mind of Negroes pushed farther and farther down and whites rising higher and higher, leaving the gap between them greater and greater. [Here he was so interested that he demonstrated with his hands, showing the white people rising and kicking the Negroes back down with their feet—his fingers pointed downwards to show exactly what he meant.] I was then about twelve years old, and I have never forgotten my resolution to do with my qualifications—whatever they may be—just what any other man would. I wish I could remember that speaker's name. He was a young man, rather tall, light-brown skin. I don't know whether he was from Washington or not, or from Howard, either. In fact, I guess I wasn't paying much attention when he was introduced. I didn't get any of the facts about him. I be-lieve that I would know him if I were to see him, and I mean some day to tell him how much he influenced me. I really have felt much better since I experienced this change. I haven't been afraid to face facts; I was born a Negro and I know it means a lot of difficulties to face, but I am willing to face them. I am glad I am no darker—darker Negroes have still harder times. I wouldn't mind being lighter, but have never wished it very seriously. I would "pass" if I could, but I don't see any special gain in doing so. People who "pass" impress me as being something of hypocrites. They are deceiving themselves. They could actually arrive, if they would only get rid of their fears. I mean arrive as Negroes. It is not necessary to "pass" to realize ambitions. I don't think I should be glad that I am not darker—because color of skin really is not important. It is what is within a man that matters. I guess I've just picked up that feeling subconciously. I know I didn't get it from mother or dad. We don't hear that kind of stuff around here.

The comment above does not indicate that this youth has a "sour grapes" attitude toward "being white." Nor is it a mere accommodation to his status as a Negro. It represents a redefinition of his role and a thoroughgoing change in his conception of himself as a person.

SUMMARY

From the data which we have been able to gather on these youth, it seems clear that social movements in the strict meaning of the term exercise practically no influence on the personality of Negro youth. This is even true of the few established organizations with programs for the improvement of the status of the Negro, but when a more particularized movement like the picketing for jobs is inaugurated, it arouses among a minority some of the latent militancy and resentment of Negro youth toward discrimination. On the other hand, there are certain ideas current in the Negro communities in border cities which seemingly influence the conception which Negro youth have of themselves as well as their attitudes toward whites. There is the general belief that Negroes do not "stick together." This idea certainly makes many individuals feel that Negroes are inferior to whites or lack certain qualities of character which whites possess. Although this belief has a vague reference, it often turns out to mean that Negroes do not support the business enterprises of the upper class. It is from the upper class that there has emanated the idea that the Negro could solve his economic problems by building a segregated economy. The upper class sees to it that the idea of a segregated economy is tied up with the Negro's growing racial consciousness. This growing racial consciousness has fostered certain ideas concerning the Negro's physical character. The idealized picture of the Negro as presented in newspapers and magazines is not that of a black man or woman but of a brown man or woman with modified Negroid features. To the darker members of the lower classes, it provides an ideal which influences wishes concerning themselves, their marriage partners, and their children. To the middle class, the majority of whom are brown, it provides a means of racial identification. Even the upper class, with a large proportion of members of fair complexion, accepts it with a variation toward the lighter shades.

Certain personalities in the Negro world exercise possibly a far greater influence upon Negro youth than the above ideals involving merely physical characteristics. Negro youth of the lower and middle classes especially are inspired with hope by Negroes who have surmounted handicaps of race and poverty, and achieved some distinction in the white as well as the Negro world. Negro youth in these two classes tend to identify themselves with these outstanding personalities and thereby develop confidence in their own possibilities. A person like Joe Louis enables youth of all classes to enjoy vicariously his victories over whites. Such satisfactions, though experienced indirectly, tend to support the ego of Negro youth who on every hand encounter so much disparagement.

PART II

TWO NEGRO YOUTH
WARREN AND ALMINA

INTRODUCTION TO PART II

THE ANALYSIS which has been presented thus far of the effects of minority status on the personality of Negro youth has shown only segments or fragments of the personalities of a number of children and youth. This could scarcely be avoided since our broad purpose was to show the influence exerted by people, groups, institutions, social movements, and ideologies upon the feelings and attitudes of many youth toward themselves as Negroes. Although in our analysis we undertook to interpret their reactions as a part of their total personalities, it was inevitable that their attitudes and behavior, abstracted from the context of their total personalities, should appear in a different light from what they would have appeared when viewed as a part of the total behavior of a living personality. In this section we hope to remedy this defect by presenting two Negro youth as living, human beings, in the totality of their relationships and interactions with the social and cultural world of which they are a part.

Of course, to present a complete description and an analysis of a human personality even over a relatively short period would require volumes of observations of his overt behavior, not to mention his introspective accounts of his impulses, wishes, feelings, and ideas. The information which we have secured on the two youth is inadequate for a thorough exploration of their personalities, but it is adequate to give us some idea of their personalities in their functional relationships with family, friends, various groups, and the organization of a larger society.

Another observation should be added concerning our study of these two youth. Since we regard personality as a complex organization which develops within the matrix of the experiences of the individual, personality may be studied from two points of view. First, it may be studied from the point of view of its growth and development over a period of years during which impulses and wishes become organized in various patterns of behavior. Second, the behavior of the individual may be studied intensively at any moment in an effort to discover the hidden impulses or motives which are not apparent in his verbal responses and overt behavior. As far as our data would permit we have kept both points of view in mind in studying these youth. We have attempted to analyze the organization of their earliest impulses and wishes and to discover whatever traits were apparent at different periods in the development of their personalities. The greater attention has, however, been focused upon their present behavior—both overt and covert. In attempting this we were naturally faced with the difficult problem of probing beneath what they said or even did. Fortunately, we were aided in this difficult task by a psychiatrist who possessed the specialized competence required for depth analysis of personality. This does not mean that we were able to ferret out all the hidden motivations or that the psychiatrist himself felt that he had solved the problem in hand. In fact, because of the extreme limitations within which he worked, the psychiatrist hesitated to present his tentative findings. However, since the psychiatrist as well as the writer viewed the whole undertaking as an exploratory and a pioneer study of the personality of the Negro, the psychiatrist agreed to supplement our analysis with a discussion of the problem.

Finally, something should be said concerning the selection of these two individuals. We did not attempt to identify an "average" or a "typical" Negro boy or girl. Warren, whose family is of middle-class status, was selected because we became very well acquainted with him and his family, and we were, therefore, able to secure much more valuable material on him than on most of the other subjects. The same could be said concerning Almina, whose family was of lower-class status. Of course, we may say that these youth are representative in the sense that they come from the two largest classes in the Negro group. But from the standpoint of their personality development, we feel that such terms as "average" and "typical" should be avoided because in so describing an individual, one leaves out what is essential in every personality—its uniqueness. Thus, although one may say that Warren's experiences and processes of adjustment are typical of youth in his class or that he exhibits certain personality traits similar to other youth, one is not warranted in making him in any strict sense a "typical" Negro youth.

CHAPTER VIII

WARREN WALL*

THE WALL family, consisting of father and mother and nine children, occupies a large, red brick, six-room house in a run-down section of Southwest Washington which is gradually being rehabilitated to serve white people. A large vacant lot has already been converted into a playground for whites, notwithstanding the fact that there are no white children in the immediate neighborhood. Although the house occupied by Warren's family is poorly furnished and the wall paper and floors are in need of repair, it is not so bad as the dilapidated structures which surround it. It is one of the few houses in the block that have modern sanitary equipment, and it is far superior to the one- and two-room huts across the street. But like other houses in the neighborhood, the small front yard is dusty and bare. Warren's brothers and sisters during their play have dug numerous holes in the yard, which is enclosed by a badly bent iron fence. The excavations are only one of the evidences of the never-ending activities of this teeming household.

Although the Wall family lives in a section of the city occupied largely by lower-class families, the family is really of middle-class status. Mr. Wall, who has a highly skilled and responsible position, is a veteran of fifteen years service in the employ of the municipal government. His regular and comparatively good income has enabled him to provide his wife and nine children with most of the necessities of life. In maintaining discipline in his family, he has not lost the confidence or respect of his children. Outside of his home he is both respected and liked because of his amiable disposition as well as his interest in civic and church affairs.

* The names used in this analysis are purely fictitious.

WARREN'S PARENTS

Mr. Wall, a large, very dark but florid man, weighing one hundred and ninety-seven pounds, is thirty-nine years old. He has been living in his present home since he was eight years of age. His father, who was a laborer, migrated from Virginia and bought property in Southwest. Moving in advance of the growing Negro population, Mr. Wall's father bought land at the present location and erected the first brick house in the neighborhood. He died when Mr. Wall was only eighteen months old and left the property to his wife, who was in domestic service, and his son. Mr. Wall was the youngest and, it seems, the favorite child. After his brothers and sisters had died or left home, he became his father's heir. Mr. Wall was graduated from the high school that Warren attends at present. After graduation he did odd jobs and later became a messenger in one and then another of the government bureaus. It was not until he married that he took a civil service examination and was appointed to his present position.

Mrs. Wall was born and reared in a rural community in Virginia. She was next to the oldest of eleven children. Her parents still run the farm in Virginia. Most of her brothers and sisters—all of whom, except two brothers, are living—have migrated to near-by states. Mrs. Wall attended only the lower grades as a child but completed the elementary course at a night school during the past year. She migrated to Washington and entered domestic service. Soon after coming to Washington, she joined the Baptist church and became a member of the choir. It was through the church that she met Mr. Wall and married him when she was seventeen.

Mr. Wall is a very amiable and good-natured person. He is popular in the neighborhood and during the summer may be found each day on the corner lot playing "community checkers" with the men in the neighborhood. Concerning the Southwest section, he said:

I rather like it down here. Most people think Southwest is the worst part of the city, but I don't think so. The trouble with this section has been that as soon as Negroes get fair jobs and get anywhere up in the world they move up in Northwest section and other sections. Of all the men working within my set-up, I'm the only one living down here. This section has always kept poor Negroes because of low rents, and as the homes and neighborhoods improve it is beginning to attract the more important Negroes from the Northwest back down here for the same reason.

Contrary to the usual beliefs, this side of Washington is pretty quiet. At least people don't bother you down here. We have a lot of common Negroes down here but when they are common, they don't care who knows it. That's a lot different from people in other sections.

But a great change has taken place in the "niggers" who live here, though; the section as a whole has improved very little. I don't suppose much change will take place until the government starts its program of building and improvement down here. I get along with them all, as anyone else could if they treat these people like they are humans and not like you're superior and all that.

His major civic activity is the sponsorship of two Boy Scout troops, one at his church and the other at a near-by settlement. He takes considerable pride in sponsoring these organizations and seems to have a real interest in youth. He remarked: "I've stuck to this Boy Scout program because I think it's worth while." He also told of having to put aside personal dislikes because he would not do "anything that would hurt the program of the boys." At home he has a rather expensive hobby, an amateur radio station. Although this hobby as well as his Scout activities creates a solidarity of interest with his children, it is probably indicative of a certain easy-going optimism in his make-up. His account was cut off at one store because he let his payments lapse and was unable to reopen it because another debt for $25 had been standing for ten years. He stated that since they had ceased to pester him about it, he "didn't bother about paying them at all."

This does not mean that Mr. Wall fails to provide his family with the necessities of life as far as his salary will permit. During one year he bought forty-seven pairs of shoes for his family. In fact, he is extremely devoted to his wife and nine children.

These children range in age from sixteen to three years. There are five boys and four girls. The color of all of them is very dark and they all have kinky hair. They are apparently a very happy and playful group. The children have the run of the house and their numerous friends only add to the confusion. Consequently, the house is always torn up and there is constant bedlam, but this does not disturb either Warren's father or his mother.

Warren's mother, a pleasant little woman, thirty-five years of age, seems satisfied with life and has never complained about the responsibilities of a large family. Her husband, she said, was disappointed because there were only five boys when he wanted enough for a baseball nine, but she has done her best! She added:

> I love every one of these children and I'd even like more, but at this late stage of the game, I guess I'd better call quit. I have to be very careful now as old as I am to keep the number at nine.

Mrs. Wall recalled jokingly that soon after she was married her husband told her that he had "dreamed he had nine children and he hoped they'd all be boys" and she had "told him if he'd told me that a couple of months ago, I would have kept my job and let him go on his way." Nevertheless, she is happy with her children, and although when the children were young she could not go to church as much as she would have liked, she is "too busy to get tired and bored of staying in."

> It is a job trying to keep this house and family together and happy. I'm busy from the time I get up till I lie down at night and then it looks as though I've done nothing. Clothes and food are our biggest problem and I'll be glad when the older children can get out, get jobs and help us with the younger children.

Although Mrs. Wall only received an elementary school education, she wants her "children to realize the value of a good education and go out and get one while they can."

Discipline in Warren's family is not entirely in the hands of his father, although when Warren was asked who administered corporal punishment in the family he answered: "I guess the chief of that department is still my dad." The father no longer, however, administers such punishment to Warren and his brother Charles, but does so occasionally to the younger children. When the two older boys are guilty of any infraction of family rules, the father just "gives them a good talk," but the mother does not hesitate to deal more severely with Warren and Charles, as the following statement indicates:

> I often have to whip the younger children but the usual system is to have one child watching the other. When Warren and Charles were small I used to let them stay up pretty late. Then when they were twelve and thirteen and joined the Boy Scouts I began making them go to bed early. Now when other people's children are roaming the streets around here, mine are sound asleep in bed.
>
> One night Warren stayed out much later than he should have and I made him stay in his room for a week and wouldn't permit the other children to even talk to him. Till today he hates that kind of punishment. Once when my father was here he marvelled at how I was able to handle these boys and he wanted to know how I managed to make them stay in their room. I said, I don't make them, I'm their mother. When I had to punish them in the summer, Mr. Wall would say I should let them come down in the front or back yard because of the heat. But I'd say, nothing doing till the week's up. They did have a swell time, though. There were a lots of good books here. They'd never stopped to read, and they read most of those. Then we had our first inkling at Warren's artistic ability. He made a beautiful carving of a Boy Scout during one such confinement, and a friend from our church saw it and encouraged us to let him take up any crafts and shop work that struck his fancy. And even now when he can get hold of tools or go to the school shop, he is at his happiest.

Punishment of any kind is of infrequent occurrence in the Wall household, since the children have acquired habits of obedience to their parents as a part of the general family discipline. The children, who are required to help their mother, have worked out a more or less regular schedule among themselves for helping with the younger children and the housework. Family discipline also includes regular church and Sunday school attendance. Warren's entire family belongs to a Baptist church in which his father holds several offices. His father usually goes alone to church and his mother, who attends "fairly regularly," goes later to the church services. Although the children do not attend the church services every Sunday, all of them go regularly to Sunday school. Recently when Charles got a paper route which would require him to work during Sunday school time, his mother informed him that he would have to change the time of his work or give up the job.

The family does very little entertaining. According to Warren:

> There's not enough room. The last party I know anything about was a birthday party I had on my-tenth birthday. I thought there was nothing finer. I got lots of presents, a big cake, and a lot of my school friends came to the party. My sister has had a club over here since and my mother entertained one of her church clubs here once or twice. But I've been sort of ashamed to have people come here and see the house looking as it does. My mother had a group of women here to dinner once and the way they looked at the place, I could have cried.

ATTITUDE TOWARD HIS FAMILY

Warren, a tall, lithe, well-built, dark-brown boy of sixteen with an intelligent face and pleasing personality, appears to be a serious youth. He seldom smiles when talking, uses no gestures, and generally gives the impression that he is getting information rather than giving it. When speaking of his family, Warren frankly admits that he, the first-born, feels handicapped by the presence of his brothers and sisters. In one of the early interviews, he spoke as follows:

> I come from a large family. My great-grandfather had twenty-one children. My father had about nine brothers and sisters, but I don't think he has more than one brother living now. I never knew my grandfather, but we used to spend a lot of time down on my grandmother's farm in Virginia, about one hundred and thirty miles from here—just on the other side of Richmond. We had a swell time there too and I wish we could live there. My father often talks about getting a place in the suburbs or in the country, but I don't see how he can ever do it. I feel that a big family like this is a holdback to me. I don't think I ever want to get married and when I do I sure don't want any children.

When Warren was born, his mother weighed only one hundred and seventeen pounds. Because of his size and weight, nine and a half pounds, his mother, in her words, "had a hard time with him, but less with the others, because they were more normal in size and weight." "Warren," said his mother, "was a terrible baby," and added,

> I was sick a lot when he was small and though I nursed him a little, we had to depend on bottles. Most of the children were bottle babies, too, but I fed some from my breasts. I had an awful time training Warren to toilet habits. He cried more than any baby I ever knew and I suppose I gave in to him more than we ever did the others.

As the first child, Warren enjoyed the attention of his parents and got what he wanted. His mother stated as much during an interview:

> Warren has been more or less the favorite of the family. He was the first child. The children are crazy about him and he's as playful with them as they are with each other. He probably remembers all too well that he fared much better before we had such family increases and often gives vent to his feelings that because of them he is deprived of so many things he likes and wants.

At another time she remarked that Warren was "a very sensitive boy—is easily hurt and I believe, as some of his teachers say, he is jealous of the rest of the children." However, it appears that Warren did not resent the presence of his brother, Charles, the second child in the family, or even the third, who was a girl. Concerning this brother he said:

> When Charles and I were small we used to have everything—go on trips, have clothes and toys but now we don't get anything. When the first two or three came along we didn't think anything about it, but after that I used to hate the arrival of all the rest. Now the family is nine and I don't know yet whether that is the end or not. It got so it didn't look like they'd stop coming. I don't think the stork stopped by here—he just stayed.

He and his brother Charles used to masturbate together. Concerning this phase of his life with his brother he said:

> My brother Charles and me used to masturbate, but we didn't

do it long. I guess I was nine years old when we started doing it. We used to sleep together and when we were left alone at night, we tried everything. But my father caught us one night and he wore us out and I don't think either of us masturbated again for over a year. It was lots of fun as a small kid, but as we grew older we found it more and more disgusting. I haven't done that since I was twelve years old.

On another occasion Warren remarked concerning his large family:

When there were two or three of us, my father used to take us camping, take us on hikes, take us on fishing trips. But now, we have so many to consider that we don't get any place. A big family seems to make hardships for all, and I suppose when I do get old enough to get a good job, I'll spend most of what I make to keep the rest of the family going. It means that none of us probably will get to college and we lost a lot of things we could have had. I remember how well my mother used to dress me when there was only a few of us—in fact, I dressed better than any boy in my school; but now I seldom get anything new. Shoes and food go mighty fast in my family. We spend as high as sixty dollars a month for food sometimes. There isn't much left for anything else.

Thus, to Warren his big family means being deprived of many things which he once enjoyed and desires at present. Moreover, as we shall see, his ambition is to go to college, but because of the huge family he sees this major ambition blocked. As the oldest boy in the family, he feels insecure because responsibility for the support of the family would fall on him if anything happened to his father. During an interview he said:

I've suddenly begun to feel the responsibility that could be mine if anything happened to my father.

Then he went on to tell of a dangerous accident which his father had with his amateur radio station.

Although Warren believes that his father is intelligent, he does not think he was "so smart" when it came to the matter of having children. Concerning his mother's attitude he said that he had asked her recently if they were going to have any more children and she "looked very woeful" and said: "I hope

not—but if they come, I'll love them like I love the rest of you."
Warren is extremely critical of his parents at times. Once he
remarked: "Sometimes I think they're both crazy as far as having
children is concerned." On another occasion he criticized his
parents for not knowing anything about contraception:

> I heard somewhere that people could control the number of
> children they wanted to have. It seems my parents should know
> something about such things. And I don't believe they're
> through yet. It makes hardships on us all and it's a wonder any
> of us would want children after you live in a house full of them.
> I don't think Negroes should have such large families. White
> people who have more than we do, don't try to have such large
> families. I don't know much about these things, but I still think
> some precautions could be taken. I'm sure going to find out
> before I get married. My father is an intelligent man, too, but
> I don't think he's been so smart!

Warren's parents take pride in the fact that their children
like to stay around home. Warren has not been an exception in
this regard. Although he is "not much at house cleaning" and
hates it, nevertheless, he does not object to sharing in the work
at home because he "gets breaks at home" and is able to go
"when and where" he wants. But, of late Warren does not "stay
home much anyway." He added: "I'm usually gone most of the
time and although home is all right and pleasant too at times,
I get sick of the noise and the crowd." In fact, Warren's main
complaint against home is that it does not permit him the
privacy which he desires.[1]

> I've always wanted some place around the house I could call
> my own. I sleep in one room with my four brothers and all
> these rooms are small as you can see down here. My mother
> and father have their own room and in their room is all my
> father's radio equipment and that takes up a lot of space. The
> middle room belongs to my four sisters. In my room I have
> an iron locker where I try to keep my few treasures or prize
> belongings. But that doesn't hold much, so I just have to do the
> best I can. Charles is probably the biggest baby of them all and
> he throws his things around, does as he pleases and actually

---

[1] On the Bernreuter Personality Scale Warren had a $(B_2$-S$)$ score of 34, which
indicates that he is not a person who prefers to be alone.

gets away with it. He sets up a howl when it's time to clean up
and it usually falls my lot to see that the room is straightened
up and that means I do the work. We have a couple of beds in
our room but there's not much room around them. And when
all five of us get in, it's darned near crowded.

There are other features about the house which cause Warren
to be dissatisfied with it. He said during the same interview:

We get disgusted with the dirt, the faded and darkened wall
paper, rough floors, and so forth. My father has been doing the
papering in our house as long as I can remember. He doesn't
have a great deal of time and less money, and before he can get
to the next job, the first one has fallen apart again. He has
always wanted a place out in the suburbs but he hasn't gotten
around to it yet. Then, too, he says he can't find a place near
enough to his work and school for us. I wish we were out in the
open. I love the country, anyway. Though, I sure don't want to
do any farming. That's out of my line.

When Warren goes into homes of people who "have much nicer
things" than his family, he wishes that his mother "could have
them"; but he suddenly remembers "the pack of children at
home" and realizes "that even if she had them, it wouldn't be
for long."

Although Warren leaves home as much as possible to escape
the crowd and the noise and its disagreeable physical features,
his contacts today as when he was younger are mainly within
the neighborhood. In these neighborhood relations, he has
never "had a serious fight even with a Negro," although he
has been in some trouble as the following statement indicates:

As a small boy and even when I got some size I used to get into
arguments that usually ended in fights. But even after a good
nose bleed or a knot on the head we usually ended up fair
friends anyway. My mother usually fussed and fumed whenever
any of us had fights no matter who they were with. My father
says we should fight for our rights—never pick fights, mind you—
no matter who they were, Negroes or whites.

Warren's mother said that preventing her children from fighting worries her more than anything else because

if they're like their father they're hotheaded. I don't want them fighting anybody—black or white. My husband often takes groups of boys in the troop on hikes. They come back and tell of the boxing and fighting they've done. I think it's terrible and I've tried to show Mr. Wall it's all wrong; that he shouldn't teach them to fight, because the average boy does enough without being taught. Of course, they probably don't hurt each other, but I think it's just wrong and when some older person isn't around they'll fight and probably hurt someone seriously.

Warren has never "run" with gangs. In his opinion "all boys like gangs" but he prefers clubs, though he thinks that "a club is just an orderly gang trying to do something worth while." His father's disapproval of gangs has undoubtedly influenced him in his attitude, but he says: "In fact, I don't believe decent boys run in gangs anyway." Warren has always "run" with two or three fellows. One of these fellows, John, has been his bosom friend since they had a fight eight years ago. As Warren indicated once, he feels closer to this boy than to his brother Charles. Warren and Charles had been very close pals until Warren "took up" with John. It happened that John also had a younger brother, and when he and Warren became friends, he broke away from his younger brother also. Both he and Warren complain that their younger brothers do not know how to act, especially around girls, or that they will attempt to show off or will tattle to their parents. It is not unlikely that Warren prefers John as a close associate because he does not regard him as a competitor. Although Warren is not a better student than Charles, he likes to belittle Charles, who, though not a good student in school, probably has a keener mind. On the other hand, John, in the words of Warren, "is crazy." On one occasion, he remarked concerning John:

> John over there is more like a brother to me than Charles. When you see him, you see me and *vice versa*. When I'm not down at his house, he's at mine and that's most of the time. We even go on dates together. He's crazy, I think, but darn good company.

On the other hand, Warren and his oldest sister, Mary, get along very well. He does not regard her as a competitor, though she is three years younger than he but in the same grade in school. Mary helps Warren with his lessons and the two are very good pals. Charles often expresses jealousy of the friendship between the two.

RELATIONS WITH GIRLS

It was through contacts in the neighborhood that Warren had his first sex experience. Warren's account of this experience is as follows:

> When I was fourteen years old, I had my first intercourse with a girl. She was a girl in this neighborhood and I thought I was hot stuff. She did much of the coaxing and I didn't need much encouragement. Well, that was a big night for me, and it happened over to her house, too. The next day something bit me like a pair of pliers. I looked and found myself almost covered with small bugs. I stole my mother's book of home remedies out of the house but couldn't find what I wanted. I was ashamed and scared, too, besides being miserable. But I took a chance and went to my father about the matter. Much to my surprise, he took me and got the necessary treatments and showed me how to relieve myself. He told me that these parasites come from the female body and told me that as I grew up I would have to be careful of the people I had sexual relations with, and that he preferred to have his boys wait until they were older and knew how to take care of ourselves.

The initial contact which led to this experience actually occurred in the junior high school which Warren attended. The story of the initial contact as told by Warren was as follows:

> The girl was in the seventh grade. She was smaller but almost as old as I was. She used to come into the study hall where I was with my grade. She wore older girls' clothes, silk dresses, tight fitting and pretty, silk hose and high heel shoes. So once when she passed me I patted her on her "fanny"—just to be fresh. She evidently liked it for she wrote me a note in the study hall and told me she liked me and that I should come over to her house to see her. I went over and it was a lot of fun. I kept going and I never bothered her at all. Then she kept calling me a "sissy" and told me she thought I was a man. There was nothing else to do so I just threw all caution and better judgment to the winds. To make a long story short, I'll never forget the experience because for weeks I was darn near eaten up. I had to go to my father and he just laughed and got me the necessary 'stuff to get rid of them. That was as near a talk on sex I ever got from my father and I know I could never go to my mother. We feel we could

go to dad if we had such questions, but somehow I think he ought to realize we'd like to know about such things before we run across such experiences.

Since this experience Warren said that he had had few sexual relations with girls.

I know a lot of girls but with most of them I'm just a big brother. I have two "cousins," and a "sister" over at school now. They are pretty kids and most of the fellows think they are really kin to me, especially the "sister." One fellow even tried to arrange a date with her through me, hoping I'd bring "my sister" up to the school dance. She lives in Virginia; so I had to lie my way out of that one. I told the boy she was living with some relations in Virginia and that it would be just as convenient for him to meet her at the Virginia bus terminal—because it costs 20 cents both ways and sister or no sister, I wouldn't pay for someone else just to keep from being made out a liar.

Warren has refrained from sexual relations with girls because as he remarked:

You see, I've always wanted to be an athlete and I know you can't use your strength on girls and expect to give your best in athletic games. My first year in high school was a very successful year at football and I was glad I let girls alone.

Furthermore, Warren has a girl friend who is the sort of girl he "wouldn't approach for sexual intercourse."

I found one girl over in Southeast who I've been keeping company with for some time. My family knows her family and has even invited her to my home since they found I was interested in her. I've taken her to movies, to picnics, and walks to the parks, but she is the sort of girl I wouldn't approach for sexual intercourse. I've kissed her, but she doesn't approve of petting and I'm glad.

Warren expressed himself as follows concerning the type of girl he preferred:

Well, I don't have much choice in the matter. It depends pretty largely on the girl. I like brown-skin girls. Smaller than I am, of course. What fool wants a woman bigger than he is? I wouldn't mind a girl having a better education than I had providing she used it to try to help me, but if she used it to just lord it over folks, then I'd prefer the dumb ones or at least those with less or no more education than I've had. I've gone with light-skinned girls but I prefer the brown-skin ones. And they must have a shape, too, that's another thing.

Warren then went on to discuss the question of his intimacies with girls and what he thought parents and teachers should do in regard to the problem of sex. It is important to note two facts: first, his relation with his father is such as to make possible discussions of sex with him; and second, he does not know whether his mother is aware of his first sex affair.

I really believe that if I had a problem along this line, I could discuss it with my father. I've always been afraid that he told my mother about the first affair. I'd like for her to know it, but I'd want her to let me know she knew it. My knowledge of sex came from the corners and bunches of boys who told things in a very petty fashion and in most cases they were boasting about the things they'd done to girls. I think a father or a teacher at school should give you firsthand information from time to time without being asked. Once at high school a series of talks was arranged on sex and health. The boys went to one, the girls to another. I knew one girl pretty well, and we promised to exchange information we got in the lectures. After she had been to hers, she refused to tell me about it. I begged her, of course, but she still wouldn't tell. First, I believe such talks can be given to mixed groups of young people. I didn't want to know for curiosity, I really wanted the information. I shouldn't think anyone, man or woman, should be ashamed of the human body. After all, sex, birth, babies and all that sort of thing are natural things and happen among birds, beasts, and man alike. I think taking each group alone makes each group just curious and in the end what has been gained with men knowing men's bodies and the care of them alone, and girls knowing women's bodies, and the care of them, and not have any information concerning each other?

CONTACTS WITH WHITES IN HIS NEIGHBORHOOD

Since Warren lives in a neighborhood which is practically entirely colored, he has had few contacts with whites. There is a Jewish store around the corner where Warren goes occasionally. His opinion in regard to the racial identity of Jews is indicated in the following statement:

I think they are just as different from white people as Negroes are. I don't consider them white. Of course, there are two kinds of Jews and I certainly consider myself better than the lower class of dirty Jews. The other and higher Jews live better than white people. One thing about Jews; they sure can save and that's more than any Negro can do. They can make money where nobody else can. I haven't had a great deal of dealings with Jews but I know all about them. On the side they prefer Negroes, but that might be mostly for business reasons. These dirty Jews keep filthy shops. Around the corner you can go in a Jew store and ask for a cake of yeast and he'll get it out of the box where beef liver is dripping down on the yeast and all those sorts of things. Believe me, we don't deal there. The old woman in the store tries to "Jew" me once in a while but I generally keep her from succeeding. When I'm broke and want a piece of candy, I go around, and if the candy sells three for a penny, she won't give me the odd piece till I've paid up. Then sometimes I go around to get a small bag for my school lunch, and often carry cleaner and larger bags we got from the Sanitary Stores. She'll take the larger ones, but want me to pay for the small ones. You can't get around them and if I owe her a cent for three weeks, she remembers it.

Warren's attitude toward Jews is evidently ambivalent because while he feels that "on the side they prefer Negroes," he has accepted many of the stereotyped notions about Jews for which he thinks he finds support in his own experiences with this particular storekeeper. An ambivalent attitude is probably the source of his statement concerning how he feels about the treatment of Jews in Germany. He said:

Well, I do feel sorry for them and probably Hitler knew what he was doing when he put them out, but I don't think he should have been so brutal about it. He could have asked them out in a nicer way and besides not rob and kill them as he did.

Although Warren said he has a few Jewish acquaintances, he considers only one a friend. This is the big, eighteen-year-old son of the Jewish storekeeper—in his words, "the son of the old Jew woman." According to Warren:

He seems to like Negroes and we get along swell. Every football season he buys football equipment and about this time of year he buys a couple of gloves, bats, and balls. He comes over after me and we go out and have a swell time playing with them. I heard he takes the money from the cash drawer to buy the things, and there probably is some truth in the story because he never actually buys the things himself but always sends some colored boy uptown for them. Once he brought a new racket over to my house and he said I could use it as long as I liked. It wasn't a very good racket but I did play with it some.

Because of the prejudice against Jews and, what is more significant, because of Warren's belief that "beneath the skin they're black, too," he thinks that Jews should be "nice" to Negroes. Jews, however, expect Negroes to treat them as if they were white, and because of the dependence of Negroes, Jews can demand the same respect shown whites:

> Jews have every right to be nice to Negroes. They are as near being Negroes as they can possibly be without being black and I believe sometimes beneath the skin they're black, too. White people don't treat them as if they were white but they sure expect Negroes to treat them so and as long as they have all the business and Negroes have to depend on their generosity, they'll get the respect they want.

Warren does not remember when he first became conscious of the fact that he was a Negro.

> I don't think I remember when I first found out I was a Negro. I felt like other folks until I got some size and learned at school that dark-skinned people were Negroes, so I came to the conclusion I was one, too. I've never tried to go places where Negroes weren't allowed to go, so just didn't try to crash where I wasn't wanted.

Despite this statement and the fact that Warren has not had contacts with white boys in his neighborhood, he feels a certain hostility toward white boys and would welcome an opportunity to engage in some form of aggression toward them or at least try his strength against them. This was apparent in his statement:

> I've never fought a white boy, but I've always wanted to. I've always thought a white boy was easy to whip.

He then went on to note the fact that the playground in the neighborhood was reserved for whites:

The playground is located in a Negro neighborhood, and it's one large city block gone to waste. The playground usually has only a few white children on it and Negro children line the fences wishing they could get in to play. I've tried my best to get one of the white boys mad enough to fight about it. It seems strange that so much space would be used for a few boys and a great number of other boys have so little. They have ball diamonds, tennis courts, swimming pools, and all. There's not a swimming pool in the whole Southwest for Negroes.

Warren's hostility toward whites was undoubtedly aroused by an experience which he had when only nine years old. His story of the incident was as follows:

We used to go on hikes over in Maryland for minnows, but the "pecks" were so mean we didn't go over there more than two or three times. We'd go over to a stream where there was a lot of minnows and twice a small white kid would run out with a bad dog and called us "niggers" and all that went with it. I used to get so mad I could bite a nail in two. The third trip we took a boy named Henry with us and skated out there. We seined and got I guess a hundred minnows when a white fellow came over and kicked our minnows over and back into the water, threw our skates in the water and told us if we wanted to make something of it there were some other white fellows near-by. We looked up and on a small bridge not far away were three half-grown white men laughing at us. I started walking away and my brother followed. Henry stopped to argue and they hit him on the head with a big rock, and left a big knot there. We got away all right—and Henry tickled me, too, because he promised to get his father some liquor and bring him back to whip the fellows. He said his father got drunk once and almost killed a man.

After reciting the story of the above incident he added the following significant statement:

I've never had a fight with a white boy but in late years I've always wanted to. At times I felt I could take on anybody but I've just itched to take a crack at a white guy just to see if he can take it like he can dish it. Even now I think I'd be ready to scrap if I could get one to meddle with me or meddle with anyone else in my presence. White people aren't going to mess with you unless they feel they definitely have the upper hand. They like to hurt your feelings and call you names and I've just been waiting to have one do it to me while the two of us can stand as man to man. Not much chance of that, I don't suppose.

Although Warren did not recall having heard any specific instructions in church concerning the treatment of whites, he felt that religious exhortations to treat all people as neighbors and with good will included whites as well as Negroes.

ATTITUDE TOWARD CHURCH AND RELIGION

Because of his family background and his relation to the church it is not surprising that his beliefs concerning God are extremely orthodox. Concerning this phase of his life, he said:

I believe in God and everything in the Bible. I go to Sunday school and church every Sunday. You learn a lot in Sunday school but as a rule it's a waste of time going to church. I go of course because I have to. Once in a while the minister will preach an intelligent sermon, one packed with information and interest. The others have me just watching the clock and wishing I was far away. And boy, am I glad when it's over!

After church services one Sunday Warren discussed his relation to the church, remarking:

It's a funny thing—almost every time I go to church I fall asleep. Not that I'm bored or because of dull services but it's usually so warm I just can't help it. So I generally miss the opening subject of the morning—I didn't hear it this time, either. I go to church now because I like to and because I know it pleases my parents. I used to go to keep them off me. I usually manage to get some thought out of the service that I try to put into practice. This morning the service was something about the similarity of bringing up youth into the church and the planting of acorns to become great oaks, and that in so doing we could become the strong oaks of the church. I enjoy the services and lessons when I can see a practical application somewhere. My father is so wrapped up in church and the lessons we don't dare question or argue with him about things we hear there.

Like the majority of these youth his religious ideas have been influenced by the pictures which he has seen. But he exhibits a certain cynical distrust of whites in speaking of these pictures. He remarked:

Christ was a Jew and I've only seen white ones, so Christ must have been white. All pictures I've seen of Him have made Him a white man. I've never seen pictures of Negro angels either, but that can be expected with white people painting the pictures. Of course, Negroes go to heaven and they become angels like anybody else. And I believe they remain colored.

PRIDE IN NEGRO SCHOOLS

Warren, who is in the first year of the technical high school, does work of an average grade. Concerning his school work he told the following:

Down in junior high school I took Spanish, so when I went up to high school I took it up again. I didn't realize you could forget so easily. I'll never forget the first term I got C in the course. A boy friend and classmate got a B. So I promised him I'd jump the B and that I'd make an A next semester. And I worked too. That semester I got C and he got B. The third and fourth semesters we both loafed and slept in class. I still got my C and he his A. So I just got discouraged and quit. I've learned how to study languages now, so when I go back this fall I plan taking Latin One and Two, and I'll romp through that—just watch.

Warren feels considerable pride in his school and thinks that colored schools are as good as the white schools.

I think the Negro schools are just as good as the white ones, and I believe the teachers are just as well trained as the white ones. Some of them even went to the same schools as the whites. I think the high schools are even better. Of course, we don't have all the up-to-date equipment the others have but for example, X School has the finest photography laboratory in the city schools. My physics teacher is interested in various things and he has taught me a lot. I like him because he actually knows a lot about everything. You don't find many Negro teachers like that or willing to help no matter how foolish the question. I think Howard is just as fine as any white college. I don't know much about it, but they say it's a grand school.

His chief complaint against the schools is that they do not teach about the accomplishments of Negroes.

I've often wondered why we didn't study more about Booker T. Washington than George Washington. No matter how much I try, I can never be a George Washington. What he did, he did for his own people—what Booker T. Washington did, he did for my people. In school, we seldom ever hear about Negroes, if it wasn't for Negro History Week, we'd know a whole lot less. We study white people and white people's history, and with all that knowledge, we don't get any whiter and they sure don't treat us like we were becoming whiter.

Warren belongs to the history club at school, which he enjoys because of his interest in history.

RECREATIONAL ACTIVITIES

Warren participates in athletics, and after his first year, he felt that he had done well on the football team. This success he attributed to the fact that he had left the girls alone. Although Warren belonged at one time to another club at school, he gave it up for the Boy Scouts, in which he finds the major part of his recreation. He dropped out of this club because "the club was made up of boys and girls and it was all too serious." Since he "couldn't have any fun or clown," he quit. In the Boy Scouts, Warren and his father are brought into close association. Concerning his father's relation to the Boy Scouts, he said:

My father was chairman of our troop committee and is deeply interested in the boys of the troop as well as in us. The other boys can't get their fathers to meetings and outings, but my father tries to make them all. So far, I haven't found any other clubs had much in them that interested me; so I've been satisfied with just the Boy Scouts.

The Boy Scouts have afforded Warren an opportunity to hold a prominent position.[2] He brought out the fact that he held the highest rank in the troop and became junior assistant scoutmaster. But Warren says that he likes the Boy Scouts for another reason which concerns his racial status.

I like the Scouts because it gives you a chance to learn a lot of things; you can compete with white boys and get the same recognition. I feel every Negro boy should some time in his life between twelve and twenty join the Scouts. Scouting started among Negro boys right here in Washington nearly twenty years ago and yet Washington has yet to produce a Negro Eagle Scout! I

[2] Warren had a percentile (B4-D) score of 81 on the Bernreuter Personality Inventory, which indicated that he tended to dominate in face-to-face situations.

met three of the Scouts from Cincinnati during the Jamboree who were Eagles. That's the height of my ambition in Scouting. I'd like to be the first Negro Eagle Scout in Washington. It's something to shoot at anyway. But somehow I'm stuck—I don't know whether it's me or the Scout leadership.

It was during the Jamboree in Washington that Warren met what he called "segregation ideas from southern boys." This, he said, "was to be expected" and went on to say:

On the other hand, boys from the West and North, and those from foreign countries treated us so nicely we forgot about the little nasty things the southerners said and did. We went everywhere they went—to Mt. Vernon and other places on the buses and hikes, and on all boat trips up and down the Potomac. I don't think I ever wanted to be a white boy as much as I did during those ten days. They had everything any boy could wish for, had the freedom of the city, and enjoyed good times in the city that even Negro Scouts couldn't enjoy here ordinarily. Scouting is one program where a Negro boy is nearly an equal, and I wish we had sufficient trained Negro leaders to help me reach the top. I've always wanted to be an Eagle Scout. So far, I've only reached Star rank. I've been in Scouting three years, and I've been a Star for almost a year now. It looks like I'm stuck!

Warren enjoys other forms of recreation. He is vice president of a recently organized social club which was originally limited to eight members but decided recently to admit girls. The dues are 10 cents a week and the meetings are to be held in their homes. In regard to dances Warren said:

I manage to get to a dance or so a month. I like dances and I like to rug-cut. I like the other dances, too, but the average girl can't even two-step but they can all clown and be jitterbugs. So I do, too. I never go to house-hops; first, because I don't get invitations and, second, because I don't like them anyway. Around people's houses they usually are drinking and smoking, and during football season I tried to keep decent hours and now that I'm on the track team, I need my rest so I just don't bother about going. I try not to miss school dances.

Warren admits that he is sometimes embarrassed around girls because of his shabby clothes. He said he did not go to many dances because

I don't have the money; true, they don't cost much but that's more than I have regularly. I've got a friend who is in the same fix but no sooner than he got a regular paper route he began making all the dances. I only get a chance to work, and do odd jobs, on week ends, and I'd prefer to save what little I can earn for a rainy day—any rainy day. My father never says anything about these house parties but I don't think he'd like it if we went to them.

Warren is also interested in a number of hobbies, concerning which he said:

When I get a chance I still collect things. Snakes, bugs, turtles, and other things that I find that interest me. I like crafts but because of my eyes I gave up those things long ago. I monkey around with my father in our radio laboratory and I work with him on electrical gadgets. Outside of these I just don't bother any more. And another reason is because in my house we don't have any place or space you can call your own to ever put anything away.

ATTITUDE TOWARD WHITES IN WASHINGTON

Outside of his neighborhood, Warren has had very few contacts with whites. As he remarked: "I don't know any white families intimately." At one time, however, he had a paper route in Southeast and all his customers were white. His account of his contacts was as follows:

They were very nice and most of them pay in advance of my report. So I had my money always by Friday and I had all my money by Monday and was able to get a discount from the newspaper office. At Christmas time, each family used to give me up to a dollar; so I usually had money to buy presents for my family. I didn't know any of them well enough to stop in their homes or visit them. None of them ever invited me over. I'd like to have white friends, though, because I think I could learn a lot from white people. They have more interests than I have—interests few Negroes have. They had the advantage of education and experience that I'd like to share. I wouldn't want any other intimacies but just their friendship. They still talk to me on the street and shake hands when they meet me on the street. Some of the boys over there are Scouts and we take great interest in such common things. We talk about such things whenever we meet and often we end up seated on the sidewalk talking Scouting and demonstrating some of the things we've learned.

According to Warren the paper route was the only job which he has had, but, nevertheless, he feels that he would rather work for Negroes than for whites.

> I'd much rather work for Negroes than whites because they treat you better, and though white people do pay you better, I'd much rather work for Negroes any day if they paid as well. I do a lot of odd jobs in the neighborhood. I have some electrical work and a screen door to mend for a colored woman across the street. I know she doesn't expect to pay much or she'd have hired someone else. Negroes are all right. They just don't have the means of doing the things they want to.

Although Warren's mother said that "questions about white people are seldom brought up in the home," Warren has undoubtedly been influenced in his attitudes toward whites by his father. He recalled:

> I've been around with my father when he did odd jobs and I've been brought up to act around white people just like he did. He got along swell and everybody liked him—so I tried, too. Around white people I delivered papers to, that I could shittle something out of, I would say, yes, mam, or no, mam, because I thought they liked it; but I hated it every time I did it.

Hence, although Warren's parents have taught him to "treat all older people with courtesy and respect regardless of color," he says:

> If you have some white person you want to cultivate and expect to get something out of them, you might lay it on a bit thick, but otherwise treat them all alike.

The most important fact which has influenced his attitude toward whites so far as his father is concerned is that he is convinced that his father would have been promoted if he had not been a Negro. It happens that his father is in a colored unit and the only promotion which he could receive would place him above whites. Therefore, he has been kept in his present position despite his merit. Promotion would not only mean an elevation in status but an increase in salary, which would in turn mean a better home and clothes and also the assurance that Warren could achieve his ambition to go to college. But the white man's prejudice stands in the way of all this.

He has heard his father as well as other people say that "Washington is kinder to Negroes than cities farther South and we actually get treated as well as Negroes farther North." Although Warren "guesses it's all right" and thinks Washington is a beautiful place, he would "sure like to see some other places" before he would say that he likes Washington, his "home town, better." In fact, his real opinion of race relations in Washington was stated as follows:

There are many crazy restrictions on Washington Negroes. White people don't like to address Negroes with Mr., Mrs., or Miss. They think by calling them by their names, they are lowering them. White people will address Negroes as Mr. and Mrs., if they are trying to get something out of them. [He pointed to a white peddler across the street, canvassing from house to house.] Take that guy across the street. He'd call you Sweetheart to sell you his stuff. Everybody is Mr. and Mrs., but just you wait until he gets on his feet or through with the sale, he's ready to call you Joe, Sam, or Mary. When people of that class call us by our names and we resent it instead of smiling and taking it or calling him by his name, that would stop some of it.

There aren't many stores in Washington that don't cater to Negroes. G———'s and H———'s are the only ones I know who ever discriminate against Negroes. I know one store over in Virginia where my mother once tried to buy a hat. She tried on several and before she got out of the store, she had to take those she tried on. Negroes don't go to white theaters except the Gem and the Gaiety. I don't go to the shows often and then I go uptown to the best ones. I've never been in the Gem Theater and with the reputation it has, I don't think I want to go. Negroes use the same waiting rooms at the stations and use the same accommodations on buses, streetcars, and taxis. White people come to our church often and seem to enjoy themselves. Negroes don't go to white churches unless they happen to be servants. We go to separate schools, too, in this city. I don't think all white people wish to segregate us. But there are too few of them. One of these days, things will change.

His paper route enabled him to have some firsthand acquaintance with white people, with the result that he lost some of his distrust of them. He remarked that he "even liked them." He continued:

I used to hear people talk about white people and the way they talked I always thought white people couldn't be trusted. Well they learned to trust me. So I trusted them. Almost every white person in the section had a dog. Some of the people used to pay me to take the dog out in the evenings and on Christmas they'd give me money and presents.

Although such contacts helped to remove some of his suspicion of white people, Warren was influenced in his attitudes toward white people more decidedly through contacts with a white professional man who became interested in him. His change in attitude was due partly to the fact that the colored interviewer told him that the white man was "all right." Concerning this contact, he said:

I learned to like and trust Dr. X and the same way thought I didn't feel as friendly toward him as I wanted to at first. And when he asked questions about racial matters and how I felt going to white places where Negroes weren't wanted, I did feel funny and uncomfortable. I don't know whether it was because he was a white man and I a Negro or just that the subjects were touchy ones anyway. I think he's sincere and will do all he can to help me as he promised and till he proves otherwise I intend to be honest with him and trust him, too. I usually get suspicious when white people get all solicitous but after you told me he was all right I was willing to take the chance. I've never known another white man like him. In fact, he was so kind and friendly like I thought he was a Negro until you told me he was white. I then got sort of scared and felt quite embarrassed for I was afraid that I might have said things I shouldn't have—things I certainly wouldn't say ordinarily to a white person.

Warren does not believe that Negroes have the same chances as whites to secure jobs although they are qualified to hold any job in the country. He remarked:

Most jobs prefer a white face to experience. That shouldn't be, of course, but the white man is in a position to choose what he wants. I think a Negro could do any job as well if not better than any white man. Somewhere in this country there is a Negro who could even handle the job of the President, and do a good job of it. I think we'd have a far better chance when more of our people get an education. In the South, where thousands of Negroes live, the white man is still able to boss them around, and they are perfectly satisfied. Our schools are getting better and bigger every day, and I guess more of us are going to them.

Concerning his own ambitions he said:

I want to go to college. I hope to go to Hampton Institute, and become a radio and electrical engineer. I know a good deal of electrical work and I like radio work. I think I can become an electrical engineer. However, if I can make more money doing something else, I'll take it in preference to the work I'm prepared to do. Of course, I'd be happier doing the work I studied to do, but I think that as a young man, a Negro should take any honest job that offered the most money. Some day I probably could make as much money in my profession, or maybe I could do it on the side, but I think my place is where the most money is. A person's job is important, but in these days, we must think of the greatest returns that can be gotten.

In this statement one notes his emphasis upon money. In fact, he said during the same interview that his greatest wish had always been to have money because "with plenty of that, I could buy anything else under the sun I wanted."

INFLUENCE OF NEGRO LEADERS

When he talked specifically concerning the handicaps of color, he said that when he thought of what men like Booker T. Washington "accomplished in spite of color, I don't feel so bad." Then he continued:

But with all the disadvantages of being a Negro put in your way, if I could be born again, I'd want to be white. I think being white would make all the difference in the world in success and failure. With my ambition to be somebody and to do something worth while, having a white face would make a lot of difference. I've seen Negroes light enough to "pass" for white. I don't blame them at all. I don't think there's anything wrong trying to "pass" if you can do it. I would if I could, and wouldn't think anything about it, either.

Warren expresses considerable disdain of those lacking in ambition. He says concerning some of his schoolmates:

> There are boys and girls I know who don't seem to get anywhere. At school some come because they have to, others come for some particular subject and still others come just to make trouble. I dislike that sort of person. It means a loss of time and sometimes privileges of those who want to learn. I dislike fresh girls and rowdy boys. I don't know any individuals I actually hate, though. I have seen lots of people whose actions would make me dislike and despise them.

Warren is acquainted with many Negroes who have achieved distinction. In concluding his comments on these leaders, he adds the significant comment:

> I think Joe Louis is important, too. I don't think he's in the class with Washington and others, but as a world champion or a champion in any field he is a credit to the race, and I think he could be listed with the rest of our famous Negroes. It hasn't been his money that has made him important; the position he holds is envied by all white men and he has proven what a Negro can do in competition with white men—and the best ones they could put against him.

His admiration of Joe Louis is obviously tied up with his desire to compete with and excel whites. This becomes clearer in the following observation:

> Since we generally have three or four radios going all the time at my house, I've been able to hear all the Joe Louis fights. I heard the one he lost to Schmeling. I was stunned and surprised. I didn't feel badly about it for in spite of what others said, I still believe Schmeling really whipped him. I heard the last one and I sure was happy he won as he did. There's no doubt now who is champion. I felt it wasn't so bad after all being a Negro, because given a fair chance, we could beat the white man at any game.

Thus, according to Warren, the Negro when given a fair chance can beat the white man at any game. Although Warren does not believe the Negro has a fair chance as a rule, he is confident some Negroes can manage to rise in the world and he hopes to be among those who at least escape from the condition of the masses.

SUMMARY

To sum up in a few words how being a Negro has influenced Warren's personality is an impossible task. Yet, from the data which we have gathered during contacts with him and his family, we feel justified in drawing some tentative conclusions. The central fact in Warren's life is that as a first child who had been the center of attention and secured what he wanted, he has lost this privileged position and has been denied many things because of the large number of brothers and sisters. He places the blame upon his father and mother because he believes that they should have known better. But Warren loves and respects his father and is confidential with him. Although he loves and respects his mother, he regards her as a frail and weak person. Though his home provides a certain amount of security and emotional satisfaction, yet it is distasteful to him because it is shabby, crowded, and noisy. He cannot have privacy and the exclusive enjoyment of his possessions. All of this, of course, could happen to a white boy as well as a colored.

There is one factor in this situation which involves Warren's racial status. Warren feels that his father is intelligent and could advance in his work were it not for the fact that he is a Negro. Advancement in rank would mean an increase in salary which would solve Warren's problems as well as those of the family. Moreover, Warren's father has told him of his handicap because of race and has instructed him concerning the way to handle white people. Consequently, Warren is suspicious of the intentions of whites and feels that he should not be absolutely honest with them. Although Warren seems disposed to resort to certain techniques to secure favors from whites, he does not like to do it and harbors hostility toward whites. His general attitude in this regard is to use white people to his own advantage.

His hostility toward whites has been nurtured by certain contacts which he has had with them. His experience in Maryland when a boy of only nine has left its impression. He has also been impressed by the way Negro children are excluded from a near-by playground which is reserved for a few white children.

His hostility toward whites impels him to seek an opportunity to engage in some form of aggression toward them, but family discipline keeps him from becoming a mere brawler seeking fights. His desire to try his strength with white boys probably issues partly from his desire to reassure himself. For though Warren is a race conscious youth and believes that Negroes can compete successfully with whites when given an equal chance, he admits that if he could be born again he would rather be white in order to escape the disadvantages of being colored.

This leads to a final observation concerning Warren and his status as a Negro. He spends most of his life in the relatively isolated world of the Negro and his outlook on life as well as his hopes and ambitions are largely oriented within this world. He has seen Negro men and women rise within this world despite the handicap of race. Warren believes that if he is not completely submerged by his family, he can do the same. If he cannot obtain the highest rungs, he can at least escape the fate of his parents.

DISCUSSION OF THE CASE OF WARREN WALL[3]

After a hurried inspection of an area in the deep South, I came as a white psychiatrist to discover what I could of the Negro in a city of the middle or border area. Some twenty contacts were made with young men from sixteen to twenty-five years of age, and of these three or four proved readily accessible and informative. "Warren Wall" of this chapter received the most attention. This was not by reason of his eminent suitability to represent the average Negro youth. Quite the contrary, he impressed one as definitely unusual. Certainly, he was the most simply communicative. This seemed to result from a personally fortunate combination of traits themselves of wide distribution, but usually organized into more secretive or otherwise inaccessible patterns. Some of the young men knew more about life in their area; some of them had far more striking personality problems that would have provided useful

[3] By Harry Stack Sullivan, M.D., of the William Alanson White Psychiatric Foundation.

levers. The particular factor that focused my principal effort on Warren was the success of his discriminating me as a person from "the white man" as a generalized object of hostility. While this did not make me by any means an object of unmixed affection, it reduced the number of illusory people concerned in our conferences.[4] Warren took me to be a probably transient phenomenon in his life, as did most of the subjects. This, in his case, however, did not mean that I was to be treated with amiable superficiality and inconsequence. He took himself, his past, and the problematic future with considerable and rather realistic seriousness. He regarded white people as both more powerful and less irresponsible "friends"—and he was very clear in his realization that, to achieve any of the objectives that he contemplated with pleasure, he would need assistance on which he could depend. His generalizations (thinking patterns) of the Negro represented them as low in capacity for durable friendship, greatly handicapped economically, and much given to envious ill-wishing. This is doubly interesting because Warren is one of the few subjects of this study who had unquestionably durable friendships with Negro compeers, and because envy of the economic and other advantages of the whites did not seem to be a great factor in his hostility. There was less of simple projection of personally undesirable traits and more of personal experience in his generalizations.

The Negro of this city would appear to be significantly different from the Negro of the deep South. I cannot vouch for the universality of the difference throughout the middle or border area, but I can say positively that I encountered no exception to the difference—among upper-class, middle-class, or lower-class youth. I saw no upper-class youth in the South, where a Negro upper class is clearly delineable. Here, I saw the only child of a family which would unquestionably be upper class among southern Negroes. The stratification is somewhat con-

[4] See, in this connection, Harry Stack Sullivan, "A Note on the Implication of Psychiatry, the Study of Interpersonal Relations, for Investigations in the Social Sciences," *American Journal of Sociology*, 42 (May 1937), 848-61, and the installment of "Psychiatry: Introduction to the Study of Interpersonal Relations," in *Psychiatry*, I, 121-34.

fused in this city of the middle area as a result of several factors
—freedman ancestry and skin color, among others. It seems to be
peculiarly difficult for a really dark-complexioned Negro to
elevate himself by intellectual or financial success and rigid
sexual morality. Contrariwise, some of the older free-born
families do not seem to be troubled by the mid-Victorianism
which characterizes the upper class in the South.[5]

Warren is dark-brown; his father and his two most intimate
friends are very dark. Both the latter are middle class, and both
are quite certain to amount to something. Warren and one of
his friends—the other is quite a "lady's man"—are unusually
continent, have "steadies" who are sisters, and have solved the
"masculinity problem" of their prevailingly lower-class environment. Most boys in the neighborhood became sexually experienced at an early age. The girls feel quite free to pursue whom
they desire and a failure to respond is interpreted—and widely
—as evidence of one's being "sissy" or "queer."

The significant difference does not appear in this sexual
freedom of the lower-class Negroes, so far as I could determine.
I believe that in this respect middle-class life also parallels the
South. Heterosexual activity seems to be one of the few un-
restricted recreational outlets. I judge that there are many
definitely promiscuous people and that this laxity arises from
factors of personality development as well as from a permissive
culture. Vividly outstanding factors in the structure of many
Negro family groups are superficially identical with those which
in whites eventuate in arrest of heterosexual development and
thus to obligate homosexual or bisexual patterns of behavior.
While homosexuality is by no means unknown in the southern
community and is apparently fairly frequent in this sophisticated border city, it would require careful, intensive personality
study of a number of Negroes to convert one of my surmises in
this connection into fact.

It has seemed that a remarkable number of the subjects
studied—including some people in the thirties—have definitely
immature personalities. In particular, their affections seem

[5] Hortense Powdermaker, *After Freedom* (New York: Viking Press, 1939), 408 pp.

shallow, if not also fugitive. This applied with as much force to friendship (isophilic) tendencies as to their relations with the other sex.[6] At the same time, some facts were to be observed in their interpersonal relations which in white subjects would be explained on the basis of persisting isophilic preferences, the handling of which entailed very little anxiety. These observations led finally to the surmise that the "promiscuity" in sexual relations and the "superficiality" in friendship relations arise from a complex of traits that we would refer to a frustration in elaborating the *good-mother preconcept*.[7] This implies a general very early distortion of personality, presumably by almost ubiquitous interracial factors. In this connection, certainty—and sound remedial formulation based thereon—would require comparative psychiatric exploration in the United States and, say, the Brazilian culture-areas.

Appeals to vague racial mythopsychologies seem to be the "intellectual" equivalent to those self-protecting rationalizations to which reference has already been made. I hope that it will be clear that psychiatry proceeds by the elucidation of differences in the patterns of interpersonal relations among people immersed in approximately uniform cultural matrices. Our particular subject, Warren Wall, while showing peculiarly distinctive patterns, showed clearly the interracial attitudes which I surmise to be quite general in the United States, but which I also surmise to show specific regional differences that are important data for science. I refer here to the elaborations of antagonism toward the whites.

The striking and perhaps most significant difference of the Negro of the deep South and of the border area shows itself

[6] I refer to their relations with other Negroes; the relationships with white people are far too complex to be relevant in this connection.

[7] The theory of personality development concerned here has been evolved over a period of years. See, for the original statement, "Erogenous Maturation," *Psychoanalytic Review*, XIII, 1-15. It was developed extensively in the manuscript "Personal Psychopathology: The Pathology of Interpersonal Relations" which was used as collateral reading in the Yale Seminar on the Impact of Culture and Personality (1932-3), a current revision of which is appearing in occasional installments in *Psychiatry*. See also the articles "Mental Disorder" and "Psychiatry" in *Encyclopaedia of the Social Sciences* (New York: Macmillan Co., 1934), Vol. X, 313-19, and Vol. XII, 578-80.

in the surface adaptation to the white. The southern Negro tends to be friendly, either diffident or elusive, and emotionally responsive. The border Negro tends to be unfriendly, antagonistic, or morose. The discrimination against the border Negro seems to be much more haphazard than in the South. There is nothing like the general etiquette derogatory to self-esteem. There are abundant educational opportunities. My informants showed a consensus of opinion to the effect that, while the physical equipment, schoolhouses, laboratory apparatus, and so forth, were "second-hand," one could secure adequate instruction in practically anything one could learn. But they all agreed also that occupational opportunities were waning. One Negro said:

> In my father's time a gifted Negro could compete with mediocre whites. That is not the case any more. It's getting to be very difficult to get a position as clerk. They want us to be laborers. I don't think it even comes from discrimination against us because we are colored. As the jobs get scarcer, they look more and more after their own people. There wouldn't be pick-and-shovel work for Negroes except that they work better than whites, and are willing to take less pay.

Rather than being at least subconsciously made to be chronically afraid, the border Negro is ignored and treated with indifference or frank contempt. I believe that the commonplace Negroes fare more ill in personality in this atmosphere than do they under the distance-fixing etiquette and caste-distinguishing system of taboos of the southern regions. I believe that there are far more contented Negroes there, despite the lower basic scale of living, the seasonal hardships, and other undesirable conditions. Gifted youth in the South comes early to suffer the limitations in educational opportunities. Gifted Negroes in both areas come all too soon to recognize the limitation in opportunity to exercise their talents. Neither area is conducive of mental health for those well above the average in endowment.

The border Negro struggles with rage where the southern Negro suffers from fear. The unconstructive wish-fulfilling fantasies that are evoked by these states are respectively malevolent and escapist. The diffuse optimism which seems ingrained in the Negro also manifests itself in somewhat different forms. The border Negro—and in this Warren is not an exception—seems to fix on goals of superiority to the whites in terms of the whites' pyramid of income and deference, in so far as it is comprehended. Reality is anything but encouraging to such ambitions; the result is anxiety, and protections against anxiety, compensatory and substitutive behavior.[8]

The tragedy of the Negro in America seems to be chiefly a matter of culturally determined attitudes in the whites, by the manifestations of which the Negro is generally distorted into a pattern of interracial behavior which permits the continuance of the attitudes without much change. This is a vicious circle, the interruption of which is an undertaking of great difficulty. In serious discussion of this problem with highly intelligent and ordinarily resourceful confreres, I have been told in essence that there doubtless are unusual Negroes, but that it takes a psychiatrist interested in the problem to find them. I have heard much about "typical Negro characteristics" and, unhappily, when my role has been commonplace instead of that of an investigator, or a friend and colleague, I have had experiences that could readily be rationalized in accord with these "typical characteristics." Even here, however, when the role is shifted and the techniques of intensive study of interpersonal relations have been substituted for those of a detached and generally pre-occupied professional man, the presumptively "typically Negro" performances have been resolved into particular instances of the "typically human." On the one hand, the social distance of the Negro and the white ordinarily conceals the personal facts; also, the Negro, well trained in the almost infra-human role, finds certain utilities in playing it out.

It is evident that, if we are to develop a real approximation to national solidarity, we must find and cultivate a humanistic rather than a paternalistic, an exploiting, or an indifferent

---

[8] A certain loud boastfulness in the presence of white bystanders belongs in the last mentioned category—and is perhaps the most unfortunate in its effect on white attitudes toward improving interracial relations. More subtle but similarly unfortunate dynamisms are seen in preoccupations which minimize the interest free for investment in activities important to white employers.

attitude to these numerous citizens of our commonwealth. As a psychiatrist, I have to speak particularly against using them as scapegoats for our unacceptable impulses; the fact that they are dark-skinned and poorly adapted to our historic puritanism is really too naive a basis for projecting most of our privately condemned faults upon them. They deserve to be observed as they are, and the blot of an American interracial problem may thus gradually be dissipated.

CHAPTER IX

*ALMINA SMALL**

APPROACHING the neighborhood where the Small family lives, a visitor would be impressed by the row of neat, well-kept houses in a block shaded by large trees. Here, in the Northwest section of Washington, live a widow, her two sons, and four daughters. Mrs. Small takes evident pride in her rented house, and the six large rooms are scrupulously clean and orderly. Ever since they came from a little town in North Carolina they have occupied this dwelling. Mr. Small found an opportunity to continue his occupation as a laborer and just before his death, three years ago, was promoted by the government bureau for which he worked. The story of the widowed Mrs. Small and her daughter Almina gives an excellent insight into the lives and the attitudes of many lower-class Negroes in Washington.

Essentially, it is the record of the influence of a mother with the cultural background of the Negro folk upon the personality of her daughter. Mrs. Small has a vague, inarticulate dissatisfaction with her status in life, and she has persistently labored to achieve a better home for her children. Economic difficulties and a low social status have been too much for her. As a result, she has become resigned to the comforting belief that the Lord will in time work out all problems for the best. What she and Almina might have achieved, had life been less harsh for them, one may only conjecture. Uneducated and superstitious, she is, nevertheless, a woman of admirable impulses who has never quite sunk to the lowest levels of lower-class Negro society. Her perspicacity and refinement are concealed under a mass of ignorant opinions and naive understandings.

* Names in this case as in the previous one are purely fictitious.

MR. SMALL

The meager information supplied by Mrs. Small concerning her husband indicates that he never had the slightest opportunity to enjoy the benefits of a cultured life, and that he often sought in drink an escape from his hard lot. Yet, for some unexplained reason, he was evidently a man who, had he been given a chance, might have maintained a pleasant home for his children. Mrs. Small, fully aware of his shortcomings, remembers him with kindness:

> I guess my marriage has been as happy as most. You know, we all have our troubles—can't expect everything to be all right all the time, but if you are just patient and lean on the Lord, He relieves you in time. My husband liked to go all the time. He was one of those "sporty" kind of men. He liked to drink and carouse and all that. He wasn't so bad about it that I knew until we was married. I guess he kinda kept it hid. But one thing, he provided for his family and kept up his home. And that's all you can ask of any man. He never brought any of his carousin' home. I wouldn't stand for that, and he provided for us. He never left us no property, but he left us plenty insurance. That is, he left us a nice little policy, but of course you know with a family money don't last long. An' I never tried to reform him. You know everybody gotta run their own race, and he ran his. He drank hisself into T.B. That's what he died of in the sanitarium. As soon as we knew he was sick with it, we had him put away 'cause it wouldn't do to have the children catch it. And T.B. is awful contagious. He wasn't sick long before he died.

With curious inconsistency he went on drunken sprees, though he was a strict churchman. Almina recalls how insistent he was that all the children attend church and behave properly:

> His death does make a difference. We have more privileges since he has been dead. He was real strict—a lot stricter than my mother. He belonged to the Baptist church; all of us do. My father went to church all the time and made us go, but my mother never goes. She believes in church, but she doesn't like to be away from home.

MRS. SMALL

After first apologizing that "there's not much to tell," Mrs. Small related the following story:

We were raised in North Carolina. I had four sisters and two brothers. Both of my parents are dead, but all the rest are living. My father died when I was small, and I don't remember him well. He was a laborer, and my mother did domestic work. She was a good woman. She used to have prayer with us and talk. . . . You have to excuse me for fanning, but I am sick and I sweat so, but I'll be better in time. Time is a wonderful thing, ain't it? Yes, time and the Lord can make anything happen. I often tell my children that—the words of my mother. I remember way back when we was children she used to say, "The times'll change. Time will come when there'll be plenty all around you, and yet there'll be people starving to death"; and it's here, ain't it? Right now! She said, "There will be things flying in the air and they won't be birds. They'll be things running on four wheels, and they won't be drawn by horses." That's true, ain't it! Time's a wonderful thing. Wonderful the things God brings to pass! . . . All of my sisters and brothers were married before I was. I wasn't the youngest or the oldest. I just decided not to get married and leave my mother alone 'cause she had done a wonderful favor by us, bringing us up like she did and her a widow. . . . I don't remember hearing my mother say much about her childhood or slavery. She was born the year of emancipation, so she didn't know anything about slavery except what she heard other folks say. She was always so busy by the time she got through raisin' us she didn't have time to talk about things like that. . . . We've all scattered now. Some live in North Carolina, some in Baltimore, and one lives here. We're all fond of each other, but we just don't keep track of each other. 'Course if any of us should get sick or die, we would go to see them.

Mrs. Small's deep religious faith had evidently been acquired from her mother to whom she was greatly attached. Although she had resolved not to leave her mother in order to get married, Mrs. Small had traveled considerably as a maid and had acquired a broader experience than many Negro women of her background. Concerning this phase of her life, she said:

I always wanted to travel—go places—and I did every chance I could. I did maid's work. I wasn't no common servant. I waited table mostly and helped the lady. That was nice work and it paid good. Whenever I heard of anybody who was goin' away and wanted a maid, I went to see them. I even had other folks looking out for them for me. I got to go all over, up and down the coast, and places like New York, Chicago, and summer resorts. I used to listen to these people talk and try to pattern after their ways in whatever they did that I liked. Ain't it good I went all them places then, 'cause now I don't get no place?

Even though she had worked as a menial, she never sacrificed her self-respect:

If I seen that they was all right, I took the job, but I always had carfare back home, so if I didn't like them I could leave.

She developed a technique for getting along with people while permitting no familiarities. Indeed, Mrs. Small is quite aloof:

It don't pay to get too familiar with people. I teach my children that—just keep back. I never have nobody walkin' in without knockin', or just goin' in my kitchen to git a drink. When you let folks get that familiar, as sure as you live, you're goin' to have a fallin' out. I never knew it to fail. Yet I don't have no cross words with nobody. I smile and speak and go about my way. I teach my children not to fight. I tell them if you see anybody wants to fight or do things they shouldn't do, don't you say nothin'—just separate yourself from 'em. You don't have to let them know you don't like it; you just leave. Whatever you do, don't fight!

Some of the defeatism, resignation, and suspiciousness of lower-class women is illustrated in the following extension of her opinions about the best way to get along with people:

That's one thing about the black man—he won't stick together. That's where the white man has him bested. Now, our folks are just like crabs in a basket. When one tries to reach up and climb out, the others pull him back. That's why we're so weak. We need to organize and stick together. Fightin' ain't goin' to do no good. I tell my children like my mother used to tell me. When white folks don't treat you right, don't try to hit back. The Negro is weak, and the white man is in power. Vengeance is mine, says the Lord, and we gotta leave it to Him to vengeance us. I tell my children that now is the time to be quiet 'cause we ain't got a thing. We're the underdog. And listen; don't pass this on; just keep it to yourself! The black man is gonna stay down as long as we got this present administration. Now don't you go tell 'em this 'cause I'm on relief and they'd put me off.

As a result of frustrations Mrs. Small tends to interpret recent social movements in the light of her folk background and paranoidal apprehensiveness:

Chile, it's awful! The way Roosevelt's got things now, we're livin' in slavery. Why, when you ration a person off and say you can't make but so much, what is that but slavery? And who is this Roosevelt after? He's after the black man, that's who! I don't care how white they come, if they got one drop of Negro blood, he's after 'em. See, Roosevelt's smart. You gotta give it to him. What does he do? He pacifies you. He knows if you give a black man a pat on the head and give him something to eat, he's satisfied. Why, those folks down to relief they say, "I'm for Roosevelt!" I tell 'em they're crazy. Roosevelt's just patting 'em on the head and holdin' 'em down. It's slavery—all but the block! The white man, he's always studying some way to keep the black man down. Now you take hardware stores; do you know any black man who owns a hardware store? I mean, who sells guns? No, you don't, and you won't, either. 'Cause guns mean power, and the white man don't intend for the black man to get guns 'cause if he does he's got power.

On another occasion she remarked:

I don't mean that Roosevelt isn't doing what he thinks is right and isn't a better man than Hoover. But you know, he's under the Robert E. Lee administration, and Lee's last words were, "Keep them [Negroes] down."

Mrs. Small said of a WPA project on which she was employed:

I worked on the WPA sewing project for a while, but I got so nervous I shook like a leaf, so I had to give it up. I got $23 every two weeks, and I was working from 3 till 10:30 P.M. Now, how could I manage off of $46 a month, me with six children!

Mrs. Small was critical and suspicious of WPA, but she was frank concerning the moral shortcomings of certain of her fellow workers:

Now, down to the sewing room they was always hintin' for an excuse to put a white woman over us colored so they'd have an excuse to pay 'em more. They went to work and invented the job of head cutter so they could give the job to a white woman and pay her more. Some of these supervisors don't know a thing about sewing. They were mean, too, just 'cause we was colored.

'Course some of those colored women did act awful. I guess you have to be tight on that kind. They'd come to the sewing room drunk and cussin' and dirty. Honest, I never did know people really lived like that! Some of 'em older than I was—otta been makin' their peace with God—down there drunk, havin' young men—real young—meet 'em, and talkin' about "my boy friend this and my boy friend that." Oh, it was awful!

Many Negroes voice the complaint that colored people simply will not present a united front against social injustice. Mrs. Small believes that "this is the whites' day; we got to be quiet now"; sometimes, however, a militant stand is justifiable:

I'm in favor of Peoples Drug Store picket. It's the only way colored folks will get any place. That's what I call stickin' together. They ought to give the colored decent jobs when they are making their living off of them. Look at all these Jews! They live all around colored neighborhoods makin' their livin' off Negroes. Some of 'em see you on the street and don't even speak. They stay here till they make their money; then they move up town and don't even want you in their stores.

Mrs. Small's militancy was expressed even more forcibly on the occasion of a parade protesting police brutality:

If I had known about that parade the other evening, I would have gone out and marched with them. The way I feel, you have to all work together. You can't be like crabs in a basket one crawling up and the other pulling him down. I have worked for white people and they talk about keeping colored down, so why can't we talk about getting something—at least let them hear us grumble so they know we aren't satisfied.

Her memories of the race riot of 1919 are vivid:

I was in Washington then. You know, that riot started over a a white woman. Don't ever give me another race riot while I'm living! Oh, it was like war; everybody was afraid to go out! White folks come in your house and say, "Who lives here, white or colored?" If they're colored, they shot 'em all up. Then the colored do the same by them. Sometimes they'd go in colored neighborhoods and just start shootin' up people. The white folks said a colored man raped a white woman, but let me tell you she was probably about to git caught and hollered. You know, white women are crazy 'bout colored men. An' white men are crazy about colored women, too. Anything dark they like, That's why you see all these white women burnin' theirselves to death on the beach tryin' to git black. They know white men like 'em brown, and a white woman'll kill herself to please a man. Well, that's man's nature, I guess—white folks tryin' to get black an' we're tryin' to get white!

Mrs. Small does not appear to have conflicts over the fact that she is a Negro. Her principal complaint has to do with her low economic status. She is, in fact, reconciled to racial segregation:

I have talked to a girl from Plainfield, New Jersey, and I have talked to girls from places where colored and white go to school together, and from how they talk I'm glad we've separate schools. They say teachers are partial, and the other students poke fun at 'em or at their clothes, and the white teachers don't say a thing. An' you don't see 'em hiring any colored teachers. I know I'd rather have my children under colored teachers.

I think it's better for colored to be by theirselves 'cause as soon as they mix with white and something happens, they say right away it's the colored who are to blame. 'Course, a lot of stealin' comes from people not having jobs. But, when a white person commits a crime, he does a dirty crime. I was readin' in the papers about some white girl sayin' she was attacked by a colored man. If a colored man attacked her, all I can say is he was jumpin' into a lot of trouble. Yes, you hear a lot about colored attackin' whites in the South, but I don't think half of it is true!

I like separate theaters better. I've always felt if you're not wanted some place, I wouldn't go there. Yes, I've heard about some stores not wantin' colored. Well, when I hear of such stores, I just stay away from 'em. The only thing I'm sorry about is that there ain't more colored businesses.

Mrs. Small has instructed her children never to fight with white children:

Have I told my children to fight if they're called "nigger"? No, indeed! Why should I tell my children to fight? When they get older and commit a crime, I'd be the one who'd told them to fight. Why, I'm an old woman, and I've never had a fight in my life. . . . No, they can't keep away from all trouble, but I tell 'em names don't hurt 'em.

Once, however, her adjurations were disobeyed:

> There's a white family down the street, and my youngest got
> in a scrap with 'em. It just looked like those folks wouldn't
> rest 'till they'd carried the case to the Juvenile Court. So I told
> the judge down there I didn't care to have my children be with
> people like that. I didn't aim to be called down to the Juvenile
> Court each week. So the Judge just dismissed the children. . . .
> How did it start? Well, they say they called each other names.

Mrs. Small had a relatively easy time when her children were
born; "most too easy," she says, " 'cause I had seven, and seven's
a lot to take care of when your husband dies." When a daughter
died two years ago, "it looked like none of us could pull ourselves together for a long time." Within the Small family the
ties of affection are strong:

> I really don't have a favorite. You know, all of 'em are dif-
> ferent, but I love 'em all the same.

Though she knows nothing about pediatrics or child psychology, Mrs. Small appears to have many sound ideas about
how to bring up children. She had been observant of the practices of white mothers and gave her own children the benefit
of this knowledge:

> There's nothing can take the place of mother's milk. I used to
> see white women all the time tryin' to get out of nursin' their
> babies. They didn't want to be bothered. Their babies be skinny
> and puny and cryin' all the time, 'cept when they'd get a colored
> woman who had milk to nurse 'em. Sometimes I think white
> women don't have no heart. I seen a white woman leave her
> two-months-old baby and go on a trip. I saw white babies gettin'
> orange juice and scraped beef and things; so when I started
> havin' babies I figgered I'd let 'em have those things. I've seen
> little children one and two years old runnin' around with their
> pants all wet and dirty. There's no need for that! It's the
> mother's fault. Mothers get impatient, and then want to spank
> their children. They should train 'em right from the start.

As her children grew older, she worked out techniques for
holding their confidence and for giving them proper guidance
for life adjustments:

> I joke with 'em and talk to 'em so they'll look at me as just one

of them. If they come in and tell me about something wrong which they've seen or done, I don't act shocked. I sort of side with it to get them to tell me the whole thing. Then, after they've told me the whole story, I say quietly—just as if I would say, "It's bed-time"—"Well, I don't think you'd better go there any more"—see? That way they won't be afraid to tell me anything. I always trust my children. I tell 'em how to act, and then I don't try to keep 'em in my pocket. I don't go taggin' 'em around. I tell 'em, "Now I've told you how to act. If you want to go some places, go, but see that you act right! If you can't, you'd better stay home like a baby." I don't believe in keeping children in. Let 'em live, go places, and see things. I want 'em to have experiences. . . . I want 'em to go with several people before they marry. Then they're in a position to know what they want. I think they ought to be at least in their twenties before they marry.

Her program of sex education seems to be more enlightened than that of many better educated mothers:

I take my girls when they're twelve years old and I say, "Now listen, my dear child; you've come into womanhood and things ain't like they used to be." I talk to 'em frank and tell 'em how you've got to be careful with yourself, 'cause if you have sex 'course you may have a baby, and it don't take but once. I make 'em know that. It don't have to happen but once, and you can have a baby. I tell 'em, "If you don't believe me, you go and try it. It's up to you, but no decent woman wants a nameless child." I tell 'em, "Now you may think boys won't like you if you don't and you won't get a husband. That ain't so. What life's got for you, time'll bring you." They listen to me, and so far I ain't had no trouble with any of 'em. I never told the children stories about babies comin' in doctors' bags. I just told 'em exactly what happens.

While Mrs. Small was working on the WPA sewing project, her older son gave her some trouble:

He started tryin' to be a man. He used to get in fights while I was away from the house. I told him, "Now listen; if you can't mind me, there's one can make you mind, and that's the court officer!" He wouldn't listen; so finally I went down to the court and had a probation officer talk with him. You know, kinda scare him! Then Dan told me he was goin' to CCC camp. I said, "Sure 'nuff? Well, good luck," like I didn't care. He went and stayed six months. He said he liked it but was glad to get back home. I think it was right good for him 'cause I ain't had no trouble with him since he's got back. Before that, though, he was goin' to "take" me. But I scare 'em all about the law. . . . Once Dan had a fight while I was at work, and he ran off and stayed 'cause he didn't want me to punish him. I let him stay out all that night. Tell you the truth, I didn't get no sleep that night myself. I was at the window peepin' out and watchin' him settin' in the yard. I didn't let him in 'cause you know boys'll take advantage of a woman if they can.

Sometimes Mrs. Small becomes discouraged and feels that "with times like they are, it don't matter how much education colored folks git, it don't do no good." Nevertheless, she urges her children "to git what education they can 'cause you never know what's goin' to turn up." Almina pays a high tribute to her mother's way of bringing up the family: "She's 'soft' but she trusts us."

She always lets me have my own way. I guess it's because I don't ever want to do anything that's real wrong. I say my prayers every night and ask God to make me a good girl. My mother tells me to always act like a lady and I do try to. She says as long as I do that, I don't have anything to worry about. She trusts me, and you know I can't go back on that!

At the time of the interviews with Mrs. Small and Almina, the mother was ill:

I'm going through the change. I guess I been goin' through it about ten years. You know, my husband died and left me with all this responsibility just when I needed to rest and be relieved. But that's life, ain't it?

Characteristically, however, Mrs. Small remained calm and patient:

I won't let nothin' make me worry about nothin'. I leave it all to the Lord 'cause He knows best.

ALMINA'S GIRL FRIENDS

Almina, who was the fifth Small child, is now a well-bred girl of seventeen. Of course, her outlook on life and her language reflect her lower-class status, but the following remarks testify to her training and are a tribute to the good influence of Mrs. Small:

> I don't like girls who act loud and common. I like decent girls. A decent girl is one who knows how to conduct herself around boys, who doesn't get drunk, who doesn't kiss boys anywhere and everywhere, and who doesn't go to extremes with boys.

> No, I don't go out and celebrate after Joe Louis wins. Maybe when I get older, I will, but in a decent way. I mean I won't go out and get drunk.

> Mother says I should never do anything wrong because my younger sister would be sure to imitate me.

Mary is now Almina's best friend; they like the same sports, go to the same high school, and belong to the same Y.W.C.A. club. At present Mary is causing her mother some concern because she is no longer interested in school or in Sunday school and church attendance. Mary prefers to go to dances. Apparently, however, Mary is unable to exert any bad influence on Almina. Sometimes they go to a dance hall on U Street, but Almina will not attend the "nickel hops" in private homes:

> They drink there! They've stopped buying whisky since port wine came out. It's only 25 cents a bottle. The girls drink it and get silly and mellow. . . . What's "mellow"? That is letting the boys do anything with them they want to. If a mother is common, she lets her daughter have her friends in while she goes out. Then the young people get mellow. She doesn't care what happens, just so she makes money off of her nickle hop. . . . I don't go to those places!

ATTITUDE TOWARD CHURCH AND RELIGION

When she was three Almina was enrolled as a member of the church, and she has never had the emotional conversion experience of many young people in her social class. She has great faith that prayers are answered:

> I think the Lord really answers your prayers when you live right. I've never asked Him for a thing that I haven't gotten it. If I didn't get it right away, I did later, or I got something even better than I asked for. Once I wanted some play suits when I was a little girl; I asked the Lord for them, and He

made it possible for me to get them. Another time I wanted Mary to go to the beach with me, but her mother wouldn't let her. I prayed, and the Lord made her mother have a change of heart, and she got to go.

Almina thinks that God is "a man with a long white beard, like the pictures in church." He is "kind of golden, between light and colored." She firmly believes in a literal heaven and hell, though she has not thought much about "whether colored people are the same color when they go to heaven." Once while looking at the moon, Almina saw the cross, but none of her companions saw it. She is uncertain whether she believes in ghosts, although she believes you can "see things sometimes." In her judgment Father Divine and Daddy Grace "rank low down," and she attends services of that type "just to see how the people carry on." Elder Michaux, however, "says some true things, and I like to hear his choir." Particularly does she approve of "some things he preaches, like how a man should treat his wife; not beat her."

RECREATION ACTIVITIES

At present Almina is unable to read very much because her eyes are bothering her. She believes that she would not look attractive in glasses. Formerly, however, she read widely in the sort of literature which usually appeals to lower-class people. Mystery tales, detective stories, and novels interest her; and occasionally she reads magazines like *True Romances* or *Love Stories*. She liked Faith Baldwin's *The Professional Virgin* and books of that sort. Apparently she reads for mere enjoyment and not to escape from reality, since she never identifies herself with the heroines of stories, nor does she "have time" for building air castles.

She greatly enjoys listening to stories on the radio. The "Amos and Andy" program she dislikes very much because she does not "like having white people talking like that." Although she found "Flat Foot Floogie" distasteful, she does enjoy listening to popular music like "You Can't Be Mine and Someone Else's Too" and "I'm Savin' Myself for You." Her preference among the better type of radio programs is for "Music Maestro," which "started me thinking." For a while she took lessons on the piano, but she "got tired of practicing and stopped." She and her sister are able to play "pretty good by ear" the popular swing and jazz music of the day.

Before her eyes commenced to give her trouble, she attended the movies at least once a week. Among her favorite players are Claudette Colbert, Kay Francis, Bette Davis, Tyrone Power, and William Powell. "I like them because of the way they act, not how they look, because I couldn't be one of them." Almina also likes active participation in sports, especially tennis and swimming. She closely follows Joe Louis' various fights, not because of her interest in pugilism, but because they afford her a vicarious thrill of achievement over the whites:

> I just know I'm going to get heart failure one of these times listening to a Joe Louis fight. It helped the colored race because he won. I went out of the room before the Schmeling-Louis fight was over! I felt sorry that he lost. I don't believe, however, that his victories will really help in solving the Negro's problems.

RELATIONS WITH BOYS

Although it is generally assumed that lower-class Negro girls enjoy considerable sexual freedom, neither Almina nor any of her girl friends have ever had sex relations, "at least, not yet." She admits that boys make advances to her, but she always says, "No!" Yet, she is not at all prudish about this matter:

> We girls often discuss boys and having relations with them. All my girl friends think about the same as I do. They don't want to have any now. I know it's natural, and I don't object if people want to do it. But, you see, my mother trusts me and lets me go with boys because she thinks I won't do wrong. I don't want to disappoint her. Anyhow, I really don't know much about it. I know that I wouldn't want a baby before I was married. So far, none of us sisters have had sex relations. I guess the reason is that mother trusts us. We don't want her to think we don't know how to act.

Apparently she esteems the good opinion of her mother more highly than the abstract virtue of chastity.

Almina is by no means unsophisticated. In discussing sex

questions, she said, "I don't think it's bad. I do say that you better know what you are doing and what it's all about before you do!" Even before her mother enlightened her, she "knew how babies were born because there were some older girls who used to talk, and I kept my eyes and ears open."

> Once I read a book on sex relations and birth control while my mother was away. When mother found out she said she didn't care if I knew those things, but she didn't want me to sneak and read them. Mother has told me some things, and I got a lot more from reading.

She is pleased that her sex knowledge was derived from her mother and from a book "most anybody could understand." When the information is supplied by other girls, "they usually talk nasty about it, and you learn it the wrong way."

Contrary to current notions concerning the sexual freedom of lower-class Negro girls, Almina exhibits the conventional inhibitions in regard to sexual freedom. During the interviews she misunderstood an answer to her question about the ethics of premarital sex relations and was greatly disturbed to think that the interviewer approved of them. She and her girl friend discussed with disapproval the notion that such relations should be considered lightly, and on a later visit she was pleased to have the interviewer correct the misunderstanding and point out her agreement with the girls' attitudes. She said, "I like my boy friend because he doesn't ever ask me for anything like that."

Almina takes a realistic view of love, even though she likes romantic stories and movies:

> I don't know much above love. I think that what most people call love I call just infatuation. I like my boy friend, but I don't think I love him. At first I did think I loved him, but I changed my mind.

Her lack of prudishness is evident in the remark that "there isn't any harm in kissing boys." Nevertheless, she hastens to add that all the boys who call always treat her "with respect." Her particular friend pays his visits regularly on Sunday and Tuesday evenings. Occasionally he comes on Friday, but "he can't come every night." He is under some restrictions:

I set the days, and my mother sets the time. Sometimes in vacations I want him to stay later, but my mother says, "No, he has to go at ten-thirty!" I don't question her order. In the winter when school is on, I don't mind if he goes earlier, because I've lessons to get.

Some Negro girls evidently supply their boy friends with money for entertainment and their own personal use. On that question Almina has definite opinions:

You know, I hear some girls talking about taking the boys places and spending their money on boys. Not me! I couldn't bear to see a boy eat up my money or buy cigarettes with it. I would rather not have company.

She believes that girls in the upper classes do supply their boy friends with money. "I wouldn't let boys ask me for money!"

DISSATISFACTION WITH NEGRO COMMUNITY

As a lower-class girl in Washington, Almina is aware of the wide discrepancy between her status and that of young people in the upper economic groups "who don't have to worry and work like some of us. Their parents foot all the bills." Her dissatisfaction finds expression in her wish to move to a different neighborhood:

I'm tired of living in the same place all the time. I wouldn't want to live in Southwest because it has a bad reputation. I'd like to move somewhere else in Northwest.

Preferably, she would like to go somewhere else, though she is not certain exactly where:

I'm so tired of Washington. It's a beautiful city, but the people are kind of funny. To go to New York and see the whole town is one of my wishes. I think I'd like Chicago to live in.

Once she became acquainted with a young man from Chicago who agreed "that he couldn't stand Washington, either." In Chicago, he informed her, the people are friendly and the opportunities for colored people more numerous. Although she has not planned definitely to go to that city when she finishes school, she believes that it is the ideal place for Negroes.

Almina appears to be constantly conscious of her exclusion

from the social activities of upper-class youth in Washington. In expressing her dissatisfaction with her status, she began by saying that "people in Washington are funny."

> It's the same among the young people. The ones whose parents are teachers or lawyers or something go to X School—sometimes they are so dumb it takes them years to get out. But they all hang together. They have lots of money to spend, can have friends in their house every day if they want, can raid the icebox any time. They can jump in a car, ride to Baltimore any time, they can go to all the night clubs 'round Washington every evening if they want to. They're always being written up in the weekly theater and gossip sheet.

Her bitter protests, however, against the upper-class youth who enjoy advantages which she is denied indicate her envy of their status.

On a visit to the country Almina found that she was just as dissatisfied there as she is here in Washington. "I don't like Calvert County, Maryland, because it's too quiet and lonesome at night, and I thought that Baltimore is just as bad as Washington." Sometime she hopes to find a locality where she will have an opportunity to participate in the social life of the Negro community. Just now she believes that Chicago is the ideal place to live.

Her specific complaint about Washington is that recreational facilities for Negroes are very poor. Glen Echo, an amusement park for whites, is very attractive to this adolescent girl, and she expresses the wish that "the colored had a place as nice as that." She criticizes the commercial amusement centers for Negroes:

> There isn't much for colored in Washington. There are no nice places for us to go and dance. The Hollywood may look all right from the outside, but inside it's too small. Colored people don't have any nice place like The Fat Boy, where you can dance on the roof.

She believes, however, that Negroes who own amusement centers are to be blamed for not improving the places. "If the colored who have money would put it into colored business, maybe that would help some." The Suburban Gardens, a Negro dance hall, "is falling to pieces, and it was better two or three years ago than it is today."

Almina does not recall when she first learned that she was colored. She said, "It seemed as if I have always known." Almina has never played with white children. She recalled that once when a small white child called her a "nigger," she had gone on her way without saying anything because she knew that "the child didn't know any better." Although Almina does not seek social contacts with whites, she firmly believes in equality of opportunity for Negroes. "The colored people should have just as much opportunity to go places and do things as the whites. White people are no better than colored people." She seldom has any contacts with white people individually. "In fact, I seldom see them on the street." She is not upset because she is excluded from motion picture theaters, but she does regret that the theaters for Negroes are not so attractive as those for white people. What vexes her is that Negroes have restricted opportunities to develop their own destinies.

As yet, her knowledge about racial disabilities is based upon hearsay. "I've heard people say that colored can't go to the theaters on F Street and that it's hard for colored to get certain kinds of jobs." In her social life, however, Almina and her mother agree that they do not "like to associate with white people." Of course, Almina and her mother are resentful that their status as Negroes deprives them of the benefits of civilized living. But they appear to be more concerned about their low economic and social status in the Negro community and about the restrictions which seem to keep them from having an opportunity to raise their cultural and economic level.

In the presence of white people Almina is quite self-conscious.

Well, I look around and if I see someone colored, I feel better. But, if I am dressed all right and conduct myself with dignity and in a lady-like way, why then. . . . It is only when colored aren't acting right that people stare.

She is disturbed because some colored people create a bad impression upon whites:

I have noticed that whites don't like these dirty old men who have been digging in the street to sit beside them on the street-cars. I think myself they should go and stand in the back. I don't like those dirty men to sit by me. I never ride on the streetcar unless I am clean and look all right; then I set any place.

She recalled with amusement the discomfort of a white woman when a dirty Negro workman sat beside her on a street-car. "It looked like she was trying to push half the side of the car out to get away from him." Almina, who always wants to appear as well as possible in the eyes of whites, added that she would not have wanted to sit by this man.

She is quite concerned about the fact that other colored people do not always conduct themselves in such a way as to reflect credit upon their race. Particularly is she disturbed about the behavior of Negro pupils in school:

The principal told us why they don't give colored new build-ings. He said we don't take care of things and keep our enroll-ment up. Many drop out of school, and those who stay there tear the place up. That's the truth, too! When the whites left X School, it was old but it still looked good. You ought to see it now! Everything's marked up. They aren't going to give colored new buildings until they learn how to take care of those they have. I think that's right! I'm not against my race! I'd like to see them have better things, but they're too destructive.

She is, however, unable to tell how to develop a sense of pride in Negro pupils from poverty-stricken homes.

Although she is more or less reconciled to the many restrictions imposed upon Negroes, she is resentful of the treatment colored people receive in certain stores:

I don't let clerks refuse to wait on me! The other day when I was in a little Jew store a white lady came in, and the clerk waited on her first. I just walked out! I'd walk a mile so I can be treated right.

She regrets the apparent inability of Negroes to develop their own business enterprises. In her judgment the solution of the Negro problem is to develop the economic life of the Negro community. She believes that there are plenty of opportunities:

Colored ought to work together, but those who have money don't like to help build up colored places. Why, we have only one hotel in Washington, and that place is no good! If only the colored would put their money into colored businesses, that would help the race.

If there were attractive stores, theaters, amusement parks, and dance halls for colored people, this Negro girl would not be much troubled by social separation. In fact, she would much prefer to have that state of affairs.

ALMINA'S DISPOSITION

Almina is a healthy, extraverted, happy young girl; she greatly enjoyed being interviewed. All her answers were given in a frank, objective manner. As a small girl, however, she was reserved:

I was quiet when I was small; never said a thing. I'd listen a lot, but never talk! I never made any friends. Now I'm the noisiest one in the family.

Now she is strongly extraverted. On the Bernreuter Personality Inventory, her answers indicate an emotionally well-balanced, confident, well-adjusted girl. Her happy disposition is illustrated by her answer to the interviewer's query, "Have you ever cried about racial discriminations?" Laughingly she retorted:

I wouldn't cry! That wouldn't help! I have never heard about anyone crying about something like that.

She has had so many happy experiences that she finds it hard to tell which one was most pleasant. Finally she told about her first trip to the beach as her happiest moment. In telling about a club which was being organized, she said that each member was to take the name of one of the Seven Dwarfs and that she would be "Happy." Certainly that name fits her personality. If she were to be born again, "I'd want to be just who I am. I'm satisfied!" She would like to have more money, but "money isn't everything; other things matter." If four wishes might be gratified, Almina would take "dresses, travel, a lovely home, and a car." She believes that "you get what is planned for you" and that no amount of wishing can alter fate. It is interesting to observe that this lower-class girl, living on the margin of economic security, is not at all depressed by social injustice. On the contrary, her attitudes are those of a healthy adolescent girl who objects to specific disabilities but who is untouched by abstract questions or social problems.

PLANS FOR THE FUTURE

Like many other young people, Almina has never had any adequate guidance in self-discovery of interests, aptitudes, and vocational choice. At one time she wanted to become a physician, "but I couldn't stand the long years of training." Now she believes that

> I would like to be a secretary or maybe a social worker. If I were a social worker, I'd go around and visit people and ask questions and help them out. I think it would be easier for me to get a job as a secretary. I like the business course at school, all but the bookkeeping. Ten years hence I would like to be settled down in a home of my own or making lots of money in a business firm.

She would also like to be a dancer, for "I'm crazy about dancing." In case of necessity "I'll take a job looking after white children." Evidently the public schools have done little for girls like Almina to help them in wise vocational decisions. The superficiality of her life plans is typical of any undirected adolescent.

She is aware of the fact that Negroes have a difficult time in obtaining satisfactory employment. For that reason she may not have been able to come to any specific decision about her life plans:

> I know a colored girl has it rather hard, particularly if she is trying to get a job which will pay her well. I used to feel mad about it, but I have learned to accept things as they are.

On completing high school, she sought in vain for a position:

> I've about stopped asking. I keep hearing how hard it is to find a summer job, and if I can't find the kind of job I want, I won't work.

She is, however, hopeful of passing a typing test, for "the man said if I passed it, he could get me a job."

Of one thing she is certain; she does not want to do housework for white people:

> If working means sweating over someone's stove or scrubbing a floor, then Almina doesn't want a job! I don't like to scrub any floors. I don't scrub them at home. I'm not going to scrub them in anyone else's house. My mother scrubs the floors at home.

She is not troubled by the fact that her mother has to do this hard work because "we have only two that need scrubbing, the bathroom and the kitchen." If, however, the day comes when she must scrub for a living, "I'll have to scrub." With the callousness of youth, white or colored, she rationalizes that it is all right for her mother to do menial work.

Although "working for whites is kind of funny," there would be no objection to a job of looking after children. She has heard that some white people ask their colored servants to change names:

> Indeed, I wouldn't change my name for any of them! I know a girl who went to work for some white people who had a daughter of the same name. They wanted the girl to change her name and to call the daughter "Miss." You know, I couldn't go around "Missing" people younger than me! The girl left and got a job with a woman whose name was the same as hers. This woman wanted Frances to change her name to Mamly! Can you imagine it? It sounds like some old name they used to call colored people in slavery.

Thus far Almina has protected herself against such humiliations, real or fancied, by not going to work in white households. With the characteristic irresponsibility of youth, she perceives no need to help by increasing the family income. The efficiency of any service she might render a white housewife is indicated by her exuberant statement:

> I wouldn't mind a mother's helper job. Then I could raid the white folks' icebox and get all their good food. [Much laughter.] I went a couple of times with my sister when she had a job working for some white people, and did I raid their icebox!

Like many other adolescent girls, she has thoughts about going on the stage. She would like to be a dancer; "I love to dance." Since the other girls in her class at the Y.W.C.A. have complimented her on her ability in dancing, she believes that she can say without conceit that she is talented. "Then, too, I can sing a little." Her dreams soon carry her away—"I have always wanted to see Hollywood." Upon further thought, she adds, "I tell you that if I could do what I want, I would dance for about five years." She has vague ambitions about working as a secretary for a year in order to obtain money for further stage training.

Actually, however, Almina thinks a great deal about getting married, though she protests that she will defer matrimony "until my late twenties." She casually remarks that "I'd like to travel all around with a female. Now, you're smiling! But I will be an old maid. That's what I want to be!" Nevertheless, she has decided that "I won't name my son Sam because nearly every colored boy you see is named Sam." She has already decided to limit her family to a boy and a girl.

She is firmly opposed to the notion of mixed marriages; "I don't see why any colored person would want to marry a white person." She has heard about

> that colored woman in Paris who sings and dances. She married two white men! The last was a Count. I couldn't stand for any white man to touch me! I couldn't eat with him, live with him, or sleep with him! Don't ask me why because I just can't explain. I could never marry anyone but a colored man.

She is in favor of intermarriages between light- and dark-skinned Negroes "because their children will be lighter." Dark pupils, she believes, have a hard time in school:

> They get low marks. The teachers choose the light ones with long, nice hair to call upon, to take part in the plays, and to do everything.

Since she has been impressed by movies and instruction dealing with venereal diseases, she plans to have her future husband undergo a medical examination. She hopes that he will not be "a man whom you can tell to do this and that and he runs to do it." Nevertheless, he will have to defer to her on the question of a family. She will not be "one of those poor people who can hardly take care of one child and yet have twelve and fourteen."

SUMMARY

In many respects Almina is much like other young girls, a paradox of contradictions. Her interests are evanescent and superficial, and she has no clear philosophy of life. She has been reared by parents who have never enjoyed the cultural advantages of upper-class Negroes. In spite of the low economic status of her family, she has received relatively good family training. She has been influenced largely by her uneducated mother, who has the cultural background of the Negro folk. Her mother believes in "leaving matters to the Lord, who in His time will bring things about as they should be." This belief has caused Almina to accept things as they are, an attitude which, significantly enough, she has learned from the "older people."

Almina, born and bred in the city, has had many experiences which have conflicted with the folk outlook of her mother. Yet she is not bitter about the fact of racial discrimination. Her lack of any clear-cut ambition is due partly to her family background and partly to the fact that she knows how limited are the opportunities for Negroes. Her confusion in regard to her future might have been cleared up by a sound guidance program in the school which she attended. Almina seems to have done some thinking about the Negro problem and to have accepted the idea that Negroes should be economically self-contained. What troubles her most is not her exclusion from white society, but rather the fact that she does not participate in the social life of upper-class Negroes.

In fact, there seems to be clear evidence that Almina's mental conflicts are more closely related to her socio-economic status than to her racial identification. Repeatedly she asserted that she does not want to associate with white people, to attend their theaters, or do business with them. Although she would prefer a satisfactory life in the Negro community, because of her lower-class status she experiences frustrations. These disturb her greatly, but she has no clear idea of how to improve her situation in Washington. Hence she has vague plans for going on the stage or moving to Chicago.

Several final observations may be added concerning Almina. First, although she does not have a prudish attitude toward sex, Almina seems to be determined to lead a chaste life. And as far as she knows, all her immediate friends have made a similar decision, "though many girls do it." Secondly, it is clear that such lower-class people as Almina and her mother do not necessarily have low ideals of family life. It is significant that although Mr. Small drank and was the "sporty" type, he provided for his family through life insurance. Finally, she does not object to being a Negro and has no desire to be white. She does desire to escape from the irritating limitations of the lower class in the Negro community.

SUMMARY AND CONCLUSION

SUMMARY AND CONCLUSION

STATED simply, the purpose of the present inquiry has been to determine what kind of person a Negro youth is or is in the process of becoming as a result of the limitations which are placed upon his or her participation in the life of the communities in the border states. Although in common-sense and everyday usage, the meaning of personality is clear, when one undertakes to deal critically and objectively with what the term actually denotes, many important problems arise. Everyone would probably agree that one's physical or biological inheritance or constitution is a factor in the organization of his personality. At the same time, probably no one would deny that one's experiences—one's family, education, and social contacts—are also a part of his personality. Then, too, because of the unlimited variations in the biological inheritance of individuals and the infinite variety of human experiences even under apparently identical conditions, scarcely anyone would deny that each personality is a unique phenomenon.

Agreement in regard to these basic theoretical assumptions concerning personality does not, however, eliminate the more practical problems which confront an investigator who undertakes to study personality development. Whereas it may be agreed that biological inheritance—stature, temperament, and intelligence—and social experience both play a part in the organization of personality, there is a wide difference of opinion regarding the relative influence of these two factors. If, as some hold, the biologically inherited patterns of response which the precultural child exhibits are decisive in the formation of personality, then the experiences of the child or the youth become the means through which he expresses his personal characteristics. But if one holds that the experiences of the individual are more important in personality organization than biologically rooted patterns of response, then he will endeavor to discover as far as possible how the experiences of the individual have influenced the development of his personality. In view of the practical implications of these two viewpoints for the investigator, it becomes necessary that anyone undertaking a study of personality should set forth clearly the conception upon which his research is based. Therefore, in stating the conclusions of this inquiry, tentative though they are, it is necessary to make clear the conception of personality which has guided our investigation.[1]

Since this study is based upon the latter emphasis, it has undertaken to discover in the experiences of Negro youth those influences which have determined their conceptions of themselves as Negroes, their attitudes toward other Negroes and toward whites, and their attitudes toward the world about them and to some extent toward the world in general in so far as those attitudes have a racial or minority group connotation. In adopting this conception of personality, we do not imply that it is the only approach to the problem. However, it was our conviction that this conception would yield the most fruitful results for the purposes of this study; namely, to determine how the failure of Negro youth to participate fully in the life of the community influences his thinking and his behavior in relation to others. The answer sought by the scientist as well as by the layman to the question, "What kind of person is a Negro youth?" is, how is a Negro youth likely to behave in certain situations? Both would want to know, for example, whether a Negro, when invited to cooperate with whites, would speak freely and act frankly, or, because of his experiences as a Negro, would be suspicious, disguise his thoughts and feelings, and act contrary to what one would normally expect from his verbal responses?

Since we were interested chiefly in the experiences of Negro youth, we endeavored first to describe the social and cultural world into which Negro youth were born and reared. This social and cultural world was approached through the study of the Negro communities in two border cities, and an analysis of

[1] See Appendix A, p. 271.

their relations to the white communities. In the border states, the social and cultural world of the Negro is isolated in important respects from the larger white world despite its economic dependence upon the latter. Even where members of the Negro community are served by the same institutions as the larger community, physical separation and other practices set up distinctions which carry an implication of inferiority and a subordinate social status. But more often the general policy followed in border cities is the exclusion of the Negro from white institutions and the establishment of separate institutions to serve his needs. Thus, from the standpoint of participation in the institutional life of the community, the Negro lives in a social world largely isolated from the white world. The institutional life of the Negro community, especially where it is an expression of Negro enterprise and leadership, as, for example, the church, reflects in its organization and aims the various cultural heritages and traditions of Negro life in America. Social values and social distinctions stem from the experiences and actualities within the Negro world. These various social values, social distinctions, and patterns of behavior are closely correlated with the class structure within the Negro community. Although this class structure rests upon an economic foundation and corresponds roughly with the occupational differentiation of the Negro population, the social stratification of the community reflects certain purely cultural and social distinctions such as family background and patterns of behavior.

In exploring the experiences of Negro youth for the purpose of discovering how these experiences have affected their conception of themselves and their attitudes toward whites, we began with their relations within the family group. Here it was found that youth in lower-class families, which comprise about two-thirds of the Negro population, were influenced in their conceptions of themselves as Negroes by their parents' acceptance of the belief that the Negro is inferior and that his subordination to the white man is inevitable. Since many of the lower-class families have a southern background, their attitudes of subordination are traditional and sometimes the children as well as the parents have learned through bitter experience not to challenge openly the white man's authority. Consequently, the parents caution their children to avoid conflicts, to ignore insults, and to adopt techniques for "getting by." These techniques include "acting like a monkey," "jibing," flattery, and plain lying.

Although middle-class children show, in their outward behavior at least, the same accommodation to their subordinate racial status as lower-class children, there are several factors in the influence of their families which differentiate them from the latter. First to be noted is the fact that middle-class families and their children show more sophistication toward their status. While it is true they believe that because the white man has power and money the Negro must accommodate himself to the white man's world, they do not believe that the white man is inherently superior. Even where the parents use the techniques of the lower class in order to enable their children to rise in the world, the children may show their disgust and refuse to accept their parents' instructions. They believe that the Negro should seek power, money, and education in order to match his wits with the white man's. Middle-class parents are usually ambitious for their children to rise in the world and their children reflect in their aspirations the ambitions of their parents. They always try to appear decent and respectable and thus not only to dissociate themselves from lower-class Negroes but to win the approval and respect of whites.

Although upper-class children are differentiated on the whole from the other two classes by their greater sophistication, a more important factor that differentiates the influence of the upper-class parents from that of the parents in the other classes is that they never attempt to inculcate attitudes of subordination to whites. They may tell their children to avoid fights or brawls with whites but this instruction is given because such behavior is unbecoming to one of their status. Upper-class families attempt to identify themselves culturally with upper-class whites and show considerable prejudice toward the middle and the lower class as well as toward "poor whites." Since many of the upper-class Negroes are mixed bloods, they may even identify themselves racially with whites. In upper-class families, the influence of family traditions on the formation of the personality of Negro youth is very effective. The youth sometimes have before them the achievements of several generations. However, upper-class parents in their attempt to shield their children from racial discrimination sometimes create conflicts in their children by attempting to keep them from learning the social implications of their racial identity. Upper-class children often build up defenses for their egos and develop ambivalent attitudes toward themselves as Negroes and toward Negroes in general.

Because of the absence of family traditions, the insecurity, and the instability of many lower-class families, the children acquire many of their ideas not from the home but from their neighborhood contacts. In the streets they are frequently exposed to the hostility of whites and consequently are often involved in fights with white children. Because of the fact that they may fight back in border cities without running the risk of mob violence, they develop in some cases considerable self-reliance. Especially in communities where the police offer little protection, Negro youth develop their own techniques for expressing their hatred toward the whites and for coping with any conflict situation that may arise.

Middle-class children also have occasional conflicts with white children, but because of their parents' instruction to avoid behavior which would identify them with lower-class Negroes, they are less likely to engage in neighborhood fights. Moreover, because of family discipline, they are less likely than lower-class children to be exposed to the discrimination of whites in the larger community. But, even so, they are not as well protected as the children of the upper-class from contacts which would give them a feeling of inferiority. Upper-class parents succeed in shielding their children from the cruder forms of race prejudice both in their neighborhood and in their larger community relations. In many cases upper-class children are taken by their parents to northern cities where they are less likely to encounter racial discrimination. Nevertheless, in the final analysis, both in their neighborhood and in their wider community contacts, upper-class children cannot escape some feeling of inferiority as to their social status.

In the border states, where the separate schools approximate more or less the white schools in equipment and personnel, education stimulates in Negro pupils about the same aims and ambitions as in the white. To some extent the schools themselves provide an opportunity for educated and talented individuals to develop their abilities and to find employment. But the vast majority of those who have acquired skills and developed ambitions through education must seek employment in a world which bars them because of color.

From the standpoint of class distinctions, the public schools exert a great influence on the personality of Negro youth because they are under the control and reflect the outlook of the small upper class of mixed blood. Because of their social status and dark complexion, lower-class youth are subject to discrimination on the part of teachers as well as on the part of other pupils. Although all teachers are not guilty of discrimination against the dark pupils, the cases of discrimination are numerous enough to cause the dark lower-class children to develop feelings of inferiority and resentment. Activities, such as Negro History Week, designed to stimulate race pride and self-respect have little mitigating effect upon this situation, because even these racial activities are usually dominated by the upper-class children of light complexion. In spite of these limitations the public school does awaken ambition in some lower-class youth and gives them a sense of personal dignity, and to some extent equips the lower-class and more especially the middle-class youth to compete with upper-class individuals in the Negro community and even in the larger community.

Paradoxical as it may seem, the Negro church, an institution which is the product of Negro leadership and cooperation, does little to give Negroes a sense of personal worth and dignity in a world where everything tends to disparage the Negro. This is due partly to the fact that the outlook of the Negro church is otherworldly and the emphasis of its teachings is upon personal salvation. Moreover, the religious ideology of the Negro church tends to perpetuate such notions as a white God and white angels, conceptions which tend toward the disparagement of things black. In the churches attended by the lower classes, the ecstatic forms of religious expression probably provide a release for pent up emotions and frustrations, but even this value has not prevented many lower-class youth from being influenced by the secularizing atmosphere of the city and deserting the church.

The most important contacts which Negro youth have with the larger world are concerned with employment and making a living. Negro youth of all classes agree that they do not have the same opportunity as whites for employment, but this does not concern the upper-class youth as seriously as some of the others since many of them are planning to enter professions within the Negro community itself. Many of the ambitious individuals in the middle class also hope to obtain similar positions after they have completed their education. But lower-class youth who have little hope of rising out of their class look with grave misgivings upon obtaining employment even in occupations traditionally held by Negroes. Many of them turn to criminal and antisocial behavior in order to survive the struggle, while others become accommodated to low types of legitimate employment.

Negro youth are influenced in subtle ways by ideas current in the Negro community, although in the border cities there are no general ideologies related to social movements as in the larger northern metropolitan areas. Rather, these ideas have come into existence both as the result of folk rationalizations and because of the influence of the upper class. This is illustrated by the current notion that Negroes do not cooperate or lack the capacity to cooperate as other racial groups. Lower-class individuals who are wont to accept the prevailing derogatory appraisals as true, naively attribute the Negro's shortcomings and economic dependence to his inability to cooperate. Upper-class Negro businessmen, whose interests are involved, propagate the notion that the failure of Negro business is due to the fact that Negroes do not cooperate or patronize the Negro businesses, despite the obvious impossibility of a segregated economy. Because of this widely accepted notion, Negro youth are critical of Negroes and skeptical of their possibilities.

Our analysis of the factors influencing personality development gave a segmental analysis of the individuals studied. In order to remedy this defect, we attempted to explore the entire personalities of two Negro youth, a boy and a girl, in order that the racial factor might be viewed in the context of the total personality organization. Although the cases chosen were not regarded as typical, they enabled us to see the personality of Negro youth in its functional relationship to the social world in which it developed. As in the case of these two youth, the personality of the Negro child develops in response to the family situation into which it is born. The culture, traditions, and economic position of the family determine not only the type of discipline to which the child is subjected but the manner in which he develops his conception of himself as a Negro. As he grows up, his contacts with the larger outside social world influence still further his attitudes toward himself as a Negro as well as his attitudes toward white people. Because of the limitations which make impossible free and easy participation in the larger community, his attitudes and overt behavior will show more or less the influence of the isolated social world to which he is confined.

APPENDICES

A Statement of the Relation of Culture and Personality in the Study of Negro Youth

In one of her shrewd comments on the numerous visitors to her Paris retreat, Gertrude Stein wrote that Paul Robeson "knew American values and American life as only one in it but not of it could know them" and added the ambiguous observation, "And yet as soon as any other person came into the room he became definitely a Negro."[1] That the Negro since his introduction into America has been in the midst of American life and culture but at the same time has been excluded more or less from participation in the life about him, has been one of the obvious facts of race relations. Only recently have students of culture and personality begun to study the effect of this paradoxical position upon the development of the Negro's personality. These studies have revealed that the Negro who has escaped from the folk culture of the masses and participated in the culture of the white world exhibits characteristics similar to those of other "marginal men" or cultural hybrids such as the Jew, the Eurasian, and other westernized Orientals.[2] But for knowledge of the personality traits of the Negro masses, chief reliance has been upon American fiction with its changing stereotypes and rationalizations of current prejudices designed to support social policy.[3]

Human personality, which Goethe regarded as mankind's most fortunate possession, has excited the interest of men from time immemorial. Theological speculation, reflecting animistic conceptions, has regarded personality as a manifestation of an immortal spiritual essence or soul. Philosophers have speculated upon personality under the concept of the self as distinguished from other objects of observation. Only during the past century has the so-called "baffling mystery" of personality become the subject of scientific study. Yet despite the age-long interest in the subject and the development of

[1] *The Autobiography of Alice B. Toklas* (New York: Random House, Inc., 1933), p. 292. By permission of Random House, Inc.

[2] Robert E. Park, "Migration and the Marginal Man," *The American Journal of Sociology*, May 1928. See also Everett V. Stonequist, *The Marginal Man: A Study in Personality and Culture Conflict* (New York: Charles Scribner's Sons, 1937).

[3] Sterling Brown, *The Negro in American Fiction* (Washington: Associates in Negro Folk Education, 1937).

scientific conceptions and techniques, "The term personality," as Professor Sapir has said, "is too variable in usage to be serviceable in scientific discussion unless its meaning is very carefully defined for a given context."[4]

It is not necessary to consider here all the definitions of personality. In the various definitions of personality two fundamentally opposed points of view are apparent, and they are concerned with the old question of the relative influence of nature and nurture. Hence, the important question which one may ask concerning personality is whether the basic pattern of one's personality is inalterably fixed by one's biological heredity or determined by the social and cultural world into which one is born. Of course, the problem is not so simple nor the issue between the two viewpoints as clear-cut as appears from the above statement.[5] But generally speaking, the psychiatrist and the sociologist have given almost diametrically opposed answers to this question. The viewpoint of psychiatry, though modified by some members of the profession in recent years, is that personality is rooted in the biologically inherited patterns of response which are exhibited by the precultural child. Though the psychiatrist recognizes differences between the behavior of the child and the adult because of the modifying influences of culture and social experience, he maintains nevertheless that the basic pattern does not change. One suspects that Miss Stein was influenced by some such idea concerning personality when she stated that Paul Robeson became "definitely a Negro" in the presence of other people. It is easy to see how such a conception of personality may lead to the conclusion that if one inherits a certain type of personality he may more readily adapt himself to certain elements in a culture. Or one may logically expect the cumulative effect of a certain personality trait to result in a specific psychological bias in the culture of a race or people.[6]

Returning once more to Miss Stein's second statement, we might assume that she was able to perceive attitudes and traits of personality which Robeson had acquired as the result of having lived most of his life among Negroes. If this were true, she merely had in mind what a white social worker expressed concerning the late John

[4] Edward Sapir, "Personality," *Encyclopaedia of the Social Sciences* (New York: Macmillan Co., 1934), Vol. XII, p. 85. By permission of the Macmillan Company.

[5] There are, of course, some psychologists who regard human personality as a system of psycho-physical reactions and do not attempt to disentangle the physiological and the psychological factors.

[6] Edward Sapir, "Personality." See also Ruth Benedict, *Patterns of Culture* (New York: Houghton Mifflin Co., 1934).

Hope whom she took for white until he "opened his mouth to speak" on an occasion which in itself did not identify him as a Negro.[7] To the sociologist it is understandable why a mulatto with a negligible admixture of Negro blood might exhibit "Negro characteristics," not because of some biologically inherited patterns of response, however, but because of his participation in the social world of the Negro. The sociologist recognizes that every human being is born into a pre-established society or group with its particular language, customs, behavior patterns, and ideas. As a result of his participation in a social world, the individual's behavior—what he perceives as well as what he does—is defined by the responses of other members of the group.[8] In this manner the behavior of the individual acquires meaning in terms of the particular culture into which he is born. Moreover, his behavior—his thoughts and actions in regard to himself as well as toward others—becomes organized in relation to the behavior of others. It is in this sense that one may speak of personality as being the role which one plays in the social organization. Therefore, in order to understand a particular personality, the sociologist focuses his attention first upon the social and cultural context in which the personality takes form.

To the sociologist the significance of such biologically inherited traits as physique and temperament "consists in the way in which they enter into the role of the individual in his social milieu."[9] But at times the sociologist has written as if such traits were the determining factors in personality formation. For example, Professor Park, who has inspired some of the most fundamental studies of the American Negro, writes that the temperament of the Negro manifests itself in

> a general sunny, and social disposition, in an interest and attachment to external, physical things rather than to subjective states and objects of introspection, in a disposition for expression rather than enterprise and action.[10]

Because of racial temperament, the Negro race according to Park,

[7] There are many jokes current in the Negro world relating to the manner in which the identity of mulattoes in positions and places forbidden to them has been revealed through some gesture or remark. In one such joke, the mulatto was discovered when he replied as to whether he would return to work on Monday: "If the Lord spares me and nothing happens."

[8] Ellsworth Faris, *The Nature of Human Nature* (New York: McGraw-Hill Book Co., Inc., 1937), p. 35.

[9] Robert E. Park and Ernest W. Burgess, *Introduction to the Science of Sociology* (Chicago: University of Chicago Press, 1924), p. 70.

[10] *Ibid.*, pp. 138-39.

has selected out of the mass of cultural materials to which it had access, such technical, mechanical, and intellectual devices as met its needs at a particular period of its existence. . . . The Negro is, by natural disposition, neither an intellectual nor an idealist, like the Jew; nor a brooding introspective like the East Indian; nor a pioneer and frontiersman, like the Anglo-Saxon. He is primarily an artist, loving life for its own sake. His *métier* is expression rather than action. He is, so to speak, the lady among the races.[11]

In view of the above statement, it is difficult to see the justification for the statement of a psychologist that the sociologist overlooks "completely the part played by biological determinants (by intelligence, temperament, and physical heredity)" and considers "the subjectification of customs and social traditions within a single human life as the whole story."[12] As a matter of fact, the sociologist does not deny that intelligence, temperament, and physical heredity play a role in the formation of personality. However, as Professor Burgess has indicated, "original differences in mentality, in temperament, and in volition enter into the determination of the form of personal behavior patterns, but their organization and fixation occurs in social interaction."[13] Hence, the original nature of the individual does not enter into the organization of his personality as a fixed quantity determining his responses to the culture but always as an amalgam of nature and nurture. Evidently Allport, who accuses the sociologist of overlooking biological determinants in the formation of personality, regards the matter in the same light. In criticizing the psychoanalyst for overemphasizing sexual motivation, he states:

Biological motives never operate singly. Sex in normal lives never stands alone, it is tied to all manner of personal images, sanctions, tastes, interests, ambitions, codes, and ideals. To put the case as crisply as possible: sexuality in its stark biological simplicity is segmental in the organism, often insistent but never devoid of mental ramifications; in these ramifications it is indeed pervasive, but it is no longer mere sexuality; it becomes diffused into the major systems of interests and traits which are themselves the *fundamental* structural and functional systems of personality.[14]

The sociological conception of the relation of biological impulses or motives to personality formation would logically preclude the

[11] *Ibid.*, p. 139.

[12] Gordon W. Allport, *Personality: A Psychological Interpretation* (New York: Henry Holt and Company, 1937), pp. 38-39.

[13] E. W. Burgess, "Study of the Delinquent as a Person," *American Journal of Sociology*, XXVIII (May 1923), 667.

[14] Gordon W. Allport, *Personality*, pp. 187-88. Allport makes a similar criticism of the biological theory of personality, pp. 119-20.

explanation of Negro personality in terms of temperament or intelligence. But in addition the sociologist realizes that the very conception of temperament is vague and experiments designed to detect temperamental differences between races have produced uncertain results.[15] When it comes to the question of intelligence, it might appear to some that the results of numerous intelligence tests provide reliable evidence to support the notion that the Negro is by nature lacking in those qualities which are necessary to the intellectual. Here too there are many weighty theoretical objections to these tests as a measure of "innate intelligence." Moreover, the data on Negroes present many contradictions which can only be explained in terms of the social environment of the Negro. In one study at least it has been shown that

> an improved environment, whether it be the southern city as contrasted with the neighboring rural districts, or the northern city as contrasted with the South as a whole, raises the test scores considerably; this rise in "intelligence" is roughly proportionate to length of residence in the more favorable environment.[16]

Consequently, there does not appear to be any reason why the sociologist or social psychologist should regard temperament or intelligence any more than other biological traits as fixed and uninfluenced by social interaction.

With the foregoing discussion as a background, we are prepared to make clear the assumptions underlying our study of the effects of minority status on the personality development of Negro youth. We have recognized first that there is no technique at present by which we can disentangle the biological from the social determinants in the formation of personality. Therefore, we have assumed that in studying motives, wishes, attitudes, and traits of personality, we are dealing with emotions and impulses which have been organized and directed toward goals in the course of social interaction. As far as possible we have ferreted out the social psychological determinants of childhood because of their primary importance in the development of personality. For example, where a child has developed a feeling of insecurity or inferiority we have searched in his experiences for situations which might have created in him feelings of insecurity or inferiority. Because of the special interest of the present study we have probed these experiences in order to determine if the responses and attitudes of others to his complexion or the social

[15] Gardner Murphy and Lois Barclay Murphy, *Experimental Social Psychology* (New York: Harper & Brothers, 1931), p. 120.

[16] Otto Klineberg, *Negro Intelligence and Selective Migration* (New York: Columbia University Press, 1935), p. 59. By permission of the Columbia University Press.

evaluation of his race have been responsible for his feelings of inferiority. At the same time, we have attempted to find out how attitudes and traits acquired as the result of his experiences as a Negro have colored his attitudes and evaluations in regard to the world in general. Since we have sought in the experiences of the Negro adolescent for explanations of attitudes and feelings of inferiority, we have naturally discarded as unwarranted such assumptions as that of McDougall, namely, that the Negro has a strong instinct of submission.[17]

We have worked also on the assumption that personality is a dynamic organization of attitudes and traits which change during the life history of the individual. According to this assumption new interests and attitudes replace older ones and new social objects come into existence as a result of experience.[18] Such an assumption, we realize, is opposed to the traditional psychiatric assumption that motives at every stage of one's development are rooted in biological impulses which are present in the precultural child. However, we feel that our conception is in harmony with the growing recognition on the part of psychiatrists of the influence of cultural factors in personality development.[19] Instead of regarding motives or personality conflicts as due to oral, anal, and genital drives of an infantile or archaic character, some psychiatrists are beginning to seek within the individual's social experience and cultural milieu the sources of motivations and conflicts.

This leads us to include one final word concerning the point of view of this study in regard to the relation of the individual to his social and cultural milieu. Though implicit in our previous discussion, we wish to make clear that we regard the process as exceedingly complex by which the individual takes over the attitudes and culture of the group and gives them that unique expression which every personality exhibits. The process we feel is much more complex than is represented in such mechanistic formulas as *conditioning* and *stimulus and response*.[20] The validity of such formulas as descriptions of processes operative in relatively simple and defined situations and under controlled conditions is undisputed. But in the study of the highly complex responses of the individual to

[17] William McDougall, *Is America Safe for Democracy?* (New York: Charles Scribner's Sons, 1921), pp. 118-119.

[18] Gordon W. Allport, *Personality*, Chap. VII, where the author discusses the functional autonomy of motives.

[19] Dr. Karen Horney, *The Neurotic Personality of Our Time* (New York: W. W. Norton & Co., Inc., 1937).

[20] Herbert Blumer, "Social Psychology" in *Man and Society*, editor, Emerson P. Schmidt (New York: Prentice-Hall, Inc., 1937), pp. 186-96.

his social world where meanings are the essential elements, it is impossible to reduce behavior to such simple mechanisms. Therefore, in order to understand the development of the personality of the Negro adolescent, we have studied the more complex process by which he has acquired a particular organization of attitudes toward himself and others as a result of living in a particular social world.[21]

In view of these assumptions, it is not strange that we should have in our study a description of the social and cultural world of the Negro. Nevertheless, a word of explanation is necessary, especially since there are conflicting opinions concerning the existence or nonexistence of a so-called Negro culture in America. First, we should make clear that in presenting a description of the social and cultural world of the Negro, we are not allying ourselves with those who talk uncritically of the survival of African cultural traits or with those who attribute the music and dancing of the Negro to some peculiar racial endowment. On the other hand, the very fact that we have felt that it was necessary to describe the social and cultural world of the Negro indicates that we do not share the opinion of those who assert that the social and cultural world of the Negro is identical with that of the whites simply because the Negro wears the same clothes and speaks the same language as the whites. Here we are concerned with the more subtle but at the same time concrete aspects of the more or less isolated world of the Negro. It is in this more or less isolated social world, with its peculiar social definitions and meanings and with its own social evaluations and distinctions, that the personality of the Negro takes form and acquires a meaning. Although this world is not completely isolated from the larger white world, for the great mass of Negroes it represents a large measure of the totality of social experience which has real meaning for them.

[21] George H. Mead, *Mind, Self and Society from the Standpoint of a Social Behaviorist* (Chicago: University of Chicago Press, 1934).

APPENDIX B

Supplementary Information on the Institutions, Social Movements and Ideologies, and Social Pathology of the Negro Community in Washington, D.C.

INSTITUTIONS

The institutions of the Negro community reflect in their organization and structure the social stratification which we have described in the text. The more important institutional aspects of Negro community life which will be analyzed from the point of view of the class structure include the family, the church, the schools, recreation, cultural associations, business enterprises, and welfare institutions.

The Family

Only among certain elements in the middle and the upper classes has the family achieved an institutionalized character. Family life among the great mass of lower-class Negroes rests upon sympathy and habit. A large proportion of these people are newcomers to the city who with their folk customs are attempting to adapt themselves to the more secular environment. One may find small enclaves in the city where in relative isolation these families are able to maintain the bonds of sympathy and affection which held them together in the rural regions. But often the city environment dissolves the bonds of sympathy and parents lose control over their children's conduct. It is among this class that one finds desertions, nonsupport, illegitimacy, and juvenile delinquency. In the middle class, family life rests upon a firmer basis. This is due partly to the fact that members of this class have a larger and more secure income, and still more largely to the fact that they possess certain social and cultural advantages. Usually they have had a longer period of residence in the city during which they could become adjusted to the urban environment; in the main, they spring from those elements in the Negro population that have traditions of stability in family relations and are integrated into the institutional life of the community. In many cases the parents strive to provide their children with a better home and education than they have had. Of course, the social striving among this group may tend to break family ties, but it often

278

means reorganization of family life on a pattern in conformity with that of the upper class.

The "old families" who were once the backbone of the upper class have suffered the fate of "old families" in every changing society. They have seen their position challenged by those who have risen through competition to the top of the social pyramid. They have seen the standards and values which they have held sacred flaunted by their own children. In some cases they have withdrawn to themselves and formed an inner circle rather than come to terms with the new world about them, and their children have migrated to other sections of the country or even gone into the white race. Nevertheless, these families have left a heritage among their descendants which has given them a sense of personal worth and dignity. In fact, the traditions which these families have built up and preserved have provided some of the ingredients which have gone into the culture of the upper class.

Yet, taking the upper class as a whole, one finds that the character of their family life does not reflect the traditions of the old stable families in Washington but the traditions and culture of Negro families drawn from many sections of the country and the aspirations and values of a group "on the make." One is struck first by the small number of children in these families, a fact which is undoubtedly connected with their individualistic outlook as well as their effort to maintain certain standards of living. For example, in a group of 65 married couples who consider themselves the elite in the upper class, 49 of the wives are employed and 36 of the couples have no children. The couples with children have an average of 1.4 children.[1] Although this group may not be representative of the whole upper class, it indicates certain tendencies in this class. In the relations of the spouses and the relations between parents and children there is, generally speaking, an absence of patriarchal authority and the presence of a high degree of democracy. In fact, among the most favored families the children are often spoiled because of the endeavor on the part of the parents to indulge their wishes and provide them with the luxuries which are considered proper in this class. The children certainly acquire the belief that they are the aristocrats in the Negro world whatever those outside this world may think of them.

The Church

Of the institutions which owe their origin and continuance to the initiative and the support of Negroes themselves, the church is

[1] E. Franklin Frazier, *The Negro Family in the United States* (Chicago: University of Chicago Press, 1939), p. 442.

the largest and most influential. It is because of this fact that the various church organizations reflect the social stratification of the Negro community in their membership, in the character of their religious services, and in their distribution as to denominations. There are approximately 150 Negro churches in Washington, over 50 per cent of which are Baptist.[2] The estimated value of the Baptist churches ten years ago was more than $3,000,000; their membership was reported as 40,000, and their yearly expenditures were reported as over $400,000. The next group of churches in importance are the 30 or more Methodist churches with church property valued at nearly $2,000,000 and a membership numbering around 15,000. About half of this group were affiliated with the Northern Methodist church and the remainder with the independent Negro organizations, the African Methodist Episcopal, the African Methodist Episcopal Zion, and the Colored Methodist Episcopal. There were three Congregational churches with a combined membership of less than 2,000 and seven Protestant Episcopal churches with a membership double that of the Congregational churches. There was a relatively large number of Catholic churches with a total membership of 9,000 to 10,000, and between 15 and 20 churches of various denominations including the Seventh-day Adventists. In 1926 the churches in the Negro community reported a Sunday school membership of 20,000, half of which was in the Baptist churches.

The numerous church congregations in Washington are housed in buildings ranging in size and character from large, well-kept edifices to small missions and "store front" churches. The majority of the larger edifices have been taken over at high cost from white congregations with the result that the colored congregations have been burdened with heavy debts. All sorts of money-raising schemes are constantly resorted to in order to take care of expenditures. It is usually the poorer members of the congregation who make the greatest sacrifices. Although, generally speaking, the lower and the middle classes worship in the Baptist and Methodist churches and the upper class in the Congregational, Episcopal, Presbyterian, and Catholic churches, a few of the Baptist and the Methodist churches have always had a goodly portion of the upper- and more especially the middle-class families. The figures which have been cited above on church membership cannot be taken at their face value as a measure of the influence of the churches, since all of the churches, it appears, are complaining of the failure of Negroes, especially the younger generation, to attend church. On the whole, their efforts to stem the tide of secularization of Negro life in the city are futile, though

[2] *Religious Bodies: 1926* (Washington: U. S. Bureau of the Census, 1930), pp. 730-31.

some churches are attempting to meet the situation by adapting their services and programs to new conditions.

The character of the religious services naturally reflects the intelligence of the minister and members, and the social status of the congregation. In some of the churches emphasis in the sermons is upon orthodox or literal interpretations of the scriptures. But in most of the churches there is an injection of comments on the status and problems of the Negro. In the Congregational churches especially, the sermons are concerned with larger social issues, and in one Congregational church the sermons which deal often with the present conflicts of capital and labor show a definite leaning toward the "left." In the churches attended by the masses, both large and small, including the "store front" churches, the emphasis is upon the ecstatic element in religion. This is especially true of the smaller, nondescript churches, the open tent meetings, and the services of the nationally known Elder Michaux.

Some of the churches have had a long history which has been bound up with the social stratification of the community. The Metropolitan African Methodist Episcopal Church, which has always been supported by the more sturdy elements in the middle class, has been one of the prize appointments in the African Methodist Episcopal church. The Nineteenth Street Baptist Church, under the leadership of the venerable Reverend Walter H. Brooks, who has served as pastor for over half a century, has been influential in the community. This church was once attended by the upper and the middle classes but the majority of the upper-class mixed-bloods withdrew years ago and established the Berean Baptist Church. The Berean Church since 1929, however, has also lost its reputation for being the church of exclusive upper-class families, and now persons of the middle class (of darker complexion) attend. The same thing is apparently taking place in the Fifteenth Street Presbyterian Church, whose pastor for years was the late Reverend Francis J. Grimké, a nephew of Angelina Grimké of South Carolina and brother of the nationally known leader in the National Association for the Advancement of Colored People. This church was for many years distinguished as a meeting place of the old mulatto, upper-class families, but with the decline of this group, the social standing of the congregation has declined also and now includes many dark-skinned worshippers. Lincoln Congregational Church, which at present has a small congregation, once flourished as the church of the intellectual elite. Today one finds the small Plymouth Congregational Church, under the leadership of a young, intelligent minister, attracting the thinking members of the younger generation who seek in the church a solution of social problems.

The Public Schools

In order to understand the role of the public school as an institution in the Negro community, it is necessary to view it in its relation to the social stratification of the community. From the standpoint of the great masses of the Negro population, the public schools of Washington provide a type of education that is far superior to what is usually given Negro children where separate school systems are maintained. The children as well as their parents are not unaware of this fact. This is doubly significant for the Negro masses who, in addition to their great faith in the power of education generally, regard it as the means of rising to the top of the Negro social world. Then from the standpoint of the teachers, the public schools provide the largest and the most secure remuneration for this important element (about one-third) of the upper class. Because of the importance of the public school as a source of income for the upper class whose standards are based to no small extent upon pecuniary valuations, many of the teachers have regarded the public schools as an economic rather than a social institution. This accounts for the keen competition for positions in the public school system. Such employment, in addition to being a symbol of economic security, has still more subtle values for the teacher who is trying to maintain status. In this connection the particular type or grade of school in which one is employed becomes important. A case is reported in which a school principal did not wish to have the correct number of undernourished pupils reported because she did not want to be known as the principal of a "poorhouse." Likewise, the intense rivalries between the high schools in athletics and competitive cadet drills have been participated in by the teachers as serious affairs involving their prestige and status in the community. Therefore, it is not surprising that the teachers as well as the children of upper-class mixed-bloods have probably been guilty of regarding the high schools as an exclusive possession of this class.

These provincial attitudes have been dissipated by changes in the community which have affected both the teaching and student personnel of the high schools. The children of the masses are so filling elementary and high schools that they contain a cross section of the Negro community, and their teaching personnel represents to a larger extent than formerly all classes in the community. As the schools have become more of a cross section of the Negro community, their character has been influenced more by the general culture of these areas. In the deteriorated districts, where considerable social disorganization exists, teaching as well as discipline in the schools presents extremely difficult problems. These problems are so tied up with the economic and social problems of the community that the public schools cannot solve them simply by methods of formal instruction.[3]

Recreation in the Community

Since Washington Negroes are excluded from the theaters and motion picture houses attended by white people, their recreational life is restricted entirely to the Negro community. The major forms of commercial recreation are provided by the motion picture houses, the poolrooms, and the night clubs. There are 13 motion picture houses for Negroes, with a combined seating capacity of about 8,000. Twelve of these houses are owned by whites, though with one exception they are managed by Negroes. The three largest houses are located on U Street. One of these, the Lincoln theater, which has a seating capacity of over 1,600, has upholstered, individual seats, reserved seat boxes, carpeted floors, large foyers and lounges, and elaborate interior decorations. The Republic theater provides somewhat similar features, while the Booker T., a much smaller house, is less pretentious. The first two houses show second-run pictures and the Booker T., second- and third-run pictures. These three houses are patronized chiefly by the upper and middle classes. The Howard theater, which runs a stage show featuring nationally known orchestras but more often vulgar and risqué comedy, attracts a less discriminating audience of Negroes and whites at midnight performances. Three other houses are fairly well equipped and offer third- and fourth-run pictures for the middle class at fifteen to twenty cents.

Practically all of the remaining motion picture houses are located in areas inhabited by the lower class. Their programs consist almost entirely of western and crime pictures and their admission fees do

[3] A word should be said concerning the place of Howard University in the Washington community. Because of the generous support of the federal government, Howard has become a national institution possessing the largest aggregation of Negro scholars in one center. However, in spite of the national character of the university, about one-fourth of the students come from the Washington community. On the other hand, though the faculty at Howard constitutes about a sixth of the professionals in the Negro community, some members of the upper class who have a middle-class outlook (that is, in the historic sense) affect a certain disdain toward the intellectual interests of Howard professors. Moreover, many of the ministers, especially those in churches attended by the masses, complain of the indifference of the Howard faculty toward the church and religion. In Louisville, the faculty members of the Municipal College enjoy greater prestige and are regarded as an integral part of the upper class. The institution occupies about the same position in the community as the Miner Teachers College in Washington, the faculty of which is accepted as a part of the great body of public school teachers.

not exceed fifteen cents. In one of these houses whites are admitted, but the races are separated by a partition running the length of the theater. In some of these houses, the patrons smoke, eat, indulge in loud talking, and sometimes annoy other patrons by snoring.

Washington also has its Negro night life, but the cabarets, clubs, and inns lack the glamour, sophistication, and cosmopolitan atmosphere which one finds in the night clubs of Harlem. The places are owned by Negroes and are patronized by Negroes, mainly the sporting fringe of the middle class. When persons of upper-class status go to night clubs they usually select more exclusive places incorporated as private clubs, though not conducted strictly as such. With a few exceptions, the night clubs are small, undecorated, dimly lighted, and poorly ventilated rooms, generally overcrowded with patrons. Entertainment consists of a "swing" pianist, usually a man, and one or more women singers. Some of the entertainers are homosexuals and are featured as such. One of the night clubs formerly offered a complete floor show to attract the economically better situated Negroes but it had to discontinue this feature and provide a place for the masses to give rein to their emotions in wild dancing. From observing most of these night clubs, one gets the impression that the patrons are mostly "emancipated" peasants who are having their first fling in the "wickedness of the city."

The poolrooms, clustered along the main thoroughfares in the Negro community, provide the chief forms of recreation and at the same time a loafing and meeting place for the lowest income group. Because of legal restrictions, poolrooms are supposed to admit only men and boys eighteen years of age and older. The general atmosphere of the vast majority of the poolrooms is such as to make them undesirable as places of healthful recreation. From a physical standpoint, they are unattractively decorated, poorly equipped, and dirty and foul smelling. Many of the poolrooms serve as a place for promiscuous drinking, and as hangouts for men engaged in "numbers" work and other illegal practices. Periodically some of the poolrooms are raided and police constantly visit them on the lookout for criminals. Even in the few properly equipped and well-regulated poolrooms a fight is not unusual.

Public facilities for the recreation of Negro children are provided in a dozen year-'round playgrounds under the supervision of the department of playgrounds, and in twenty-one summer playgrounds under the supervision of the Community Center division of the Board of Education. These playgrounds are patronized on the whole by the children of the middle and lower class. The year-'round playgrounds are fairly well equipped for the limited programs they undertake, but they lack provisions for youth and employed adults who are only free after the playgrounds are closed. These playgrounds have been in operation for a number of years, and most of the supervisors, being acquainted with the children, are able to exercise considerable control over their behavior. But the summer playgrounds, beyond providing an enclosed play area, offer very little else in the form of adequate recreation. Since all playgrounds are located on property used by the schools during their regular session, the available space varies with the size and location of the school. The grounds are shadeless, lack equipment, and are generally congested. Moreover, provisions for the comfort and recreation of children depend upon whether the principal is in sympathy with the summer program. Despite the fact that many of the boys carry knives and various cutting weapons and there are occasional attempts at sexual contacts between the boys and girls, the playgrounds are, on the whole, free from serious problems.

Cultural Associations

There are some institutions and organizations in the Negro community which may be considered as primarily of a cultural character. There are the local chapters of the college Greek-letter fraternities and sororities and the Boule, an exclusive organization composed of men of the upper class. The once well-known Negro Academy, in which scholars from various parts of the country read papers and discussed the race question, has all but disappeared. The Mu-So-Lit Club, which once flourished as an exclusive upper-class organization for the enjoyment of music, literature, and the society of one's fellows, has lost much of its influence and distinction in the community. The fraternal organizations, the Masons, the Odd Fellows, and the Elks, might also be considered along with the cultural institutions since their insurance features have been supplanted in the city environment by Negro insurance companies. The Elks, with their more secular outlook and various "departments" of education and civil liberties, has become a type of fraternal organization more congenial to the temper of the urbanized Negro masses. One of the most important indices to the changing community is the growth in the circulation of the Negro newspaper. *Flash,* a picture magazine, has come into existence during the past three years. The *Washington Tribune* has recently increased the volume of its news and added other features of human interest. But more important still, the *Afro-American,* with its large national circulation, has established a Washington edition which is widely read and is influential in molding public opinion. The Negro newspaper is only one among the business institutions which will next engage our attention.

Business Enterprises

In respect to business enterprise, the Washington Negro community ranks lower than a number of northern and southern cities. But like other cities its principal enterprises, about 70 per cent, are small retail establishments including restaurants, drugstores, grocery stores, coal and wood yards, and meat markets. The proprietors of most of the stores operate them with no help; in fact, the total number of employees in Negro stores is smaller than the total number of proprietors. The volume of business is likewise small, amounting in all to about $1,500,000 a year and the annual payroll around $150,000. Negro insurance companies operating on a national scale have local offices in the community. The real estate and collection agencies represent most of the business enterprise of a speculative type. The sole remaining Negro bank, which has a white as well as a Negro clientele, is the most important business institution in the community.

Welfare Institutions

The Y.M.C.A., the Y.W.C.A., three settlement houses, and the Freedmen's Hospital, under the federal government and connected with the Medical School of Howard University, are the chief welfare institutions operating under Negro leadership. There are, of course, other welfare agencies but they are branches of organizations serving the larger community. The Twelfth Street branch of the Y.M.C.A. enjoys the distinction of being the first Negro branch in America. It was also the first branch to receive one of the $25,000 gifts which Julius Rosenwald made to 25 colored branches of the Y.M.C.A. throughout the country. This Y.M.C.A. has five departments: Boys, Business, Physical and Health, Activities for Adults, and House. The building provides for 95 men in dormitories, and is equipped with a gymnasium, a swimming pool, a cafeteria, and rooms for various activities. Its membership is about 1,100, of whom approximately 600 are 21 years of age or younger. The Phyllis Wheatley Y.W.C.A. was established in 1905 in the Southwest section by the "Booklovers," a women's literary club. This branch of the Y.W.C.A., which is not affiliated with the local Y.W.C.A. but with the national office, was given a grant of $200,000 in 1918 by the War Work Council to be used for "a demonstration building in Washington for colored work." Because of its unique relationship to the parent organization, this association developed around a number of aging personalities who have failed to carry out the purposes of the organization at large. Although the association has had a paid-up membership of 1,500, this number includes very few young people. The recently elected executive, who possesses exceptional competence and experience, is developing clubs and other activities for young women. The three settlements, the Southwest Community House, the Northwest Community House, and the Southeast Settlement House, are in the poorer areas of the Negro community and provide various types of programs, including adult education and mothers' clubs, for 2,500 or more persons. The civic associations in different parts of the city are attempting with some success to enlist the support of the residents in the various neighborhoods represented in programs for general welfare.

SOCIAL MOVEMENTS AND IDEOLOGIES

Compared with Harlem in New York City and the South Side in Chicago, Negro communities in border cities are quiet and drab. They lack the ferment of ideas and movements which ceaselessly agitate metropolitan communities of the North. Occasionally the Negro communities in border cities are stirred slightly by reports of police brutality or by picketing for jobs but such incidents are surface phenomena leaving the depths of the community untouched. For example, the noisy celebration on U Street in Washington after a Joe Louis victory cannot be compared to Harlem, where the whole Negro community pours into the streets to celebrate. Even the religious movements which grip the Negro masses in the metropolitan areas of the North only make a slight stir among the masses in the Washington Negro community. The general tone and atmosphere of the Negro community in the border city reminds one of Mencken's description some years ago of Maryland as "the Apex of Normalcy."

Some of the older residents of Washington report that there has been more militancy in the community since the first World War than before. And they usually attribute this militancy, at least during the second decade of the present century, to growing restrictions upon the civil rights of the Negro. In fact, following the World War and the Washington riot, the community as a whole was aroused, and agitation and protest found organizational expression in the local branch of the National Association for the Advancement of Colored People. For a time the Washington branch of this organization was one of the largest and most active, but after a period the membership of the local branch gradually declined and the Association ceased to be really a vital organization in the community. At the time of this writing, efforts are being made to revitalize the organization.

Militant Organizations

The depression has given a new orientation to the problems of the Negro which has found expression in such organizations as the

New Negro Alliance and the National Negro Congress. The Alliance is a movement designed to secure the employment of Negroes in white-collar occupations which are generally closed to them. Although the movement is led by upper-class Negroes, it seeks supporters mainly from among the middle and lower classes. Specifically, the program of this organization was designed to secure jobs as sales clerks in stores with a large Negro patronage. Picketing and boycotting of stores refusing to hire Negroes as clerks were the chief weapons of the Alliance.[4] Appeals for support were constantly made to the race consciousness of the masses who were the chief patrons of these stores. After this movement had achieved some success among the grocery stores in Negro neighborhoods, they began a campaign against the Peoples Drug Stores. At the time of this writing, pickets are parading before two of these drugstores in Negro neighborhoods. The Peoples Drug Stores have attemped to keep their Negro patronage by advertising the number of Negroes employed in unskilled labor, but Negroes have continued to picket and members of the upper class have gained recognition for their help on the picket line.

Another movement of a different character is represented in the Washington Council of the National Negro Congress. This organization, which has been accused of communist affiliations, does not attempt to supplant any organization but undertakes to give expression to "the struggle of the Negro on all fronts, such as civil and political liberties, labor, social service, politics, fraternal and church interests" through existing organizations. In keeping with its broad program, the Washington Council has attempted to arouse the masses to protest against wrongs which could be dramatized. While its mass meetings have seldom brought the masses out, members of the Council through skillful publicity and working in cooperation with labor unions and other organizations have been able to influence to some extent the thinking of a large number of Negroes. In the calendar for December 1938 were included: a mass meeting protesting persecution of Jews; a regular meeting at which a play entitled "Peace in Demand" was presented by WPA actors; a mass rally for Negro government workers; picketing of Peoples Drug Stores; and a mass meeting of the Alliance.

Current Ideologies

Even a brief account of the movements in the Negro community must take notice of the current ideologies which reflect the relative

[4] A recent United States Supreme Court decision has upheld the right of Negroes to picket stores for jobs.

isolation of the Negro world. One aspect of this isolation is shown in the lack of consistency in ideals and values expressed by the different movements. The Negro upper class, as we have remarked, has an essentially middle-class outlook (that is, in the historic sense), but in their philosophy and behavior one finds all forms of antiquated aristocratic attitudes toward work and expenditures as well as a "sporting complex." On the other hand, this class places great emphasis upon success and conspicuous consumption. Because of their isolation, members of this class overemphasize the importance of their position in the Negro world and speak contemptuously of poor whites (who incidentally include public school teachers). They exhibit an almost childish awe toward professional men, especially physicians. The confusion in ideals and values is also vividly represented in Negro newspapers. These news organs are intensely race conscious and exhibit considerable pride in the achievements of the Negro, most of which are meager performances as measured by broader standards. In addition to carrying a large number of advertisements of products designed to conceal Negro characteristics, these papers constantly play up the slightest recognition shown the Negro by whites. The confusion in ideologies is shown in other respects. For example, a casual reader of the *Afro-American* might get the impression that this newspaper is far to the "left" and espouses working class ideals, but a regular reader would find that upon occasions it is likely to play up the activities of Negro "society" or voice some reactionary religious or economic ideal.

In spite of its apparent isolation, the Negro community shares the current prejudices and the dominant outlook of the white world. For it should not be forgotten that, since the Negro world is not completely isolated, it gets most of its ideas and prejudices from white newspapers, magazines, and other contacts. For example, the anti-Semitism which one finds in the Negro community is not due entirely to their relations with Jewish shopkeepers, but generally to the notions which they have taken over from the white world.

In the border states, the circulation of radical ideas is extremely restricted. They may find acceptance among a small group of academically minded people or among the intelligentsia because it is fashionable, and Negroes with a real working class outlook are to be found in the labor unions and working class organizations, but the great masses of the Negro population are without any philosophy of social salvation. Many of them are still influenced by the otherworldly outlook of the church. Others accept the middle-class ideals and prejudices (that is, in the historic sense) of the Negro upper class and dream only of rising to the position of the latter in the Negro world. The confusion in ideologies, though reflecting to some extent the various interests in the Negro world, is primarily indicative of the incomplete assimilation of the Negro in American life.

SOCIAL PATHOLOGY OF THE NEGRO COMMUNITY

The Negro community in the border city exhibits all the characteristic pathological features of social life which one would expect among a racial minority of rural background and low economic status, and subject to all forms of economic and social discriminations. There are, however, certain less obvious and not so easily classified pathological features which should be considered briefly before discussing the generally recognized problems of poverty and dependency, family disorganization, and crime and juvenile delinquency. The first of these rather unusual features is the considerable excess of females over males in the community. Though the excess of women has declined since 1910, there are still about nine women to every eight men.[5] The excess of women has affected the relations of the sexes in that it has given the men a decided advantage in their relations with women. It appears that in all classes women have been compelled to compete for the attentions of men. Among the lower classes it has probably contributed to loose family ties and sex relations. Even upper-class women who would normally be discriminating in their choice of mates and follow conventional codes have been compelled to sacrifice ideals or go without mates. Then, too, married women tend to exhibit a marked anxiety in regard to their own marriages as well as an uncommon hostility to single women in the community.

The other pathological feature of the Negro community is of a more general character and grows out of the fact that the Negro is kept behind the walls of segregation and is not permitted to compete in the larger community. This produces an artificial situation in which inferior standards of excellence and efficiency are set up. Since the Negro is not required to compete in the larger world and to assume its responsibilities and suffer its penalties, he does not have an opportunity to mature. Moreover, living within a small world with its peculiar valuations and distinctions, he may easily develop on the basis of some superficial distinction a conception of his role and status which may militate against the stability of his own little world. This is manifested not only in the activities of racketeers who are known as such, but also in the behavior of those who because of color or "good looks" or education maintain a professional or upper-class "front" while engaging in antisocial practices.

[5] In Louisville, the excess of females is slightly smaller, 92.4 males to every 100 females.

Dependency, Delinquency, and Family Disorganization

Turning now to the more usual pathological features of the Negro community, we find first of all that a large portion of the population is extremely poor and during a crisis is easily swept into the ranks of those dependent upon charity or relief. In Washington nearly three-fourths of the families on relief rolls are Negroes. These dependent families constitute nearly a fourth of the Negro families in the community. The incidence of poverty and dependency varies, of course, according to classes and sections of the community. For example, taking the five broad zones marking the expansion of the Negro community, we find that on the basis of the 1930 population over a fourth of the relatively few Negroes in the central business area were on relief. In the second and third zones where three-fourths of the Negroes are concentrated, a fifth and a seventh, respectively, of the Negro population were dependent upon relief. In the fourth and fifth zones, the proportion of the population on relief decreased to about one-tenth.

Because of the general poverty of the community, a large proportion of the married women must share or bear the entire burden of supporting their families. More than half of the married women and over two-thirds of those widowed and divorced were gainfully employed in 1930. The large proportion of employed married women is responsible in part for high delinquency rates among Negro children. Of the 840 boys committed to institutions and placed on probation in 1937, 630 or 75 per cent were colored. Five-sixths of the delinquent children come from the second and third zones. During the same year, Negro children also constituted the majority (about 55 per cent) of the 280 dependent children handled by the juvenile court. In both Louisville and Washington slightly more than a fourth of the Negro families had a woman head. This was not due solely to widowhood or divorce, but also to the large number of desertions on the part of the male. According to census returns, almost one out of every five women fifteen years of age and over has been made a widow through either desertion or unmarried motherhood. Washington has had a conspicuously high rate of illegitimacy among Negroes over a long period. The number of illegitimate births has declined slightly from about one in four births fifty years ago to one in five today, although in the second zone it is still one in four. Another factor influencing unfavorably the integrity of the home and the family life of the Negro is the large proportion of homes with lodgers. In Washington a third and in Louisville a fifth of the Negro families have lodgers.

Criminality

Criminality among Negroes in the District is high as measured both by the number of arrests and by the number of inmates in the Lorton Reformatory. In 1937, over four-fifths of the inmates of this institution whose residences were in the District were colored.[6] Among the colored inmates of this institution, a comparatively large proportion (about one-sixth) were from 16 to 21 years of age. More than half of the colored inmates were committed for housebreaking and robbery. About a fifth of them were guilty of larceny and auto thefts. An even larger proportion were guilty of crimes against the person, including cases of homicide. The proportion of Negro inmates charged with homicide was 50 per cent higher than that among the white inmates. The high percentage of inmates charged with crime against the person is related to the relatively large amount of violence in the community. In Louisville, the homicide rate for Negroes (that is, deaths due to homicide) was twenty times that for whites in 1937.

Disease and Death

Yet the menace of violent death is small in comparison to the ravages of disease, due to ignorance and poverty, which carry off large numbers each year. Although the crude birth rate among Negroes in the District is almost 30 per cent higher than that of whites, their death rate (crude) is 65 per cent higher than that of whites. Tuberculosis, though not taking as high a toll today as formerly, is still the chief cause of death. The tuberculosis death rate among Negroes is still over five times that of the whites. One finds the same in regard to heart diseases and pneumonia, the latter causing more than twice as many deaths proportionately in the Negro group as in the white. A large number of the deaths recorded as due to heart disease were probably caused by venereal infection. Even so, the records indicate that deaths from venereal diseases are seven times as high for Negroes as for whites. The infant mortality and stillbirth rates, always associated with poverty and ignorance, are more than twice as high among Negroes as among whites. Louisville shows similar differences in death rates from various diseases among whites and Negroes, though on the whole tuberculosis and other death rates are not so high as in Washington.

[6] The residences of 215 of the Negro inmates were outside of the District.

APPENDIX C

Statistical Tables

TABLE I

DISTRIBUTION OF BOYS AND GIRLS INTERVIEWED ACCORDING TO AGE

Age	Total	Washington, D.C.		Louisville, Ky.	
		Boys	Girls	Boys	Girls
9	2	2	0	0	0
10	3	3	0	0	0
11	3	3	0	0	0
12	14	8	4	2	0
13	17	9	7	1	0
14	31	10	15	3	3
15	26	8	10	1	7
16	32	8	19	2	3
17	46	16	21	2	7
18	22	4	16	0	2
19	25	7	6	5	7
20	17	7	2	7	1
21	19	7	6	5	1
22	2	1	1	0	0
23	1	1	0	0	0
Unknown	8	0	5	1	2
TOTAL	268	94	112	29	33

TABLE II

DISTRIBUTION OF BOYS AND GIRLS INTERVIEWED ACCORDING TO SOCIO-ECONOMIC CLASS OF PARENTS

Socio-Economic Class	Total	Washington, D.C.		Louisville, Ky.	
		Boys	Girls	Boys	Girls
Professional	28	15	11	1	1
Public service	15	4	10	0	1
Trade	12	3	8	1	0
Clerical	8	5	2	1	0
Skilled	26	7	13	4	2
Semiskilled	17	6	9	1	1
Personal and domestic	95	31	34	12	18
Laborer	59	23	23	7	6
Unknown	8	0	2	2	4
TOTAL	268	94	112	29	33

TABLE III

DISTRIBUTION OF BOYS AND GIRLS INTERVIEWED IN
WASHINGTON, D.C., ACCORDING TO ZONES

	Total	Zone I	Zone II	Zone III	Zone IV	Zone V
Boys	93	0	31	54	8	0
Girls	111	0	43	55	9	4
TOTAL	204[a]	0	74	109	17	4

[a] One boy from Virginia and address of one girl unknown.

TABLE IV

DISTRIBUTION OF BOYS AND GIRLS INTERVIEWED IN WASHINGTON,
D.C., ACCORDING TO LOCATION IN FOUR SECTIONS
OF THE DISTRICT OF COLUMBIA

	Total	Northwest	Northeast	Southwest	Southeast
Boys	93	47	4	20	22
Girls	111	71	12	14	14
TOTAL	204[a]	118	16	34	36

[a] One boy from Virginia and address of one girl unknown.

Staff

E. Franklin Frazier, Ph.D.   Director
Harry Stack Sullivan, M.D.   Consultant
Charles H. Parrish, A.M.   Supervisor, Louisville, Ky.
Miss Zulme S. MacNeal   Secretary

WASHINGTON, D.C.

Miss Laura V. Lee, A.B.   Interviewer
Dennis D. Nelson, A.B.   Interviewer
Miss Ruth Bittler, A.B.   Research Worker
Thomas E. Davis, A.M.   Research Worker

LOUISVILLE, KY.

Mrs. Thelma L. Coleman, A.B.   Interviewer
D. Gardner Kean, A.M.   Interviewer

PART-TIME WORKERS IN WASHINGTON

John C. Alston, A.B.   Interviewer
Mrs. Isadore W. Miles, A.M.   Interviewer
Miss Bernice A. Reed, A.M.   Interviewer
Miss Lauretta J. Wallace, A.B.   Interviewer
Miss Jean P. Westmoreland, A.M.   Interviewer
Mrs. Leora H. Nesbitt   Typist

INDEX

Accommodation, of lower class, 41-46; of middle class, 55-56; of upper class, 61-64

Alley Dwelling Authority, 8

Bethune, Mary McLeod, 177, 178, 183

Bond, Horace Mann, 4

Border states (see also Community), differentiated from the South, 3-6; Negro illiteracy in, 4; Negro birth rates in, 5; Negro families in, 5; urbanization of Negro population in, 5-6; number of Negro adolescents in, 38; neighborhood contacts in, 70-72; separate schools in, 91; social movements and ideologies in, 168

Capital View, D.C., 14

Carver, George, 176, 177, 178, 183, 190

Chicago, Ill., 10

Children, influence of family traditions on, 41-44; revolt against parental instructions regarding race, 46-48

Church, Negro, as Negro's own institution, 112; attitude of lower class toward, 112-15; religious ideas of lower class influenced by, 115-20; and the present world, 120-22; attitude of middle class toward, 122-27; influence upon middle class, 125-27; attitude of upper class toward, 127-30; influence upon upper class, 127-32

Color distinctions (see also Families, Negro, Ideologies, Lower class, Middle class, Schools, Upper class), 51-53

Community, Negro, in border states, Chapter I: character of population in, 3; social organization of, 18-28; relation to whites, 29-38. Appendix B, 278

Conversation of three youth, xv-xxi; influence of race upon, xxi-xxiii

Delaware, 3, 4, 5

DePriest Village, D.C., 14

District of Columbia, 3, 4, 5, 6; growth of Negro population, 6-8; Negroes in alleys of, 8; areas inhabited by Negroes in, 8-14; distribution of Negroes in census tracts in, 10 n; zones of Negro expansion in, 10-14; Southwest section in, 11-12; Northwest section in, 12-13; number of Negro adolescents in, 38

Divine, Father, 51

Douglass, Frederick, 100

DuBois, W. E. B., 61

Dunbar, Paul Lawrence, 100

Employment, concern of lower class about, 134-37; chances of lower class for, 137-39; attitude of lower class toward "passing" to secure, 139-42; experiences of lower class, 142-45; attitude of lower class toward, 145-48; ambitions of lower class for, 148-50; attitude of lower class toward white and colored employers, 150-52; attitude of middle class toward white and colored employers, 152; chances of middle class for employment, 152-54; attitude of middle class toward "passing" to secure, 154-55; experiences of middle class in, 155-56; ambitions of middle class for, 156-58; attitude of upper class toward, 158-59; chances of upper class for, 159-61; experiences of upper class in, 161-63; attitude of upper class toward "passing" to secure, 163-65; ambitions of upper class for, 165-66

Family, influence upon personality, 40

Family, Negro, in border states, 5; influence of traditions in, 41-44; among lower class, 41-55; influence of stereotypes in, 48-49; parents instructions in, 49-51; rationalizations in, 54-55; among middle class, 55-61; among upper class, 61-67; attitudes of upper class, 61-62; influence on attitudes of children, 62-64; dilemma of upper class, 64-69; Appendix B, 278

"First" families, 20

Frazier, E. Franklin, 10 n

Free Negroes, 19-20

Garfield Hospital, 37

Holy Rollers, 112

Howard, O. O., 7

Howard University, 12, 108

Ickes, Honorable Harold L., 37 n

Ideologies, influence on lower class, 168-82; influence of police brutalities on, 169-70; N.A.A.C.P. and lower class, 170-71; picketing and lower class, 171-73; lack of cooperation among Negroes, 173-76; and ideas of lower class concerning leaders, 176-80; brown skin as ideal of lower class, 180-82; influence on middle class, 182-85; influence on upper class, 185-93; attitude of upper class